AFTER BLAIR

POLITICS AFTER THE NEW LABOUR DECADE

AFTER BLAIR

POLITICS AFTER THE NEW LABOUR DECADE

Edited by Gerry Hassan

Lawrence & Wishart
LONDON 2007

For Eddie and Isobel Rice, Lyndsey, Kimberley and Emma.
With love and hope for the future.

Lawrence and Wishart Limited
99a Wallis Road
London
E9 5LN

First published 2007

British Library Cataloguing in Publication Data.
A catalogue record for this book is available from the British Library

ISBN 978 1 905 007 41 7

Text setting E-type, Liverpool
Printed and bound by Biddles, Kings Lynn

Contents

Introduction: after Blair, after socialism and the search for a new story

Gerry Hassan

> The historian's puzzle is why the Labour Party lasted so long: what could more perfectly illustrate the principle of social inertia? Like democracy itself, the Labour Party was a reaction against the feudal tradition. It arose out of the old working class as it was called, which had such solidarity because its name belied it: it was not so much class as caste.
>
> Michael Young, *The Rise of the Meritocracy*, 1958: 139

The political weather of Britain is clearly changing – with the hollowing out and exhaustion of New Labour, the arrival of David Cameron's new look Conservatives, and Tony Blair's long, lingering, goodbye. Behind these changes are more profound issues: the malaise at the heart of British democracy after the brief hopes of 1997, a loss of trust across the general public about politicians and political processes, and the culture of fear, anxiety and anxiousness aided and abetted by post-9/11 and 'the war on terror'.

This book attempts to look at the current and future prospects for progressive politics in the UK; the ways in which New Labour has changed the political environment for good and bad; and the issues and dilemmas this leaves for the centre-left. It aims to do this by beginning with the some of the major questions raised by Eric Hobsbawm and Stuart Hall, well over twenty five years ago, writing in *Marxism Today* in the immediate run-up to Thatcher's victory in 1979 (Hobsbawm, 1981; Hall, 1979). Their two key texts – 'The Forward March of Labour Halted?' and 'The Great Moving Right Show – have stood the test of time, challenging conventional shibboleths and laying out longer-term prospects. This tradition was also drawn on in *The Blair*

Agenda and *The Moderniser's Dilemma*, in their attempts to understand and critique the politics of post-Thatcherite New Labour
(Perryman, 1996; Coddington and Perryman, 1998).

The Hall and Hobsbawm essays pose questions which transcend the
immediate concerns of their time: how do centre-left parties, forged
out of a certain politics of the industrial revolution, respond to a very
different economic and social order? How can the left meet the rising
individual aspirations of a large part of the electorate and deal with the
new inequalities and dynamism of capitalism? Are the forces of the
new right innately better disposed to nurture the new culture of individualism? These are questions Labour has been grappling with ever
since. And these are the issues that contributors to this book try to
address in the following chapters. The remainder of this introduction
aims to outline some of the main questions that arise in trying to
answer these dilemmas.

THE PARADOXES OF NEW LABOUR
New Labour has been the most electorally successful phenomenon in
Labour's history. Yet, paradoxically, the result of three terms of Tony
Blair's premiership cannot be said to have been anything but ultimately
politically disastrous for Labour and the centre-left. Two points illus-
trate this paradox. Tony Blair became the longest serving Labour Prime
Minister in August 2003, and if he remains in office until May 2007 will
have served a decade in office – something his predecessors, and
perhaps, successors, might view with envy.

At the same time New Labour has become, post-9/11, a force
shaped by, and embracing, the politics of war and security. Tony Blair's
liberal imperialist adventure with the US in Iraq which began in March
2003 has now run for three and a half years, with no foreseeable end in
sight, surpassing the Korean war.[1] Thus, New Labour's unprecedented
length of time in office must be offset against its constant sense of fear
and insecurity: fear that the electorate were really Conservative-
minded and 1997 an aberration, and then the fear of not being tough
enough on asylum, immigration and terrorism, and in the process,
becoming a prisoner of their own nightmares.

New Labour was born out of a realisation of the need to change to
counter Conservative dominance in the twentieth century, and centre-
left weakness. It is certainly true that, before Blair, Labour was
amnesiac about this weakness, due to its obsession with the myths of
1945. But with New Labour this shifted to the opposite end of the
spectrum, as Blair, Mandelson and Gould became fixated about the
centre-left only having won three full-terms in one hundred years:

1906, 1945, 1966. They noted the electoral success of the Conservatives across the twentieth century, but not that it included difficulties and serious challenges. As Andrew Gamble has argued, the four long periods of almost uninterrupted Conservative rule were each separated by shorter periods of Liberal and Labour rule, from which the Conservatives always recovered (see Table One). The story of 'the Conservative century' is a complex one: of Conservative pragmatism pre-Thatcher and constant renewal, and of progressive failure to seize opportunities.

Table One: Dominant Parties in British Politics 1886-

1888-1906	Conservative
1906-1916	Liberal
1916-1940	Conservative
1940-1951	Labour
1951-1964	Conservative
1964-1979	Labour
1979-1997	Conservative
1997-	Labour

Source: Gamble, 2003: 169

New Labour has become trapped in its own history: the near-history of the 1980s and Labour's civil war, and longer-term, in the inability of Labour prior to 1997 to win elections. It has made a fetish of winning and retaining power above all else. New Labour sees itself in Finlayson's penetrating analysis, as 'a movement leading Britain out of the "old ways" of hierarchy, tradition and entrenched power, and into a new fluid world of networks and opportunity for all' (2003: 203). In practice it has been very different.

ASSESSING THE NEW LABOUR LEGACY

There is still even at this late hour confusion about what New Labour is, partly because of the mixed messages it transmits. Polly Toynbee has called this 'the best Labour government in the last 50 years', and has declared Blair 'a political genius – three times victor – creator of a left-of-centre economically solid and socially progressive.' She admits, however, that many of the 'good stories [are] not part of the narrative' – issues such as Sure Start, tackling child poverty and the national minimum wage (2005). What she does not recognise is that these and other progressive advances have not been ignored by the Blairites by acci-

dent; it is because they are not part of their central narrative of what
New Labour is.

Michael Rustin, a usually critical but nuanced commentator on New
Labour, similarly showed significant degrees of confusion. In a post-
election piece that shifted back and forward between optimism and
pessimism, he commented that watching Blair's progress across the
country during the 2005 election reminded him more of 'his achievements and virtues than of his failures and vices.' He went even further,
arguing that 'New Labour's success has created some space for a more
progressive politics' (Rustin, 2005: 116), a fascinating comment given
how far the Blairites have travelled to the right on a host of issues. Both
Toynbee and Rustin seem to have been sufficiently mollified by the
subordinate, weak social democratic element of the Blair agenda to
overlook the broader picture of the government's trajectory, which will
be discussed in more detail later.

At least three distinct interpretations can be identified of New
Labour:

- *New Labour as Labour:* This account does not see New Labour as
  breaking particularly new ground. It stresses that the Blair government is the most successful Labour government in the party's
  history and has advanced many traditional progressive goals: using
  a sustained period of economic growth to increase public spending
  and engage in redistribution. A number of party loyalist perspectives have emphasised this, as have several academic accounts of
  Labour history (Fielding, 2003).
- *New Labour as New:* This is the Blairite 'official' account of what
  New Labour stands for: a break with the 'Old' Labour state socialism of the past and free market conservatism of the new right.
  Instead, New Labour's 'third way' combines economic efficiency
  with social justice, and is uniquely suited to deal with the challenges
  of globalisation. This account has been consistently associated with
  the writings of Giddens (1998).
- *Neo-Labour:* This sees the Blair government as the continuation of
  Thatcherism by other means. Social democracy, which still informs
  some of the government's policies, has been diluted and slowly
  supplanted by the logic of neo-liberalism. The phrase, 'Neo-
  Labour', invented by Neal Lawson, has been persuasively examined
  by Hall (2003) and Finlayson (2003).

One fact we can be sure of is that New Labour will be remembered
differently in history from how it is seen today. The Attlee government

is seen by most within Labour as the high point of labourism, establishing full employment, the welfare state, NHS and much more. However, in its immediate aftermath it was viewed by many as a major disappointment, conservative and unimaginative in many of policies, unable to engage in transformative socialist policies, or renew itself in office (see Crossman, 1952). The Wilson administration of 1964-70 has in recent years been the subject of renewed interest and an attempt at revisionism, with people looking at its policies on comprehensive education, expansion of higher education, and avoidance of being drawn into the US-led Vietnam war. At the time, and for many still, the Wilson years were seen as a period of disillusionment and betrayal, where Labour abandoned its policies of economic growth and higher public spending, and could not address the causes of British economic decline (see Ponting, 1989).

Furthermore, the whole period from 1945 to 1976 is often subsumed into the idea of 'the post-war consensus'. For some commentators there is now a much more defined and unified conception of the 1945-76 period than there was at the time when people were living through it. However, all of the shifting attitudes outlined above, while making the case that the Blair government will be seen differently in history, can also be seen as part of a wider picture, namely of the retreat of left hopes and the diminution of its hopes. Those who make the positive case for New Labour often tend to ignore this long-term shift.

THE LEFT'S LACK OF A STORY

One reason for the sometimes confused views on what the Labour Party currently represents is that the left has lost the sense it once had of a defining project and story, centred around progress towards the idea of socialism. This had a number of sub-stories and themes within it. First, there was a notion of political economy, based for most of the post-1945 era on Keynesian demand management and planning, and the need to redistribute income, wealth and power (Thompson, 1996). This was related to the second strand of the story of socialism: the belief in the power of the state to do good and be a benign, progressive force making peoples' lives better and fairer. The central state was seen as the best instrument for change and redistribution between classes and regions.

Third, it also had a powerful concept of agency, rooted in the organised working class and trade union movement. This idea of 'the labour movement' as an inevitable, incremental, partly invincible force of history and progress informed all of the actions, thoughts and compromise of Labour in office. Small or even significant retreats or defeats were all part of a wider picture and higher cause. Thus, the over-arching story of socialism gave Labour politicians and members a sense of values and mission, and a belief that even small scale incremental change might be worth supporting as a step in the direction of transformative change.

If we examine the state of centre-left politics under New Labour all of these elements have disappeared from the scene. The over-arching narrative of socialism has long disappeared, but so have the sub-stories of political economy, the role of the state and sense of agency. As Bauman has pointed out, the left 'has yet to learn to live without an historical agent' (1986/87: 93). The consequences of this have barely begun to be understood. In a world after socialism – after the original 'project' – what does a Labour government stand for, what makes all the compromises and diversions worthwhile, and what makes politicians, activists and members believe in the cause?

The state of American politics is a warning of what can happen to a left in retreat. Despite the Clinton Presidency and the efforts of the New Democrats, the Republicans are now the dominant political party of the US – having won seven out of the last ten Presidential elections, controlling both Houses and having a conservative majority on the Supreme Court. As Michael Walzer, editor of *Dissent*, has pointed out the US right wing have a defining story, historical – some would argue messianic – mission, and sense of agency: the power of free market capitalism and belief in God (Walzer, 2005).

The American left, on the other hand, have no sense of story, mission or agency, which has led them into the dangerous terrain of arguing every policy issue-by-issue, while their right wing ideological opponents can lay claim to a higher moral ground and authority. Walzer argues powerfully that this leads the left into a profound sense of malaise and self-doubt. This is a world where the left explores each policy after an issue-by-issue moral examination and forensic debate, so that people are for military intervention in one situation, against it in another, or simultaneously pro-choice, pro-gay, pro-gun control. As he writes: 'No one on the left has succeeded in telling a story that brings together the different values to which we are committed and connects that to some general picture of what the modern world is like ... The right, by contrast, has a general picture' (2005: 37). This leads to an exhausting, incoherent, tactical politics where one side – the centre-left – argues elaborate, complicated, evidence-based politics, while the other side – the right – have 'a world historical project' in the way that Marxism did.

Walzer is not proposing that the left should have the same kind of moral certainty and fanaticism as the right; nor is he ignoring the contradictions in the American conservative movement between free marketeers and evangelicals. And of course the experiences of the US and the UK are very different. The British left is unlikely ever to have to face the American levels of evangelical and religious opposition. But what is common between the two countries is the politics of what Walzer called 'the near-left', which he characterises as filled with doubt, moderation and qualification. Walzer states that: 'Most of us on the near-left live in a complex world, which we are not sure we understand and we move around in that world pragmatically, practising a politics of trial and error' (2005: 35). It seems that the politics of the near-left is suited to a number of situations, mostly as a tactical response in a hostile climate, such as the 1980s and 1990s. But as a permanent strategy it is debilitating and demoralising. Clinton and Blair, leading politicians of the near-left, have proven this: illustrating the perils of permanently operating on the terrain of your opponents.

THE STATE OF LABOUR AFTER BLAIR

The search for a new story for the left and progressives has to begin with an honest assessment of Labour as a champion of progressive values. Two extreme positions have largely defined this debate. On the one hand there is the dismissal of any criticism of the Labour Party on the basis that it is the only vehicle we have, and that there is no viable alternative. On the other hand there is the view that Labour has always been fundamentally flawed because, in Miliband's words, its 'parliamentary socialism' led it to put its commitment to parliamentarism ahead of socialism (1972). This has been very persuasive on the left, particularly outside Labour. The truth, not surprisingly, lies somewhere between these two polar opposites and changes over time.

Labour's effectiveness as a vehicle for advancing progressive values and humanising British capitalism has been a mixed one. Significant points where Labour has shaped the political weather and culture of the nation have been rare: the period 1940-51 is perhaps the only inarguable example. Wilson's dominance of domestic politics for over a decade left a poisoned chalice and little positive legacy. Despite recent revisionist accounts, the road of Wilson's failures leads inexorably to Thatcherism's door. Strangely enough, Blair's contribution to Labour looks surprisingly similar to Wilson; an undoubted political brilliance and ability to tactically wrong-foot opponents has bequeathed a sad, sordid legacy to his party and successor. A wider case for Labour's effectiveness than could be adduced for any specific administrations could be argued, however, advancing that the emergence and rise of Labour brought about a response from the British establishment, which incorporated Labour and changed British society in a progressive direction. Labour's long story and contribution to changing the UK contains much of which the party can be proud, liberating and transforming the lives of millions of people, but it is also a politics which never went far enough.

Social democratic politics and thinking have informed and shaped Labour for most of its history. However, it has recently been subject to retreat and dilution, so that it is relevant to ask whether the renewal of social democracy as the main philosophy of progressives is a worthwhile goal, or the best we can hope for. Social democracy's whole raison d'etre is slowly eroding in Western Europe. It has been assaulted in the UK, Australia and New Zealand by neo-liberalism, and characterised by institutional stasis elsewhere. '"New" social democracy is failing to prove itself as a distinct political model ...' in the face of neo-liberalism (Thomson, 2000: 189). Only in the Nordic group of nations has it become the governing credo, and proven capable of renewal across several generations and in the harsh international order of the last few decades. Social democracy is likely to remain an important part of the left's repertoire, but it will not survive unless it adapts to the new challenges and circumstances.

Related to this crisis of social democracy are questions of the 'realm of manoeuvre' available to any Labour government in the UK. It is fascinating to note that the Labour government of 1974, elected on 39 per cent of the vote, and with a tiny majority of three which soon disappeared, was called an 'elective dictatorship' and seen as a threat to British democracy. Whereas thirty years later the third Blair administration was elected on a mere 35 per cent of the vote, while being rewarded with an over-generous majority of 66 seats, without ever having its legitimacy or democratic credentials questioned. The difference between the two was that the first posed a threat to some of the vested interests who hold power in Britain, whereas Blair's New Labour has consistently chosen to govern with the grain of British society, meaning those who have power and influence in society. New Labour has chosen to answer whether or not Labour can govern, by operating a self-denying ordinance and not threatening the existing economic and social order. However, the dilemma of Labour throughout its history will remain for future progressives. Any progressive government worthy of its name will have to go against the grain of power and thus risk being challenged by power-ful vested interests.

Labour has also historically been shaped by a culture of labourism. This defined the Labour Party as a party which gave direct expression, and was organically linked to, organised labour and the trade union movement (Nairn, 1964a; 1964b). This culture of the party played a far-reaching role in differentiating the 'doctrine' of the party from its 'ethos' (for this distinction see Drucker, 1979). Whereas the party's doctrines were about its focus on policy, programme and positions, its ethos was its culture, codes and informal attitudes. If the idea of doctrine was about formal politics, ethos was informed by 'a shared past, a series of folk memories of shared exploitation, common struggle and gradually increased power' (Drucker, 1979: 31). However confident the voices of transformation and the coming of a new social order may have been in party documents, the party's ethos has been informed by a sense of unsureness and defensiveness. Labour's sense of ethos have been assaulted by the Blairite revolution to the point that it barely exists, except as some kind of collective memory. What future beckons for a party once so shaped by its ethos, but where it is now so weak?

One of the central faultlines in the new capitalism is between the winners and losers, with the former better organised, more vocal and better placed in the media, think tanks and political classes, so that they can propound their self-interest into a worldview. This faultline, for David Marquand runs through the heart of New Labour. Labour historically was a party concerned about the plight of losers in society and redressing this (Marquand, 1999: 236-37). However Blairite New Labour has degenerated into a party which believes in winners: cele-brating wealth, success and acting as the advance guard of the post-democratic international class (Crouch, 2004). There are undeni-ably problems in today's world in associating a political party or project with the idea of society's 'losers'. However, the solution cannot be to abandon such people, or the abolition of the idea of a society without significant losers.

NEW PUBLIC INSTITUTIONS, SPACES AND CONVERSATIONS

A significant part of the left's legacy has been the institutions it has constructed which embody the idea of the public realm and which nurture progressive ideas. In the pre-Thatcher era, there were many grounds for criticising the practice of many of these bodies: their centralism, top-down nature and lack of imagination and sensitivity.

New Labour has bought into this critique, but from a Thatcherite, rather than a progressive perspective.

There is a need for a new institutional framework for progressive politics which reimagines the idea of the public at the level of party, wider currents and governance. Looking at the Labour Party, it is easy to pour scorn on the Tony Blair/Hazel Blears concept of a Labour Supporters Network, as a means to dilute and neuter the troublesome party membership who want to have a say. This is the ultimate Blairite fantasy: the party reduced to the role of cheerleaders, similar to Berlusconi's Forza Italia. The longer-term issue, however, is that the old institutional coalition of Labour is now significantly weakened; party membership has more than halved since 1997, and trade union membership is still the preserve of public sector workers.

There is a desperate need to think about the kind of institution building the left should do. The state of US politics offers a salutary warning for the kind of future to avoid. For the last thirty years, the American conservative movement have engaged in a never-ending, creative exercise in creating a movement, from think tanks and pressure groups to lobbying bodies, faith groups and churches. The Democrats over the same period have been outmanoeuvred and outresourced to the point that post-2004 they have realised the need to begin to address this imbalance.

What kind of institutions does a progressive movement need to sustain itself, grow and challenge prevailing ideas? Compass is one response, but it is only one small organisation, and there is a need for many more bodies and groups, including some that address the issue of the new generation of 'netroot' activists. When Labour asked this question after its third election defeat in 1987, it looked at the influence of the Thatcherite think tanks in creating a fertile climate of ideas; this led to the creation of IPPR in 1988 and Demos in 1993. Both proved enormously successful in generating new ideas, thinking and creativity. However, there is a now a sense of think tank fatigue setting in, as the limitations of this model become apparent, with its emphasis on corporate funding, access to politicians and media coverage (see Leys, 2006). Some supposedly progressive think tanks, such as the New Local Government Network, have become leading advocates of privatising public services, which is not surprising given that the weight of their funding comes from the corporate sector.

What is needed – but Labour has failed to develop – is a distinct progressive economic and social agenda. Some sympathetic observers of the Blair government see the development of a 'new "Anglo-social" welfare model, incorporating and reconciling economic performance and flexibility with equality and social justice' (Dixon and Pearce, 2005: 81). This combines the 'economic dynamism' of the US and the 'social equity' of the Nordic model (Pearce and Paxton, 2005: xiii) in an approach focused on supply side measures where addressing massive incomes, wealth and power is not even on the agenda.

The Blair government has invested massively in public services and has pushed public expenditure as a percentage of GDP up from 37 to 42 per cent. However, there has been a profound paradox at the heart of the Blair administration in relation to public services. After a colossal and impressive programme of investment the idea of the public realm – of a sector of society which operates on a different logic from the private sector – has never been weaker or under more pressure.

The last decade has seen no real sense of championing the idea of 'public goods', of areas like education and health as being seen as so important that they have to be free, shaped by an egalitarian impulse, and run by principles different from those of the market. The exception have been the annual homilies from Gordon Brown, at the Labour Conference or TUC Annual Congress, praising public service in an evangelical way as 'a calling', and as being about 'service' not 'self-interest', which does not fit with the main Blairite or Brownite views of the public sector (see for example, Brown, 2002, quoted in Hassan, 2004: 208).

Brown's inability to find a convincing way of linking economic liberalism to the idea of the public good can be seen in the consistent failure to recognise that the idea of the public realm needs to be artic-ulated, nurtured and nourished, and given the encouragement and love to be able to self-generate and withstand the encroachments of indi-vidualist, acquisitive capitalism. Unfortunately the Blair government has taken the opposite approach, introducing marketisation into the public sector, sometimes even privatisation.

The Blair government's mantra of choice and contestability, and its consumer agenda in the public sector, may be wrong, but has to be seen not just in the context of New Labour, but the wider historic failure of the left to be creative and imaginative about public services. Blair and company have drawn directly from the rich stream of new right ideas and in-vogue business ideas. There have been few alternative models to draw from or challenge the Blairites with. Labour's decentralist tradi-tion was quickly marginalised as the party's strength grew and it became a governing party. The only real exceptions to this have been the decentralist ideas of guild socialism in the 1920s, and the brief Bennite flowering of workers' co-operatives of 1974-75.

It is time to go back to the future, and re-examine the rich fertile ideas in Labour's self-governing, decentralist tradition. The centralist, uniformist model no longer works, while the privatised, finance driven world of the Thatcherites and Blairites leaves people even more power-less. The experience of devolution to Scotland, Wales and London, has shown the emerging nature of a UK politics with different political centres. It has also shown the potential of very different social democratic politics from New Labour: universal free care for the elderly in Scotland, a more traditional approach in Wales, and congestion charges in London. These three examples all have limitations in their politics, but they do show that there are alternatives to Blairism, that play a part in contributing to a very different UK.

A recent response to the decline and hollowing out of political parties has been the emergence of independent citizens initiatives such as The East London Community Organisation (TELCO), an umbrella organisation which has brought together numerous community groups, refused to take corporate funding, and which in the run-up to the Olympic decision to award the site of the 2012 games decided to exercise its significant leverage about local jobs and contracts (Howarth and Jamoul, 2004).[2] Another has been the Glasgow 2020 programme facilitated by Demos, bringing together twenty leading public agencies in the city in a project which has given voice to the non-institutional view of the city, and use the power, imagination and creativity of story and narrative to shape different views of the city.[3] Glasgow 2020 was a first in the UK, and possibly anywhere, which attempted to reimagine a city through the stories people tell about it, and to think in very different ways from traditional policy.

The experiences of TELCO and Glasgow 2020 point to a desire to create a very different notion of public space and conversation. This is a public space shaped by local people, not corporates or developers. It is a conversation which touches some of the deep issues of life – such as the search for meaning – has a philosophical side, and is characterised by a very female-friendly, feminised politics.

In a UK state that, despite devolution, is one of the most centralist in Europe, this is about the importance of the local. The centralisation of UK politics has sucked the energy and interest out of it, and a new kind of localism, not necessarily focused on councils or mayors, seems to be where people want to locate more politics and power. It also points to the new forms of organisations and institutions which are needed in the future – neither the 'old' public, or the 'new' corporate driven public. Instead, new agencies will need to be informed by the shift from the first modernity's 'logic of structure' to the second modernity's 'logic of flows' (Beck and Willms, 2004: 27).

BRITISH POLITICS AFTER BLAIR

British politics after Blair could contain a number of possible futures:

- *Continuation of the Conservative century:* The Blair government will come to be seen as a unique but transient force, a blip in the continuity of Conservative dominance. Labour's three election victories would then be viewed as more the product of Blair and the appeal of his personality than the merits of Labour. A Labour Party post-Blair will return to conventional British politics, based on competitive two-party politics and a renewed Conservative challenge.

- *A new progressive consensus – the Europeanisation of British politics:* The Blair government becomes part of the foundation of a new consensus, which would include a return to a progressive Europeanism. This was indeed the original inspiration of 'the project', opening up the progressive coalition to Labour and Lib Dem co-operation. Such a perspective could take the Labour-Lib Dem coalition in Scotland and briefer experience in Wales as models of the way forward. However, to gain added impetus at Westminster this will require proportional representation, and for Labour to lose its majority at the next UK election.

- *Post-democracy:* New Labour's embrace of post-democratic elites and the international corporate class continues after Blair. Political parties continue the process of hollowing out, while memberships are reduced to the role of cheerleaders. Political power continues flowing out of traditional party politics and into other arenas: from the corporate world to NGOs and community activism. All the main parties collude in this process and do not challenge the orthodoxies of post-democracy.

- *Labour implosion: Australianisation of British politics:* Labour, after being in power for over a decade, is exhausted and tainted by various scandals. The serious point arrives when the party loses its reputation for economic competence, and a weakened, demoralised party is replaced by a new Conservative ascendancy. With few resources left, the party faces a long period in opposition. This is the story of Australian Labor after Bob Hawke and Paul Keating, and could be the future of New Labour post-Blair and Brown (adapted from Gamble, 2006: 308-12).

The above four possible futures are all possible. What happens will be dependent on a number of factors ranging from the nature of Blair's end period of leadership, whether party discipline remains or disunity re-emerges, and the manner of the succession of the post-Blair leadership, their style of governing and agenda. A host of external factors will be crucial – from what David Cameron's Conservatives does to the attitude of that influential Blairite, Rupert Murdoch.

FROM THE NEAR LEFT TO THE NEXT LEFT: STORY, SONG AND HEROES

Defining the politics of the next left involves looking beyond the dying embers of the Blair government and abandoning the politics of 'the near-left'. This requires a number of activities. First, it necessitates the need for a new progressive story. What are the over-arching narratives of the centre-left in Britain today? What kind of society do we want Britain to be, and what road maps have we for getting there? Clearly the UK cannot become Sweden overnight, but what sort of progressive values do we want to embed and entrench in institutions with the aim of nurturing a different political culture? Is the social democratic impulse strong, radical and robust enough for the challenges of government and global capitalism? Is British social democracy capable of renewing itself, or has it become hopelessly compromised by neo-liberalism?

Second, any progressive story needs a musical soundtrack to capture the mood of the times: namely a sense of song. All forms of popular culture matter to progressive politics, art, film, theatre, but the power of song touches a deep resonance. It is revealing of the political era across the Western world that despite the massive international protests against the Iraq war, for 'Making Poverty History', against the G8 and for environmental and trade justice, that the musical reference points of political change are still largely rooted in the myths and folklore of the 1960s. Indeed, the tyranny of the 'swinging sixties' and the self-congratulatory nature of the baby boomer generation has become profoundly conservative and nauseating. Bob Dylan, the Beatles and the Stones have been canonised and revered in a manner which misrepresents the past and limits future creativity. A radical social movement needs songs, music, concerts and collective moments of celebration, passion and connection. It does not need pop stars becoming part of the post-democratic establishment in the way that Bono and Bob Geldof have done.

Third, the left desperately needs to have a few heroes and even a few villains. Who are the heroes of the left today? Bono and Geldof are too individualistic, self-promoting and not connected to a wider constituency. Some people might laud Bill Clinton, but he remains a character too flawed with an ambiguous record. The only obvious eligible candidate is Nelson Mandela. He is the last universal hero the left has across the world: someone with international appeal with a record of real change, and a moral dimension and compass. Perhaps we need to rethink what constitutes a modern day hero or heroine.

Given human nature, the left needs a few villains as well, as political movements are defined by its advocates and enemies. Surveying the state of Britain and the planet some of the enemies of the progressive cause should be obvious. These include the corporate elites who press at every opportunity for flexibility and deregulation for the majority, while advocating rewards and remuneration for themselves, the fundamentalist marketeers who inhabit large parts of our public life and institutions, and the advocates and apologists for post-democracy in the media and elsewhere who constantly tell us 'There is no alternative'.

If any of the above is to be realised then progressives need to rethink and reimagine a sense of agency. The unproblematic romanticising of 'the labour movement' is no longer tenable, and the idea of the British state as a force for good has also been irrevocably weakened. Instead, we face the challenge of a more pluralist, unpredictable, messy, post-labourist politics, which has been brought into being by long-term economic and social changes, and aided by Blair's marginalisation of the labour and trade union movements. And the left has to recognise it cannot appease the forces of neo-liberalism as Blair and Clinton have done. The rise of anti-politics and political disillusion has been fed by the idea of an individualised, solipsistic world which reduces politics to a personalised world without collective agency: the ultimate neo-liberal fantasy (Stoker, 2006: 203).

Finally, the next left needs to have a sense of time, to think about politics and ideas in the short, medium and long-term. Short-term policies, over the life of one Parliament, respond to immediate problems and build support for wider, deeper change. But, as Bernard Crick argues, they need to be consistent with middle-term theories about how to achieve long-term goals – such as an egalitarian society. Middle-term strategies need to be oriented to trying to change attitudes and values, either by persuasion or by changing institutions that are obstacles to change; their time span is thus likely to be over the period of a generation. Lastly, long-term values have to be articulated about the kind of society progressives want (see Crick, 1984: 36-37).

Many commentators have long argued that Blair's legacy will be to make Labour safe for those with power, and to remove the potential threat of socialism. This is undoubtedly true from where we currently stand, but it is equally possible that the post-Blairite inheritance will stretch out and evolve in ways as yet unpredictable, as New Labour's decade of dominance becomes political history.

A post-Blairite progressive politics will find itself in a landscape shaped by a post-labourist politics, where the forces of Labour tribalism and chauvinism, once the anchor sheets of Labour, are no longer the defining forces. Such an environment has all sorts of possibilities for a more creative, pluralist politics, but it could also open the way for those who want to make New Labour a permanent party of the post-democratic establishment. Such an outcome could see Labour abolished in the way Michael Young foretold in his account of a future, individualised society quoted at the beginning of this introduction (1958).

The Blair government's record has had many major successes, from record investment in public services, to addressing child and pensioner poverty, the national minimum wage, and Scottish and Welsh devolution; but it has, overall, weakened and diminished the prospects for progressive politics. A post-Blair centre-left politics faces many challenges including:

- Is continued economic growth viable and sustainable and is it the best way to advance progress and the idea of the good life and society?
- The fairness agenda – what degree of poverty and inequality is tolerable in an affluent society?
- A public sector reform agenda – democratic and decentralist – not shaped by either marketisation or 'producer capture'
- The challenge to bring about a new era of corporate responsibility and accountability, and to end the 'corporate capture' and commercialisation of large swathes of public life
- The decentralisation agenda – to begin to overcome the excessive centralism of British political life and the state
- The challenge posed by European integration
- The foreign policy agenda – rethinking the obsession of the British political classes with Atlanticism.

More profound than all of these is the question of what the centre-left is about. Will people have the courage and conviction to abandon the politics of 'the near left' that they have inhabited for the last twenty plus years, and to strike out onto new terrain? In an age which has been shaped by social democratic retreat, are our hopes now confined to a defence of what has already been achieved, with a little tinkering and a few measures of reform? If this is the case, the British left will forever remain a prisoner of the conservative political culture, its best option reduced to that of governing in a hostile, unfriendly climate. Can we aspire to a politics of transformation, with a new story and project, which seeks to remake the political weather on our terms? There can be no going back to the cosy, comfortable assumptions of British politics pre-Blair. Blair's brutalism, and humiliation of so much of what 'the labour movement' has held dear, means that there can be no return to 'normal service'. That might seem a little scary, but it could also, ultimately prove a liberation for progressives.

NOTES

1. The Iraq war began in March 2003 and has now run for three and a half years. The Korean war was fought from June 1950 to July 1953. Britain's involvement in Afghanistan began in October 2001, and it qualifies as Blair's longest military intervention.
2. For further information on TELCO: www.telcocitizens.org.uk.
3. For further information on Glasgow 2020: www.glasgow2020.co.uk.

REFERENCES

Bauman, Z. (1986/87), 'The Left as the Counter-Culture of Modernity', *Telos*, No. 70, 81-93.

Beck, U. and Willms, J. (2004), *Conversations with Ulrich Beck*, Cambridge, Polity.

Coddington, A. and Perryman, M. (eds) (1998), *The Moderniser's Dilemma: Radical Politics in the Age of Blair*, London: Lawrence and Wishart.

Crick, B. (1984), *Socialism Values and Time*, London: Fabian Society.

Crossman, R. H. S. (ed.) (1952), *New Fabian Essays*, London: Turnstile Press.

Crouch, C. (2004), *Post-Democracy*, Cambridge: Polity.

Dixon, M. and Pearce, N. (2005), 'Social Justice in a Changing World: The Emerging Anglo-Social Model', in Pearce, N. and Paxton, W. (eds), *Social Justice: Building a Fairer Britain*, London: Politico's Publishing in association with IPPR, 62-87.

Drucker, H. (1979), *Doctrine and Ethos in the Labour Party*, London: Allen and Unwin.

Fielding, S. (2003), *The Labour Party: Continuity and Change in the Making of New Labour*, Basingstoke: Palgrave Macmillan.

Finlayson, A. (2003), *Making Sense of New Labour*, London: Lawrence and Wishart.

Gamble, A. (2003), *Between Europe and America: The Future of British Politics*, Basingstoke: Palgrave Macmillan.

Gamble, A. (2006), 'British Politics After Blair', in Dunleavy, P., Heffernan, R.,

Cowley, P. and Hay, C. (eds), *Developments in British Politics 8*, Basingstoke: Palgrave Macmillan, 295-314.

Giddens, A. (1998), *The Third Way: The Renewal of Social Democracy*, Cambridge: Polity.

Hall, S. (1979), 'The Great Moving Right Show', *Marxism Today*, January, 14-20.

Hall, S, (2003), 'New Labour's double-shuffle', *Soundings: A Journal of Politics and Culture*, No. 24, 10-24.

Hassan, G. (2004), 'Labour's Journey from Socialism to Social Democracy: A Case Study of Gordon Brown's Political Thought', in Hassan, G. (ed.), *The Scottish Labour Party: History, Institutions and Ideas*, Edinburgh: Edinburgh University Press, 195-218.

Hobsbawm, E. (1981), 'The Forward March of Labour Halted?', Marx Memorial Lecture 1978, reprinted in Jacques, M. and Mulhern, F. (eds), *The Forward March of Labour Halted?*, London: Verso, 1-19.

Howarth, C. and Jamoul, L. (2004), 'London Citizens: Practising Citizenship, Rebuilding Democracy', *Renewal: A Journal of Labour Politics*, Vol. 12 No. 3, 40-50.

Leys, C. (2006), 'The Cynical State', in Panitch, L. and Leys, C. (eds), *The Socialist Register 2006*, London, Merlin, http://socialistregister.com/sample/1

Marquand, D. (1999), *The Progressive Dilemma: From Lloyd George to Blair*, London: Phoenix Giant 2nd edn.

Miliband, R. (1972), *Parliamentary Socialism: A Study in the Politics of Labour*, London: Merlin Press 2nd edn.

Nairn, T. (1964a), 'The Nature of the Labour Party 1', *New Left Review*, No. 27, 38-65.

Nairn, T. (1964b), 'The Nature of the Labour Party 2', *New Left Review*, No. 28, 33-62.

Pearce, N. and Paxton, W. (eds) (2005), 'Introduction', in Pearce, N. and Paxton, W. (eds), *Social Justice: Building a Fairer Britain*, London: Politico's Publishing in association with IPPR, ix-xxiii.

Perryman, M. (ed.) (1996), *The Blair Agenda*, London: Lawrence and Wishart.

Ponting, C. (1989), *Breach of Promise: Labour in Power 1964-1970*, London: Hamish Hamilton.

Rustin, M. (2005), 'Sailing towards the Icebergs: New Labour's Third Term', *Soundings: A Journal of Politics and Culture*, No. 30, 111-23.

Stoker, G. (2006), *Why Politics Matters: Making Democracy Work*, Basingstoke: Palgrave Macmillan.

Thompson, N. (1996), *Political Economy and the Labour Party: The Economics of Democratic Socialism 1884-1995*, London: University College London Press.

Thomson, S. (2000), *The Social Democratic Dilemma: Ideology, Governance and Globalisation*, Basingstoke: Palgrave Macmillan.

Toynbee, P. (2005), 'The Birds Have Flown', *The Guardian*, 3 June.

Walzer, M. (2005), 'All God's Children's Got Values', *Dissent*, Spring, 35-40.

Young, M. (1958), *The Rise of the Meritocracy 1870-2033*, Harmondsworth: Penguin.

New Labour and old debates

Andrew Gamble

When Eric Hobsbawm delivered his Marx Memorial Lecture in 1978, 'The Forward March of Labour Halted?', a minority Labour government was still clinging to office (Hobsbawm, 1981). Within a year it had been forced out and the long night of Thatcherism had begun. It was to be eighteen years before Labour returned to government. In 1978 many agreed that Labour had lost its way and had become increasingly divided and bereft of purpose. Hobsbawm however argued that Labour's problems were not recent, but could be traced back thirty years. The forward march of the Labour movement had been halted since 1948, the high point of the Attlee government, rather than since 1978, or even since 1968. Hobsbawm set out this analysis just before the election of the Thatcher government, which was to change the terrain of British politics and the British Labour Party in fundamental ways, unleashing major debates on the nature of Thatcherism and the future of the left. After losing office in 1979 Labour went through some of the darkest days in its history, experiencing a crisis which came close to destroying it. The party however did survive. It modernised and eventually returned to government. By 2008, the thirtieth anniversary of Hobsbawm's lecture, Labour will be close to completing a third consecutive full term in office, unprecedented in the history of the party, and almost twice the length of its previous longest period in government.

Does this mean that the forward march of Labour has been resumed? Since Hobsbawm's lecture was published the terms of debate on the left have changed almost beyond recognition, and many now believe that the Labour Party of today is no longer the Labour Party of the past. Yet despite some important and obvious differences there are many continuities between old Labour, the party of the forward march, and New Labour, the party of New Times. The forward march in the sense Hobsbawm understood it no longer exists and neither does the labour *movement* in the sense in which it was once understood. But there is still a recognisable left of centre progressive tradition in British politics and the Labour Party remains its main political expression. Labour has so far had three dominant leaders, Attlee, Wilson and Blair, and three extended periods in Government: 1940-51; 1964-1979 (interrupted by the short-lived Heath Government); and 1997-2009/10. They make up around one third of the time since the end of the first world war. The other two thirds are filled by long periods of Conservative dominance: 1918-1940; 1951-1964; 1979-1997. In 1978 when Hobsbawm delivered his lecture, Labour had completed two thirty-year cycles – 1918-1948, and 1948-1978 – but while in the first, despite the great setback of 1931, the underlying trend had been one of advance, in the second cycle the underlying trend had been one of decline. At the start of the third cycle, which began in 1978, Labour was to plunge to a defeat in some respects even worse than 1931, but then it recovered to record electoral successes even greater than in 1945. But as the end of the third thirty-year cycle in Labour's history since 1918 approaches, a key question is whether the same fate that overtook the party after Attlee and after Wilson is about to overtake the party after Blair.

THE FORWARD MARCH OF LABOUR HALTED

The thirty years from 1918 to 1948 were years of advance for Labour. Following the introduction of universal franchise there had been steady progress, the formation of two minority governments, and, despite the major setback of 1931, a gradually increasing share of the vote and growing confidence that the future belonged to Labour. This period culminated in the first ever majority Labour government in 1945. But this did not inaugurate a long period of Labour ascendancy, as many expected at the time. After 1948 the reforming zeal and energy of the Government weakened, it never realised its potential, and disillusion in Labour's ranks became widespread and intense (Crossman, 1965). The party lost office in 1951, and was out for thirteen years, losing again in 1955 and 1959 by increasing margins, and seeing its vote drift inexorably lower. This downward trend was halted in 1964 when Harold Wilson won a narrow majority on a programme to modernise Britain, converting this eighteen months later into a substantial majority. Hopes were aroused once more of Labour picking up from where it had left off in 1951 and becoming the normal governing party in place of the Conservatives. In the fifteen years between 1964 and 1979 Labour was in office for eleven of them, but it achieved much less than had been hoped, and in general these were years of disappointment, disillusion and mounting problems. After the rise in the party's vote share in 1966, its percentage dipped again in 1970, and then in the two elections in 1974 it fell below 40 per cent, the first time this had happened since the 1930s. It was not to rise above 40 per cent again until 1997. The party appeared defensive, and increasingly divided about the way ahead.

Hobsbawm's lecture brought many responses, from all parts of the labour movement, and it became one of the central reference points in the debate on Thatcherism which preoccupied the left in Britain through the 1980s, and still in some respects preoccupies it. But Hobsbawm's gaze in 1978 was not fixed on the right at all. Thatcher was not mentioned. What he wanted to understand was why the progress of the labour movement seemed to have stalled. He captured a particular moment, when it was still possible to identify a labour *movement*, and still use class categories of analysis for describing its policies, its goals, its support, and its prospects. He argued that the strength of the labour movement had been built on the organised working class. The ability of the unions gradually to recruit more and more workers in Britain increased the reach and salience of the movement, and promoted an identification between being working-class, joining a trade union, living in a working-class community and voting Labour. The 'Forward March of Labour' was the gradual and inevitable uncoiling of the power of organised labour, step by cautious step, since the great majority of the British people lived in towns and cities, and were working-class by occupation, education and outlook. Britain was not so much a class divided society as a status divided society, and the status of being or not being working-class became one of the key forces moulding British democracy. The rise of the Labour Party reflected a growing acceptance that political identity was defined by 'class'. Labour was always a class party in that sense.

Labour's problem, according to Hobsbawm, however, was that the party could no longer rely on this pattern. Changes in the structure of the British economy and of occupations, the growth of white collar jobs and services, the rise of consumerism and youth culture, had all begun to erode Labour's automatic support. It could no longer count on there being an automatic built-in advantage for the party just by being the Labour Party, and expecting that in time more and more people who were objectively working-class would come to see that their interests were best represented by the party of organised labour. Sociological and economic trends, which once had worked for the party, were now against it. If Labour's working-class base, far from growing, was actually contracting, Labour had more than ever to construct a broader progressive movement, forging alliances with sections of society which did not automatically identify themselves as Labour, such as the progressive middle class. It also had to curb the tendency for sectionalism in its ranks, and the pursuit of narrow trade union interests rather than broader socialist objectives.

THE GREAT MOVING RIGHT SHOW
What few appreciated in 1978 was the depth of the British crisis, which was about to blow apart the post-war settlement and the uneasy series of compromises which had been reached between the parties. Changes in global capitalism were already rapidly transforming Britain's social and industrial landscape. Labour was slow to respond, and came to be seen as part of the problem, vulnerable to a swift war of manoeuvre which outflanked and ultimately overwhelmed its positions. Labour had become fixed in a set of Maginot line defences – protection of the status quo in industrial relations, nationalised industries, local government, and the public sector in general. In his seminal article first published in 1979 Stuart Hall showed how the right-wing onslaught, heralded by a sustained ideological bombardment orchestrated by a new breed of right-wing ideologues, think tanks and intellectuals, had prepared the ground for Thatcher (Hall, 1979).

The boldness of the Thatcher government took the labour movement, as well as many Tories, some of them in the Cabinet, by surprise. The radical phase of the earlier Heath government had been brief, and quickly reversed, so it was widely believed that there could be no rolling back of the gains of the labour movement. Many on the left declared the policies of the Thatcher government to be economically irrational for British capital, and doomed to fail. More perceptive observers such as Ralph Miliband saw them as politically rational, the attempt to inflict lasting defeats on the labour movement, and reshape the balance of power that had been established after 1945 (Miliband, 1982). Stuart Hall did not disagree with that, but focused attention instead on the novel feature of Thatcherism, its success in creating space for its policies by changing the political discourse, establishing a new commonsense about markets and the economy which systematically pilloried the left and organised labour, and opened the way for a host of initiatives which championed free enterprise and individualism.

In retrospect one of the surprising things about Thatcherism is how easy its victories proved to be. The labour movement suffered a succession of major industrial and political defeats. The Labour Party split, and its support plummeted, despite the Thatcher government presiding over a steep recession which left Britain with three million unemployed for most of the 1980s, and led to the disappearance of great swathes of traditional industry and the communities which depended on them. In 1983 Labour went into free fall, achieving only 28 per cent support in the general election, almost being overtaken by the Liberal-SDP Alliance. This dramatic shift of the centre ground of British politics to the right stranded Labour and made it look for a time irrelevant. Labour fought the 1983 election on the most left-wing manifesto it had ever adopted, and achieved one of its worst ever general election results.

The shock was profound, and set in motion the debates and the changes which eventually led to a slow rebuilding of the party. But the blows of the Thatcher era left their mark, and the labour movement was never the same force in British politics again. The unions lost their role as a corporate partner in government, their membership dropped sharply, and militancy declined to very low levels (Marsh, 1992). Following internal party reforms the unions remained an important element in Labour's coalition but were no longer the fulcrum of Labour politics. Labour emerged in the 1990s after four consecutive defeats as less of a *Labour* party than it had ever been, and for the first time more like a European social democratic party. Some even thought a change of name appropriate. The idea was considered but discarded. Instead the informal label of 'new' Labour was used to indicate that this was no longer the old Labour Party.

New Labour was a progressive party rather than a working-class party, reviving older elements of the progressive and socialist traditions (Diamond, 2004). The 'Big Tent' sought the cross-class alliance which Hobsbawm had advocated as the way back to power for Labour. It re-established Labour's link with the professional middle class, and with many other groups which had not normally voted Labour. But the Big Tent was never envisaged as a class alliance, led by a class-conscious political vanguard whose aim was to effect the conditions for a transition to socialism. New Labour lacked the class basis of old Labour, a united labour movement with both industrial and political wings, committed to replacing the existing social and economic order with an alternative one. That whole language and perspective of left politics had become obsolete.

Re-reading the interview in *Marxism Today* which Hobsbawm conducted with Tony Benn in 1981, at the height of the latter's influence in the Labour Party, reveals the extent of the transition that has taken place in the standard discourse of the left (Benn, 1981). It would be impossible to have the same conversation today with any leading figure in the Labour Party. Hobsbawm probed Benn's position, focusing on what he regarded as its main weaknesses – its preoccupation with changing the internal organisation of the party – but praising Benn's determination to develop a left strategy for Labour, to break with the old strategy of compromise and caution which had characterised the Labour leadership in the past.

Stuart Hall's critique of Labour led in a different direction from that of Hobsbawm. He believed that the left had to change its politics by finding a new language to address popular concerns. Above all the left had to get rid of its habit of assuming that all arguments could be settled by invoking the ultimately determining nature of class. It had to abandon all forms of Leninism and vanguardism and learn instead to build social movements from below. Only in this way, thought Hall, might it be possible to wrest back the initiative from Thatcherism and begin to create openings for radical politics, developing a left common sense and a democratic populism to counter the authoritarian populism of the right. *Marxism Today* throughout the 1980s followed the lead which Stuart Hall and Martin Jacques provided, questioning many deeply held assumptions and perspectives of the left – about class, capitalism, trade unions, and actually existing socialism in the Soviet Union and elsewhere, culminating in the *Manifesto for New Times* (1990). *Marxism Today* was radical and iconoclastic about the assumptions and beliefs that had once filled its pages, seeking a new left politics, which would not be bound by the shibboleths and ties of the past, and could come to terms with the rapid economic, cultural and social change.

THE FORWARD MARCH OF NEW LABOUR

The *Marxism Today* project was seen by its left critics as the ultimate revisionism, worse even than the revisionism of the Gaitskellites in the 1950s. Many expected the advocates of 'New Times' to become devotees of Tony Blair and New Labour. But while some of the key contributors to *Marxism Today* such as Geoff Mulgan and Charlie Leadbeater did move in that direction, Martin Jacques and Stuart Hall did not. They soon began expressing deep misgivings about Tony Blair and New Labour, and in 1998, one year into the new government, they contributed to a special one-off issue of *Marxism Today*, headlined 'Wrong'. Stuart Hall delivered a passionate denunciation of New Labour and everything connected with it, refusing to recognise it as in any sense a legitimate exponent of the new politics which he had advocated in the 1980s. New Labour was dismissed by Martin Jacques as having a project for the party but not for the country, exactly the criticism used by Perry Anderson against Wilson in 1964 (Anderson, 1965).

New Labour appears therefore as something of an abandoned child. No one is prepared to admit paternity. Even the social democrats in the Labour Party, both those who left the party like Shirley Williams and David Marquand, and those who stayed like Roy Hattersley, became disillusioned with New Labour, particularly when they found they had been outflanked on their right by Tony Blair and his eager cohorts. Having spent a lifetime fighting against the Labour left, they now found themselves branded as old Labour along with Tony Benn and Arthur Scargill, defenders of policies and positions which were no longer relevant (Mandelson and Liddle, 1996).

The forward march of New Labour has been hard to resist, however, because until recently it was crowned with such electoral success, and the opposition to New Labour was so disorganised and often inept. That Labour could move from the depths of despair in 1983 to the extraordinary triumphs of 1997 and 2001 was remarkable. But, as has often been pointed out, the triumph had quite shallow foundations. The voting system greatly exaggerated Labour's actual support by giving it a disproportionate number of MPs for a relatively modest share of the vote. Under Blair Labour has never matched the vote share that Labour achieved in 1950 and 1951 or even 1966, and with the collapse in turnout in 2001, repeated in 2005, Labour's total number of votes has also been historically low. Having recovered a little in the mid 1990s to over 400,000, individual party membership has collapsed to below 180,000, significantly under the level of the 1980s. The party claimed over a million members in 1952. The modernisers have failed to hold Labour's core support or maintain the Big Tent. Lots of voters and members started slipping away, especially after Iraq. Labour still won comfortably in 2005, but only because of the bias of the British electoral system that rewards the party that wins the largest plurality of votes. Its actual share of the vote was down once more below 40 per cent, back to the levels it had achieved in 1974.

THE FUTURE OF PROGRESSIVE POLITICS

In a long historical perspective, how will the events of the last three decades come to be seen? Hobsbawm has been proved substantially right in his view in 1978 that the forward march of Labour had halted. What he did not foresee was that within a few years it would no longer be possible to talk in terms of a forward march at all. The labour movement was a shadow of its former self, and progressive politics was substantially recast, and class as a key reference point for the politics of the left was abandoned. In this recasting, many hopes which New Labour briefly raised were dashed. Hobsbawm's conception of a new self-confident socialist leadership of the labour movement, reaching out beyond the movement to reconstruct a broad progressive alliance, but retaining the movement at its core, foundered. Likewise Hall's vision of a new progressive populist politics from below, with the imagination and energy to reshape political agendas and discourse also did not materialise. Disappointed too were many of the older revisionists in the party, who thought for a time that Tony Blair might be the heir of Gaitskell and Crosland.

Some of the fury directed at New Labour from the left reflects the disappearance of the labour movement as the rock on which progressive politics could be built. Its loss has been disorientating for socialists, similar in some respects to the loss of the Soviet Union as the guarantee that there was a working alternative to capitalism, however flawed. Many now question whether the Labour Party is any longer a credible vehicle for progressive politics. We have been here before (Marquand, 1991). The Labour Party has never had a monopoly of the progressive cause, and this is particularly true today. Yet it remains the only political formation on the centre-left currently capable of winning general elections and forming governments.

New Labour's achievements in government are often derided, but their contribution as a form of progressive politics is underestimated. Just as the reputations of previous Labour governments have tended to grow the longer the period has elapsed since they were in office, so the same is likely to happen to the Blair government. In time it will be recognised for having defined a new centre ground in British politics, rather than simply accommodating itself to its Thatcherite inheritance, although it did a lot of that as well (Driver and Martell, 2002; Hay, 1999; Heffernan, 1999). The constitutional revolution over which it has presided, although incomplete, will have a lasting effect on how the United Kingdom is governed. The successful management of the economy in the first ten years allowed a significant rehabilitation of public spending and the public services through a substantial increase in the share of public spending as a proportion of national income. A new agenda for social justice has been developed – including the minimum wage, tax credits, and the child trust fund – as well as further progressive social legislation. There are many negative things on the other side of the balance sheet, especially British participation in the Iraq War, the erosion of civil liberties, and the regime of audits and targets in the public sector. But despite its many failings New Labour has a considerable progressive legacy to hand on, not least its fumblings towards a new model for the public services, combining public funding with modes of delivery that promote diversity and higher standards, and which, like Bevan's 1948 NHS compromise, may be the best hope of preserving a universal welfare state and avoiding privatisation.

Is this progressive legacy also a social democratic legacy? There are undoubtedly some social democratic elements, particularly the substantial increase in public spending, which has seen it climb as a share of national income from 37 per cent to 42 per cent, with a doubling in real terms of spending on the NHS and education, the New Deal, and the attack on child poverty. But New Labour has not pursued a traditional social democratic programme and has not developed a social democratic or even a progressive narrative to describe its achievements. There are also many other elements in the mix, such as the reliance on new public management techniques like the internal market and audit culture first deployed under the Conservatives; and there has been no challenge to neo-liberal assumptions about industrial policy, corporate governance, or macroeconomic policy. Ministers have generally refused to talk about redistribution or to accept that reducing the gap between rich and poor is an objective of policy.

Disillusion with New Labour follows a familiar pattern. There was intense disillusion with the performance of the Attlee and Wilson governments, and it contributed to their demise. During the 2005 election and its immediate aftermath there was a strong sense that New Labour had become exhausted. It had broken the mould of British politics by ending Conservative rule and marginalising the Conservatives in a way that Labour had never managed to do before. But it had also made many mistakes and alienated much of its support. Its political position remained precarious even after three election victories. The power of the British media to rig the political agenda and the dominant political discourse against Labour, demonstrated to such effect in the Thatcher years, was still present. New Labour at best neutralised the media for a time, but at a high cost to its reputation for honesty and trustworthiness. By 2005 several of the Tory tabloids, notably the *Daily Mail* and *Daily Express*, had resumed their all-out war against Labour, with only the Murdoch papers still staying their hand. Conscious of the deeply conservative attitudes of the British electorate on many issues, from the EU to asylum seekers, the Labour government took many steps to placate them, so earning the enmity of the liberal media, particularly the BBC, *The Guardian* and *The Independent*. Like its predecessors, the Blair government found itself embattled on two fronts, with few allies.

The challenge for progressive politics after 2005 was whether the pattern of previous Labour governments would repeat itself or whether a new direction could be found; whether Labour could renew itself in office, or whether it would be forced to regroup again in opposition. The party faced substantial problems. Labour Party membership was lower than ever before, while turnout at general elections had dropped to the lowest levels since the suffrage was extended. Prospects for the economy were steadily worsening, and the chances of a serious financial squeeze of a type familiar to past Labour governments, and so far avoided by this one, increased after the election. Labour faced a much more difficult period in which to govern and keep delivering improvements in the quality of public services on the back of a stable economy. For the first time since 1992 a Conservative revival was widely predicted, with the party now led by its modernising wing under David Cameron, and accepting the new emphasis on social justice and public services established by the Blair government. Social democracy is in trouble right across Europe, with only a few Scandinavian oases left. Big economic challenges lie ahead, particularly from the rapid modernisation of China and India, which are likely to cause another new wave of major restructuring in the rest of the industrialised world. Even greater challenges come from the impact of climate change, global poverty, and the remorseless advance of the security state.

There is plenty here for a radical agenda for progressive politics. New Labour has reshaped British politics in the last ten years in ways which are not yet fully appreciated, but it has also fallen short in many areas. It remains to be seen whether New Labour will eventually be recognised as a stepping stone to a renewed progressive politics in Britain, or merely as an interruption before Britain's long Conservative political hegemony resumes again. Which it proves to be is not fore-ordained. New Labour has made many things possible which would not have been possible, and were not imaginable twenty years ago. But it has failed to create much sense of a forward march or a new politics amongst many of its supporters. There can be no going back to older forms of left politics, yet the new forms have proved increasingly disabling. As so often with governments of the left, it is the disconnection with progressive opinion which ultimately erodes the ability to govern. The fault lies on both sides. The chasm is not yet unbridgeable for Labour, but it is beginning to yawn.

REFERENCES

Anderson, P. (1965), 'Towards a Socialist Strategy', in P. Anderson and R. Blackburn (eds), *Towards Socialism*, London: Fontana, 221-290.

Benn, T. (1981), 'An Interview with Eric Hobsbawm' in E. Hobsbawm (ed.), *The Forward March of Labour Halted?*, London: Verso, 75-99.

Crossman, R. (1965), 'The Lessons of 1945', in P. Anderson and R. Blackburn (eds), *Towards Socialism*, London: Fontana, 146-58.

Diamond, P. (ed.) (2004), *New Labour's Old Roots*, Exeter: Imprint Academic.

Driver. S. and Martell, M. (2002), *Blair's Britain*, Cambridge: Polity.

Hall, S. (1979), 'The Great Moving Right Show', *Marxism Today*, January.

Hay, C. (1999), *Political Economy of New Labour: Labouring under false pretences*, Manchester: Manchester University Press.

Heffernan, R. (1999), *New Labour and Thatcherism: Political Change in Britain*, London: Palgrave-Macmillan.

Hobsbawm, E. (ed.) (1981), *The Forward March of Labour Halted?*, London: Verso.

Mandelson, P. and Liddle, R. (1996), *The Blair Revolution: Can New Labour Deliver?*, London: Faber and Faber.

Manifesto for New Times: A strategy for the 1990s (1990), London: Lawrence and Wishart.

Marsh, D. (1992), *The new politics of British Trade Unionism: union power and the Thatcher legacy*, London: Macmillan.

Marquand, D. (1991), *The Progressive Dilemma*, London: Heinemann.

Miliband, R. (1982), *Capitalist Democracy in Britain*, Oxford: Oxford University Press.

Making Labour safe: globalisation and the aftermath of the social democratic retreat

Alan Finlayson

Those wishing to understand or characterise a government often choose to look at the problems faced by an administration, and to evaluate the effectiveness, wit or intelligence with which it responded. Eden's handling of Suez, Wilson's of devaluation or Heath's of industrial action; Callaghan and pay-restraint, Thatcher and the Falklands, Major and the ERM: for each we can look at how they prepared or failed to prepare for a crisis; evaluate the speed and skill of their response; consider how they succeeded or failed to make political capital out of the situation; and assess their management of the governmental machine. This makes for exciting political histories full of narrative momentum, rich characters and unexpected plot twists, but it misses out some of the back-story.

Governments are only partly defined by the way they respond to the problems presented to them. Over-concentration on Macmillan's 'events' obscures the important ideas, philosophies and ideological presumptions that we put into government along with parties and prime ministers. To illuminate these we have to understand that governments are defined not so much by the problems they face as by the problems they identify. Political theories and ideologies help us pick from the flux of social and economic life phenomena that are then made intelligible as issues which necessitate certain sorts of solution: the problems of politics are 'invented' by politicians and political activists. This is not to endorse the fashionably cynical view that politicians fabricate threats, enemies and crises in order to create a 'culture of fear' that justifies extensions of state power. It means only that when we survey the fractured and hard-to-read landscape of contemporary Britain we can identify only a few of its salient features; and our vision is directed by intellectual, ethical and ideological presumptions that perceive some things more easily than others and identify only certain kinds of problem. This is not always a bad thing. Coming to see poverty as a social problem rather than a natural fate was a great political achievement of the nineteenth century. Redefining the 'problem' of homosexuality as the prejudice and discrimination against it rather than its 'corrupting' influence is a contemporary achievement. Politics is often all about how we identify and describe things as problems.

Consider the 'drug problem'. Drugs themselves do not announce to us their own problematic nature. They can be a moral, intellectual or criminal problem, with policy responses developed accordingly: propagating evangelical religion as a cure for addiction (proposed by George W. Bush in his 2003 State of the Union address); demanding better counselling to boost self-esteem; funding education so that people are properly informed; strengthening laws and increasing the funding of zero-tolerance taskforces. How a phenomenon is turned into a problem, an issue requiring remedial action, can vary widely. For contemporary government problems must be defined in ways that make clear how agencies of the state can be deployed in order to address them. Specifying the problematic nature of poverty, anti-social behaviour or terrorism (in ways moral, intellectual and criminal) is central to contemporary political argument. In characterising New Labour we need to do more than tell stories about the interaction of certain personalities, tactics of media management or paranoid image control. We need to find out what problem its advocates believe New Labour to be the solution to.

For many, New Labour first appeared to be an answer to the problem of Labour's unelectability: to a bad image and a hostile media (see Gould, 1998). But there is more to New Labour than this. In addressing policy areas such as constitutional reform, the organisation of the health service, education and welfare it draws on a range of intellectual, political and ethical traditions that help it diagnose particular problems and prescribe cures. Let us look, then, at what its leader says – here is Tony Blair from his conference speech of September 2005:

> The world is on the move again: the change in the early 21st century even greater than that of the late 20th century. So now in turn, we have to change again. Not step back from New Labour but step up to a new mark a changing world is setting for us ...

This was part of a justification for public service reform, an argument that '... now, as before, our values have to be applied anew in changing times', and Blair answered his rhetorical question 'So what is the challenge?' thus:

> It is that change is marching on again. Perhaps our children more readily understand this and embrace it than we do. How quickly has the ipod entered the language and the reality of our lives? With what sense of near wonder was the fax machine greeted, just a few years ago, and already overtaken? A baby is born. The father takes a photo on his mobile. In seconds relatives around the world can see, and celebrate. A different world to the one we were born into. Faster, more exciting, yet with that come threats too. The pace of change can either overwhelm us, or make our lives better and our country stronger. What we can't do is pretend it is not happening.

Change is consistently central to the problems New Labour believes it must address, by adapting values, institutions and individuals to it. At conference in 1994 Blair declared that: 'Today's politics is about the search for security in a changing world'. The precise nature of this change is not always clear, but it often has something to do with new technologies. At conference in 1995 Blair said: 'a spectre haunts the world: technological revolution'. He listed its sources as 'Global finance and Communications and Media. Electronic commerce. The Internet. The science of genetics ... every year a new revolution scattering in its wake, security, and ways of living for millions of people'. Our problem was that 'we live in a new age but in an old country', and so he pledged to bring the 'information superhighway' to every school, library and home. In 1997, at conference again, he said that we 'face the challenge of a world with its finger on the fast forward button; where every part of the picture of our life is changing'.

New Labour has a tendency to think a technological fix is always a good solution (see also ID cards), but this is only an element of a more general conception of change. In his 1998 pamphlet *The Third Way* Blair outlined several ways the world had been transformed: global markets and culture, technological change and the information revolution, the transformed role of women and changing political structures (Blair, 1998: 6). These were the causes of changes in attitudes, aspirations and identities as well as economics, and meant that the modernisation of party, state and society were long overdue. The Third Way was the name given to this diagnosis and prescription (Giddens, 1998). Under the label 'modernisation', public services, central and local government must renew themselves and, in line with the now passing fashions of management science, the Blair government has taken on the task of 'change management', re-engineering and re-training state and society.

It is surely right to think that institutions and individuals ought to adapt practices and attitudes in the light of social and technological change – particularly if it affects the economy or something so deeply significant as the social role and personal identity of women. But we must be clear on the nature of the change, and its causes, and take time to think about how we should respond. The fact that things have changed does not of itself tell us how we need to adapt. The climate, for instance, would appear to be changing, and it seems clear that we must do something in response. But should we prioritise tax breaks for the installation of solar panels, incentives to oil companies for developing new fuel technologies, fitting carbon filters onto all factory chimneys, the building of heat-shielding bio-domes or the availability of sunscreen free on the NHS? This is exactly what is up for debate.

However, Blair tends to go no further than saying that things are changing and we need to change along with them. In fact he often argues his case 'backwards'. Policy is announced and then justified by reference to the imperative of change rather than shown to derive from it in any convincing way – an argumentative failure made up for only with insistent conviction, contributing to New Labour's appearance of arrogant vacuity but in truth expressive only of the intellectual weakness at the core of the project. Here is another part of Blair's 2005 conference speech, this time concerning crime:

> For 8 years I have battered the criminal justice system to get it to change. And it was only when we started to introduce special ASB laws, we really made a difference. And I now understand why. The system itself is the problem. We are trying to fight 21st century crime – ASB, drug-dealing, binge-drinking, organised crime – with 19th century methods, as if we still lived in the time of Dickens.

He wanted 'to allow law-abiding people to live in safety' and this required a 'complete change of thinking'. Blair explained that three things work: a 'radical' extension of summary powers; a 'uniformed presence on the street in every community'; and giving young people a place to go off the street (adding that we should give head-teachers full disciplinary powers, identify problem families early and give a unified agency full power to 'effect change or impose sanctions' with regard to them).

This is typical of Blairite argument. Firstly, the claim is aggressively made (using combative metaphors) that the criminal justice system is stuck in the past and must change radically. Exactly how it is out of date is not made clear (unless we imagine that hooliganism, drug use, alcoholic excess and criminal gangs are unique inventions of the new century and that the system has no previous experience of them). A series of proposals is listed but their derivation is obscure and they are conspicuously lacking in innovation, largely concerned with enhancing the power and effectiveness of the central state when intervening into people's lives. More detail, and occasionally more of interest and value, can be found in policy documents concerning criminal justice, but even here most of the reforms are of bureaucracy or concern the introduction of IT. Compare the highly traditional proposals of Blair to those of, on the one hand, the so-called 'new model conservatives' who, in the name of direct democracy, argue for the development of a British version of the district attorney or, on the other, the Howard League for Penal Reform which recommends new training and support systems for young men in prison to prevent their re-offending. Blair does not ask us to reconsider our nineteenth century jails nor does he reconceptualise 'crime' – a crudely blanket term that obscures a multitude of problems – for a changing world. In the same speech, Blair argued that: 'Today is not the era of the big state but a strategic one: empowering, enabling, putting decision making in the hands of people not government'; but he actually proposed only refinements of traditional state power. This section of the speech ended with an 'amusing' anecdote (not found on the printed text):

> Talking of anti-social behaviour I must tell you this one. Polling day, Manchester, a member of my staff canvasses a young man, nineteen years old, and asks if he's going to vote. 'I'd like to vote Labour, I really would' he said, 'that Tony Blair, he's really sorted my life out'. 'Come on', she said, the polling station's just around the corner'. 'I can't' he said. My ASBO covers the school grounds … true story!

How the disenfranchising of a citizen fits into a twenty-first century legal system is not clear to me, but I suspect Dickens would have found it familiar.

But this is not all there is to the political philosophy of Tony Blair, and on the 2005 speech he stated the mission quite bluntly: 'Some day, some party will make this country at ease with globalisation. Let it be this one'. Blair's 'problem' of change is a codeword for globalisation and the knowledge economy (Finlayson, 2003). In that same speech he employed a nature metaphor of a kind he uses often: 'I hear people say we have to stop and debate globalisation. You might as well debate whether autumn should follow summer' (see also Fairclough, 2000). Globalisation is an unstoppable natural force. There is, to coin a phrase, no alternative. Blair has described the transition to the knowledge economy as 'the fundamental issue' of our time (Blair, 1999), and in 2005 he argued that government regulation to protect a workforce, a company or an industry won't work today because '... the dam holding back the global economy burst years ago ... [Britain's] purpose is not to resist the force of globalisation but to prepare for it, and to garner its vast potential benefits'.

Blair's problem, then, is that Britain is not ready to face the irresistible natural force of change known as globalisation. But he knows what we have to do: 'In the era of rapid globalisation, there is no mystery about what works: an open, liberal economy, prepared constantly to change to remain competitive. The new world rewards those who are open to it'. Back in 1991, writing in *Marxism Today*, Blair called for a 'new agenda' involving the application of technology and the better education of workers, the liberation of 'untapped potential' (Blair, 1991: 32). At conference in 1999 he referenced Rousseau: 'People are born with talent and everywhere it is in chains ... Every person liberated to fulfil their potential adds to our wealth. Every person denied opportunity takes our wealth away. People are the contemporary resource that matters'. Education would 'set free' the nation's knowledge, skills, intelligence and talents, and the public services be set free and opened up to new investors and 'partners'.

Such arguments, centred on change, technology and globalisation, and leading to assertions about reforms of the state and state services, are not found in just one or two speeches, here and there. I have been quoting from Blair's speeches and writings from 1993 to 2005 and could fill up much of this book with yet more examples. Belief in all-embracing and irresistible change, the knowledge economy, new technologies with far-reaching social effects and globalisation are core elements of the Blairite 'philosophy'. The change that matters is global economic change and New Labour's mission is to adapt us all to it. In the knowledge economy, it is believed, wealth resides in individual people, in their talents, skills and potential, which must be allowed to circulate as multiple acts of entrepreneurialism. For Blair 'talent is twenty-first century wealth' and 'the future is people'. The state must develop these kinds of people; it should be an 'enabling', 'generative' or, in Giddens's formulation, 'social investment' state, that assists and rewards people who understand that they are the most valuable of all forms of capital, and are prepared to invest in it – refining it until it reaches the best price possible on the labour commodity market. From university funding to the organisation of welfare to work, the social investment state, in the name of fairness and efficiency, formulates policies that actively individualise people in this way (see Buckler and Dolowitz, 2004; Finlayson, 2003b). The incentive structures of public funding are changed so that it is dependent on the presentation of business plans and development strategies, forcing public servants to think like commercial operators. Market 'discipline' is introduced in the belief that competition will force public sector workers to see their service valuable not for use but for exchange value. University tuition fees and the calculation of funding by reference to the individual modules students take require university teachers to market their courses as attractive commodities, and students to see their choice of course as an investment of their limited funds that requires a return only in the form of qualifications that enhance labour-market value. The welfare claimant must understand him or herself as in need of retraining, reskilling and re-branding so that they can get back on the market. The Child Trust Fund invites parents to see their babies as future human capital, saving in order to invest in its subsequent enhancement, and it ties the child into the banking system and into financial education almost from the moment of their birth.

The problem to which Blairism is the answer is that of how most effectively to subordinate first social policy and then more and more areas of social life to market commodification, in the belief that this enhances freedom, fairness and equality. It imagines that commodities are free (unconstrained they circulate, combine and recombine) and therefore other things should become commodities and compete in the market place so that they too will be free (especially single-mothers and other 'socially excluded' persons); that keeping things away from the market (as old-style Social Democracy did) is tantamount to imprisoning them; that globalisation and new technology have enabled the market to roam throughout society creating more forms of capital (human, social and intellectual), and that we should celebrate, facilitate and enhance this process. Under Keynesianism the economy was understood in terms of the relations of demand and supply – as a chain of production and consumption – and this constituted a clear domain of action and a set of potential policy instruments. For New Labour the knowledge economy requires a new regime, a new kind of state and new policy tools. For traditional social democracy the individual was first and foremost a producer, a worker who should be managed and educated accordingly. For New Labour, in the knowledge economy the individual is a buyer and a seller and the state must help retrain us. Thus, in his 2004 speech *Reforming the Welfare State*, Blair located his social policy vision within the context of a move from 'the traditional welfare state to the opportunity society'. The third term, he said, would aim to 'alter fundamentally the contract between citizen and state'. Mass industrial production has been left behind, he said, and so too must be the mass production of the state. The central focus of a new welfare service would be the individual, with the government seeking to 'empower not dictate ... in place of rigidity and uniformity comes flexibility and adaptability'. This would make it fit to deliver twenty-first century social justice, reconceived as putting 'middle class aspirations in the hands of working class families and their children'. This sounds great – but it means that the citizen must become a consumer and the public servant an entrepreneur, while the aspiration of becoming middle-class in fact means full participation as buyer and seller in the commodity economy. The 'social investment state' needs refined mechanisms for creating consuming and self-capitalising individuals, able to integrate themselves into an economy centred on individualised skills, information and knowledge. This is a supply-side policy where everything is on the supply side: culture, values, attitudes and above all people.

New Labour has not simply capitulated to neo-liberal marketisation. But in seeking to reinvent the state for the neo-liberal era it has failed to think beyond it, and has come to understand freedom and equality in market terms. Its project is to create the conditions and the people appropriate for its vision of new economy capitalism, and it identifies resistance to modernisation only as a problem to be overcome. For New Labour there is no choice about this change. It is not something that politics can take us through or warn us away from. Change is an independent force in politics as natural and inevitable as the seasons. The problem New Labour thinks it must solve is not that of dealing with any particular change but with adapting to permanent change, and it defines political positions in terms of their relationship to it. Old left ideology about the need to seize and direct history has been turned into a need to accommodate to a history that has no particular purpose, to develop a *modus vivendi* with regard to change, what Blair in his third-way pamphlet called 'permanent revolution'.

Innovation certainly can be a good thing, although it is not always necessarily so. Sometimes an organisation or an individual needs not innovation but refinement – the perfection of existing practice and capability rather than the installation of entirely new ones. If one installs a principle of market competition into the public sector, one will get self-seeking market behaviour rather than the improvement of what we already had. It would be better, surely, to regard innovation

and refinement as the outcome of non-mechanistic processes of nurturing and encouragement, seeking to improve service on the basis that the
people who deliver it want to improve it. The evidence suggests that
resistance to public sector reforms derives not from idle workers feath-
ering their nests but from professionals who remain unconvinced that
the reforms will lead to improvement (Taylor-Gooby, 2000). But we
lack the kind of communicative process through which a consensus
about change (and the commitment to it) can be developed. The UK is
unfortunate in having allowed the intermediate institutions that might
serve as locations for such dialogue (unions and professional associations for example) to become dislocated from such processes, leaving a
vacuum between state and people occasionally filled with mutual disregard, mistrust and distaste.

The contemporary political challenge faced by social democrats
involves changing our perceptions of the problems we face. Blairism
observes the technological, social and economic change of recent
decades and decides that the rest of social life is sluggish and indifferent by contrast, and thus is the problem to be resolved, by forcing it to
subordinate itself to 'change'. It fails to see that such changes were
accompanied by the rejection rather than the reform of social democracy, and that this has led to an erosion of important boundaries
between parts of social life. The space between the private activity of
market exchange (self-oriented and instrumental in its approach to the
world) and the public activity of society-making (other-oriented and
ethical in approach) is becoming lost. Society as a whole needs the
dynamism of selfish market activity, but if left unconstrained this has
corrosive effects. The subordination of social to commodity relations
(a process evident not only in the public services but in aspects of artistic culture, or in the wilful exploitation of individual pain by
newspapers and their readers) necessarily leads to the spreading of
instrumental and self-oriented behaviour across society – to literally
anti-social behaviour (Marquand, 2004). Social democrats must do no
more or less than assert the virtue of human relations based on non-
market interactions, and seek to develop policies through which
democratic control can be regained over our social life: supporting and
fostering all kinds of non-profit and non-market organisation; democ-
ratising relations in workplaces; involving community and campaign
organisations in political and legislative processes (Bentley, 2005). Such
things can be small expressions of 'traditional values in a modern
setting', rooted as they are in the sort of sentiment found in the
Manifesto of the Labour Party of Great Britain from 1923, when it
asked voters to: 'believe in the possibility of building up a sane and

ordered society, to oppose the squalid materialism that dominates the world today, and to hold out their hands in friendship and good will to the struggling people everywhere who want only freedom, security and a happier life'.

REFERENCES

Bentley, T. (2005), *Everyday Democracy*, London: Demos.

Blair, T. (1991), Interview in *Marxism Today*, October.

Blair, T. (1998), *The Third Way*, London: Fabian Society.

Blair, T. (1999), *Speech to the TUC*, September, London: Labour Party.

Buckler, S. and Dolowitz, D. P. (2004), 'Can Fair be Efficient? New Labour, Social Liberalism and British Economic Policy', *New Political Economy*, 9 (1), 23-38.

Fairclough, N. (2000), *New Labour, New Language*, London: Routledge.

Finlayson, A. (2003a), *Making Sense of New Labour*, London: Lawrence and Wishart.

Finlayson, A. (2003b), 'Squaring the Circle: New Labour and the New Ignorance Economy, *Mediactive*, 1 (1), 25-36.

Giddens, A. (1998), *The Third Way*, Cambridge: Polity.

Gould, P. (1998), *The Unfinished Revolution: How the Modernisers Saved the Labour Party*, London: Abacus.

Marquand, D. (2004), *The Decline of the Public*, Cambridge: Polity.

Taylor-Gooby, P. (2000), 'Blair's Scars', *Critical Social Policy*, 20, 3, pp. 331-348.

New Labour and the problem of democracy

Colin Crouch

Much of what has made New Labour new can be understood through the idea of the post-modern; or, as it sometimes called, the 'second modern'. Its approach to democracy partly follows this model, but with some striking exceptions. On closer inspection these exceptions merely reveal problems within the idea of the post-modern or second modern itself; from this we can derive some deeper under-standing of why New Labour has been an inadequate response to the needs of a progressive democratic politics in the early twenty-first century. We also derive further lessons about the political opportuni-ties that present themselves to those who see themselves as constituting the centre left. However, ambiguity remains, as it is difficult to deter-mine how valid and viable is the idea that we are living in a post-modern era.

Each of those five sentences is enigmatic or problematic. The rest of this essay will be spent in unpicking them, culminating, as the last of them promised, with some lessons for action. First, the issue must be set in a wider context. In a recent little book (Crouch, 2004) I defined a state of 'post-democracy', a situation where, although the formal institutions of democracy continue and might even be strengthened, the heart goes out of it; there is a wearying of democratic energy. The signal event that triggered the idea was the almost total lack of concern that US citizens showed when George Bush was declared to have 'won' the 2000 presidential election with the aid of extraordinary electoral manipulation in Florida, the state governed by his brother, and highly partisan behaviour by the Supreme Court. This cynicism of the American people contrasted so strongly with the eagerness to take advantage of their infant democratic opportunities, and to be concerned that they were 'clean' opportunities, by people in South Africa and many parts of central Europe.

Partly this question can be seen as a probably unavoidable process of democratic entropy, but it seemed to me that there are also some more contingent social changes in progress at the present time that speed the process in the settled democracies of the western world. The broad social divisions of class and religion on which twentieth century mass democracy in this part of the world was founded have changed as we move from an industrial to a post-industrial occupational structure and from Christianity to secularisation. (The latter change applies to Europe but not the USA, and it is notable how a resurgent Christianity is refuelling political enthusiasm in the latter country.) In particular, new classes of lower- and middle-income groups being formed by the services economy have not found many means of autonomous political organisation. The established parties try to process identities for them, but top-down, using marketing techniques rather than real engagement, and on the basis of their own existing preferences rooted in the industrial past.

Meanwhile, the globalisation of capitalism has changed the balance of power between business and governments, releasing the largest and most powerful firms from dependence on and commitment to any particular polity or territory. They become footloose, making it necessary for government to be increasingly attentive to their desires if they want their investment.

The social bases of mass democracy becoming uncertain and the demands of multi-national capital becoming clearer and more insistent, parties and governments responsible to mass electorates respond in the only way that we should expect. They draw closer to the world of big business, allowing their structures to overlap as they seek to close the latter in an embrace, and ever more anxious to provide policies that will please business interests above all others. In turn, the mass public becomes remote, dimly understood, and an object of manipulation through electoral marketing strategies that vary little from party to party. This hardly describes a vibrant democracy, but it is not undemocratic either, as all the institutions and structures of democracy remain in place. It is post-democracy. Among its consequences are some that look distinctly pre-democratic. In particular, political parties return to the role that they played until (in the UK) the late nineteenth century: rival cliques of persons seeking political office, places at court, responding to no distinctive social bases or ideals, but to the same power pressures, and differing little in goals. David Marquand (2004) has captured this in his insightful distinction between court politics and republican politics.

My book was not describing a situation that I considered to exist anywhere already, but one towards which the political systems of several countries were moving. It was a dystopia, and the purpose of a dystopia is to warn rather than to predict. The book was also cast at a general level. Although its concerns with the growth of international business power were rooted in a leftist perspective, it considered parties and politics across the spectrum, and in a number of countries. In what follows I shall bring this analysis home, and concentrate on the particular case of Britain and New Labour.

I am therefore concerned here with the role of a party in democracy, rather than democracy as such. The image of the future political party that emerges from *Post-democracy* resembles that of the old Austro-Hungarian Empire, which became known as 'the prison house of nations', locking up the aspirations for self-determination of people across central and south-eastern Europe. The post-democratic party is the prison house of political principles. Parties continue to monopolise the articulation of political contest, and those who aspire to use democracy to put principles into practice within a society have no choice but to route themselves through a party; but parties, returning to their old role of cliques of courtiers, keep those aspirations trapped within their out-dated shells. Does this image have echoes in the current state of British Labour?

NEW LABOUR AND THE POST-MODERN

First it is necessary to understand what New Labour is about. Some critics complain of its lack of coherence, its appearance of determined energy and drive being little more than rushing about in many directions. I think that this is mistaken. If one takes, first, the situation of the post-democratic party described above (uncertain about its social base; very certain of the demands of business interests), and, second, the idea of the post-modern, one can make sense of more or less everything that New Labour stands for. The second, the idea of the post-modern, needs elaboration.

Deriving originally from architecture, the idea of the post-modern has very useful wider political and social implications. Modernist architecture (which interestingly mainly developed within the Austro-Hungarian Empire) was that early twentieth century style that emerged in reaction to the heavy ornateness and nostalgia of the late nineteenth century. At first, it meant clean, clear lines, simplicity, functionalism. While some of its best achievements were in domestic architecture, it was ideally suited to the large structures increasingly needed to house the manufacturing processes and public and private bureaucracies that were to become the overwhelmingly characteristic institutions of the twentieth century. Over time, it lost its freshness; clarity and functionalism became drab uniformity and an unappealing adaptation to the needs of large organisations. Massive metal, concrete, and glass towers became just as oppressive and monotonous as late nineteenth century Gothic, without the latter's warmth and detail.

Gradually clients and general publics began to rebel and demand something less uniform, more varied, less ostensibly hierarchical and rigid. Eventually the challenges to modernism produced something that came to be called the post-modern. Buildings would comprise a jumble of styles from various periods and with no overall uniting theme. By the 1980s the idea spilled into the general culture: artistic creation took what it wanted from wherever it wanted, creating ever shifting and flexible novelty, mixing up motifs and themes from various periods and styles.

This was a theme that could hop across from culture into politics, as dissatisfaction with characteristic mid-twentieth century institutions matched much of the dissatisfaction with the buildings that housed them. The big, rigid, hierarchical enterprises of the industrial period were in crisis, as were the public bureaucracies of the welfare state and trade unions associated with inflexible, top-down regulation of the labour market. People were demanding more freedom and choice than these structures allowed, whether it was Fordist industry's 'you can have any colour so long as it is black', or the 'one size fits all' welfare state. There was therefore a strong desire for a politics that was a contrast to all this: for light, non-hierarchical, networked structures that could frequently change; markets instead of top-down bureaucratic and professional allocations; flexibility, constant novelty. Similarly, there was no place for monothematic ideologies pitted like dinosaurs against each other and presenting stark alternatives of state versus market.

The most articulate popular exponent of this interpretation of the late twentieth century was the German sociologist, Ulrich Beck (1991; 1997), who preferred the term *'zweite Moderne'* ('second modern') to 'post-modern'. This was accurate, as in their political meaning the new developments were not departing from the *longue durée* of the growth of rationalism and purposive design that have been the historical hallmarks of modernism in its long triumph over traditionalism and acceptance of fate. The idea of this being only a 'second' modern works all right if one starts, as did the architects, with the modernism of the early twentieth century. If however one is reflecting on the whole period of modernity and rationalisation that seems to have started in the early sixteenth century, then this should count as more like the eighth or ninth modern. The caveat is important when confronting those who talk about 'in the past' as though all the past centuries were a seamless web until the sudden break and launch into a new future which the speaker associates with his or her own life time.

Within the UK Beck's ideas were developed by Anthony (Lord) Giddens, a leading articulator of New Labour ideas (Beck, Giddens and Lash, 1994; Giddens, 1990; 1998). These concepts spoke directly to the condition of the New Labour reformers, who were in rebellion against what they saw as an old Labour heritage that embodied all the heaviness of 'old' modernism. One New Labour writer, Charles Leadbeater (2000), echoed the post-modernist slogan 'everything vanishes into air' in the title of his book describing the new economy of light structures: *Living on Thin Air*. Also, restructuring would be a permanent state of being, not an occasional upheaval of a stable normality. 'What works' would become the political equivalent of the 'anything goes' of pick and mix post-modern style.

Many late-twentieth-century corporations had followed the same pattern, with delayered and apparently flat hierarchies, and a tendency rapidly to change organisational forms, brand names and products, as masses of capital combined, separated, and recombined. Their workforces could not expect jobs for life or to pursue a single professional career; instead they would accept frequent change and reskilling. New Labour found kindred spirits in this corporate world.

Once one grasps the central energising force of these readily available guidelines for countering what had become an uncongenial and now dysfunctional past set of mid twentieth century institutions, one has very little difficulty in understanding what the New Labour governments have been about. Most apparent inconsistencies disappear; one or two exceptions to that will be discussed below. Given the problems of the terms post-modern and second modern for a political movement that defines itself as modernisation, I shall here use the terms 'old modern' to indicate the stereotyped 'heavy' institutions of the mid-twentieth century, and 'new modern' for the kinds of innovations associated with the New Labour project. In some respects, though, New Labour is truly post-modern. Just as post-modern architecture features odd bits of medievalism and other motifs from earlier centuries, New Labour's idea of 'modernisation' can extend to little historical throw-backs like reducing the rights of habeas corpus and encouraging schools that teach creationism.

THE NEW LABOUR APPROACH TO DEMOCRACY

I indicated one of the exceptions to the new modern in New Labour in my second sentence: 'Its approach to democracy partly follows this [new modern] model, but with some striking exceptions'. True to a new modern approach to democracy in the government's record have been:

- the challenge to hierarchy in the Freedom of Information Act;
- a number of innovations in parent, patient and other consumer involvement in public services, but with a preference for the market as a means whereby democratic choice is exercised;
- an informal, approachable style;
- the experimenting with various semi-formal types of governance, mixing public and private actors, as in the inchoate structure of the English regions, which is neither democratic nor integrated with other levels of government;
- the willingness to entertain a diversity of structures as with devolution to Scotland, Wales, (when it behaves itself) Northern Ireland, and in a different way London;
- a half-reformed House of Lords;
- the creation of waves of quangoes with uncertain relationship to the main edifices of democracy;
- a form of cabinet government that comprises series of informal and unminuted conversations among unrecorded small groups of ministers;
- the more or less permanent restructuring that has affected most branches of public service.

Readers may evaluate the efficacy and democratic quality of these in diverse ways; but they are innovations; they are consistent with the idea of the new modern; and at least some have improved the quality of British democracy. Rather than discuss their relative merits, which would be a complex task offering no easy answers, I want to concentrate on some characteristics of New Labour's approach to democracy that are at first sight difficult to reconcile with the general image of the new modern. I refer to:

- the extreme centralism of government itself, with 10 Downing Street dominating the functional ministries (its means of doing this have been informal, but the outcome is as rigid as anything associated with the old modern);
- the rigid behaviours centrally imposed throughout public service by narrow forms of performance measurement;

- continuation and acceleration of the long-term shift in power from local to central government, that might well have been regarded by New Labour as a hallmark of old modern government (again, the means are new; targets, indicators, contracts, but the outcome is an intensification of central control);
- the manipulative and centralised approach to communication embodied in the concept of 'spin';
- the relegation of the parliamentary party and the party in the country to channels for top-down communication from the centre rather than for two-way goal- and policy-formation.

In these respects New Labour has been an apotheosis of top-down, hierarchical old modernity rather than its nemesis. Also uncomfortable to New Labour's democratic record is its predilection for plutocracy. Particularly in its programmes for the marketisation of public services, it has drawn heavily on a small group of rich individuals and firms who advise government, second staff as advisers to ministries, and then sometimes pick up lucrative contracts. This is matched by the flow of political advisors back through the revolving door into the privileged circle of firms – a feature of post-democracy. This may be a different kind of elite circle from those of the past, but it is elite, exclusive, and highly centralised.

In other words, the new modern agenda is being implemented by highly old modern means, carrying forward many of their undemocratic characteristics and adding some new ones. Neither the wider democracy nor the structures of the party are invited to join the new flexible world of horizontal relations and loose, flexible networks that bind the new politico-corporate elite together.

NEW LABOUR AND THE PROBLEM OF POWER

However, completely true to the new modern ideal is the slogan 'what works'. If plutocracy 'works', then what is wrong with plutocracy? If structures should be infinitely malleable, what is wrong with firms and government departments being mutually penetrable? This brings us to my third opening sentence: 'On closer inspection these exceptions merely reveal problems within the idea of the post-modern or second modern itself; from this we can derive some deeper understanding of why New Labour has been an inadequate response to the needs of a progressive democratic politics in the early twenty-first century.'

New Labour writers have never confronted the issue of what happens to power in a world of dissolving and recombining structures. The impression given by many, including Giddens and Leadbeater (but not Beck), is that in the new form of amoeba-like financial capitalism, power vanishes into thin air. Power and worry about it were part of the world of big, solid, hierarchical enterprises of the industrial period and their attendant oppositions, and are no longer problematic.

There are two difficulties with this. One is that capitalist power has not disappeared at all. True, capital regroups to form new firms; firms themselves are frequently restructured and lose their identity in extended and infinitely flexible sub-contractor and out-sourcing chains; logos and brand names change frequently, the rebranding skills of marketing experts being seen as more reliable than solid reputation for the products themselves. But behind the apparent lightness and malleability lie very solid, powerful concentrations of wealth, often with a global reach. Some sectors that, during the Fordist period, could sustain a national diversity of middle-sized producers – like motor vehicles, newspapers, steel, retail trade – are now concentrated globally in a small number of giant enterprises. Although at one level we live in a more market-driven economy than thirty years ago, in many sectors it is a market dominated by heavy concentrations of power, that are then highly active in political lobbying.

New Labour has no positions from which to confront this. Obsessed with the threats posed to both democracy and efficiency by old modern approaches to lobbying – business associations, industrial enterprises seeking protection – it cannot see the different but equally problematic dangers presented by its new forms. It no longer perceives – as did the eighteenth and nineteenth century fathers of liberal capitalist ideas – the tension that should exist between firms and the institutions of politics, to check the deficiencies of the market and corporate power.

The second problem is that the New Labour state has itself resembled new capitalism, in both its constant restructuring and rebranding, and in its concealment of a centralised concentration of power behind all the informality and networking. It has been preoccupied with becoming part of a form of society which, with considerable accuracy, it believes to be emerging; and with (rightly) avoiding trying to fight features of that society with instruments and institutions of the past.

However, this does not mean that it is an easy matter to establish the basis for a democratic challenge to the new concentrations of power in global capitalism. As I tried to show in *Post-democracy*, the challenge is severe, and the social base on which it could be mounted is weak. The problems of contemporary democracy go deeper than some mistakes made by a generation of political leaders.

WHERE DO WE GO FROM HERE?

My final opening sentence was: 'We also derive further lessons about the political opportunities that present themselves to those who see themselves as constituting the left in contemporary society.' The most obvious, too obvious, lesson is that democracy must be allowed to join the new modern, and be shaken free from the heavy old forms of monolithic parties, manifesto mandates, and centralised government of which New Labour remains an unreformed part. That way it might somehow find its own level, discovering the flexibility and new institutional forms that it needs to meet the new challenges. To return to my analogy of the Austro-Hungarian Empire: has the time not come to break out of the prison house of the party and let new political principles of the centre left find their place in the changed society?

The same goes for interests as for principles: the interests of the under-privileged, those on moderate incomes, those who find it a struggle to manage work in a 24/7 environment while bringing up children who must behave well and succeed educationally, but who have been unable to find autonomous forms of political expression and articulation, are held captive by New Labour with nowhere else to go, while it swings to the right of the spectrum in order to gather and please new bases of support. Would not new movements, or trade unions that did not feel an obligation to avoid rocking the boat, be better able to find new ways of grouping and articulating these interests?

This alternative is of course already partly there, in the form of social movements and cause groups that have become the foci of demotic political energy in our society far more than the parties. This is where the critique is being developed of global warming, of the conduct of multi-nationals in the third world, of problems of human rights and working life. These constitute the authentic new modern forms of political activity. Let us assume that parties, as I described in *Post-democracy*, go back to their old pre-modern role as more or less meaningless organisers of cliques of seekers after office. In that case their relationship to democracy changes from being (as they were for most of the twentieth century) its main articulators and shapers, to being the recipients of its pressures. Those seeking office will still need votes, and social movements and civil society groups who are well organised will be able to try to lend them, temporarily, the votes of their supporters – without becoming trapped in their prison house. This is more or less how American parties and pressure groups function already.

But this can be deceptive. Social cause groups, particularly those of the left, are rarely strongly placed to challenge the centralised powerhouses of government and business power, especially when these are united. Pressure groups of the right are usually better funded and better placed in the relation to the mass media. Once again we encounter the failure of concepts of the new modern to deal with power. The analogy of the Austro-Hungarian Empire also contains a warning. For at least the first eight decades that followed their liberation from its prison house, the nations of central and south-eastern Europe did not have a great experience. Other giant forces – Nazi Germany, then Soviet Russia – were waiting to gobble them up; or, as in Yugoslavia, they failed to resolve their own internal hatreds.

Of course, this is only an analogy; it does not follow that a collapse of the Labour Party as its best activists deserted it for cause groups and social movements would mean disaster. However, a part of the analogy rings uncomfortably true. The problem for the nations liberated from the Hapsburgs was that the rest of Europe did not comprise just a set of smaller entities like themselves; there were other big beasts out there. Behind the apparently light and frothy structures of the new modern there usually lie some hard structures – a post-modern building uses reinforced concrete just as much as a modernist one. A new politics needs to acquire the same toughness, and it is difficult to see how this can be done without parties, which remain the core institution connecting government to democracy.

The ideal-world solution to which this conclusion leads is for the Labour Party to engage on a further self-renewal from within, just as it did through New Labour in the first place. However, the task was easier in the 1980s, for two reasons. First, old Labour had demonstrably reached the end of its road, and a complete change of direction was essential for mere survival. This is not the case today. Second, the changes introduced by New Labour amounted to 'kicking with the pricks', moving in directions that would be rewarded by global capitalism and the conventional wisdom of neo-liberalism; and it was deserting a power base among the poor and weak to seek one among the rich and powerful. Today the interests which need to be embraced are weakly articulated, and serving them requires challenging precisely those forces to which New Labour appealed.

Internal renewal of the party will happen only if there is a severe external challenge from the forces I have identified. The party itself will not wholeheartedly embrace such issues as the threat to the environment, work-life balance, or the dangers of a partial privatisation of the welfare state spinning out of control. It will make gestures towards these themes, but it will want to keep control, to prevent them from being articulated autonomously, because they are too dangerous.

Matters will only go further than that if there is a massive haemorrhage of support from the party to minor parties and movements that do articulate these causes robustly and without being reluctant to embarrass. We need both those working within and those without, but the latter must keep their independence from the former.

The vote in the House of Commons in February 2006 to ban smoking in most internal public spaces serves as a small but optimistic prototype of what such a new politics might deliver. Tireless campaigners in pressure groups worked away at this issue until the political elite of both Conservative and Labour Parties saw public support draining away from their prior positions. Finally they rushed to embrace the new popular mood, even though this meant upsetting some business lobbies, and despite in Labour's case a contrary manifesto commitment.

I have not followed the path of what should be expected from an essay on reforming democracy. This is supposed to talk about making it easier to vote, about extending the use of the internet for two-way communication, improving the level of political knowledge, etc. By themselves and operating within the context of present structures, these reforms just shore up the outmoded organisations of the main parties, making it less necessary for them to reform. In present circumstances low electoral turnout could be a healthy signal, as it demonstrates that the way the parties are organised, articulate interests and address citizens are not working. And this might force them to re-examine themselves in a more profound way.

HOW VALID IS THE POST-MODERN IDEA?

Most of the above arguments have taken for granted as valid the idea that modernity (or post-modernity) has entered a new historical phase characterised by frequently changing structures – though I have strongly contested the frequently associated idea that somehow inequalities of power and institutions that wield power have ceased to be important. But is the institutional instability and frequency of change that we see around us a new state, or does it just mark the fact that we are in a period of transition? If the latter, transition to what? And can we yet determine the shape of new types of structure, new modes of doing politics?

There are certainly signs that an incredible lightness of being is not the sole characteristic of our times. The new prominence of military activity, a growing apparatus of security and recourse to incarceration, clear trends towards the restrictions of rights, all suggest an alternative future. These are hardly light, fluffy institutions. Further, as already noted, capitalism is increasingly dominated by a small number of multi-national corporations; the entry of private firms into the provision of public services is likely to see a similar kind of structure once it settles down. The decline of trade unions leaves a growing majority of the workforce with no autonomous collective voice to set against an increasingly professional and bottom-line-driven management. In the UK, though not everywhere, government is becoming more centralised, local government being reduced to monitoring private contracts, the terms of which are determined in Whitehall.

A new period of institutional heaviness and growing inequalities of power may well constitute the emerging next stage of economic and political development, temporarily concealed by the emphasis on change. There is a warning here to those of us enthusing over the flexibility and adaptability of new social movements. This is fine if it is seen as a transitional period of ferment, while we learn what causes and organisational forms are viable. Beyond that lies a need to work out the lineaments of new strong forces. Further, as the ecology movement and the social movements that have developed around the World Trade Organisation already well understand, it is pointless developing movements that have only national reach. The real, enormous democratic vacuum is at the level of global regulation. That is why these new oppositional movements try to combine local roots with global reach; it is a tall order, but they are on the right path.

Many people in established social democratic parties and trade unions are wary of movements like those that emerged at Seattle and Genoa, because of the unruly and anarchistic elements that are clearly part of them. They sometimes seem to be undermining all those decades when left-wing movements struggled to get out of the streets and into the corridors of power. But what are those corridors worth now that globalisation and the ossification of the party system have weakened so many of the routes to effective power? And what will happen if the forces of the centre left confine themselves to an increasingly courtly politics of place-seeking, leaving the articulation and mobilisation of discontent, not so much to anarchists within the social forum movement, but to the racist populists who have their own interpretation of what is wrong with globalisation?

Over forty years ago George Woodcock, general secretary of the Trades Union Congress, told unions that they needed to get out of Trafalgar Square and into the corridors of Whitehall. Today, the unions are largely excluded from those corridors again, while it has become very difficult to demonstrate legally in Trafalgar Square.

REFERENCES

Beck, U. (1991), *Politik in der Risikogesellschaft*, Frankfurt am Main: Suhrkampf.

Beck, U. (1997), *The Reinvention of Politics*, Cambridge: Polity.

Beck, U., Giddens, A. and Lash, S. (1994), *Reflexive Modernization: Politics, Tradition and Aesthetics in the Modern Social Order*, Cambridge: Polity.

Crouch, C. (2004), *Post-democracy*, Cambridge: Polity.

Giddens, A. (1990), *The Consequences of Modernity*, Cambridge: Polity.

Giddens, A. (1998), *The Third Way*, Cambridge: Polity.

Leadbeater, C. (2000), *Living on Thin Air: The New Economy*, Harmondsworth: Penguin.

Marquand, D. (2004), *Decline of the Public*, Polity: London.

Britain after Blair, or Thatcherism consolidated

Zygmunt Bauman

The years of Tony Blair's premiership will probably be recorded in British history as, first and foremost, the institutionalisation (entrenchment, normalisation) of Thatcherism. Whether explicit or implicit, presumptions of the Thatcherite model of government have become the *doxa* of Tony Blair's rule (*doxa*: ideas 'thought *with*', though seldom if ever thought *about*, let alone through). During these years, Margaret Thatcher's 'rugged individualism' and hotly contested disavowal of the social state have become an undebatable principle of state policy, a 'there is no alternative' creed, the benchmark of *modernity* – that supreme value in Blair's policies, meant to replace those of social justice and solidarity.

At a deeper level, Blair's years will probably be noted as the completion of Thatcher's substitution of *homo oeconomicus* for the *citizen*. The Thatcherite philosophy of the polity as primarily an 'order of egoism' (to borrow John Dunn's recently coined phrase (2005)) has been finally fixed and confirmed as the state religion, this time pretending to represent 'the way the things are' rather than postulating 'as things should be'. To Thatcher's revolution Blair's years have been the time of retrenchment, conservation and consolidation.

Consolidation of the Thatcherist 'order of egoism' has been conducted, bafflingly, under the codename of 'modernisation'. 'Modernise' has been Blair's answer to all problems presumed to require successive crisis-management operations. Blair has indeed been an obsessive and compulsive moderniser; as the years have gone by, few areas have escaped the modernising zeal; and few institutions have retained the pristine form in which the new Blair management inherited them from Thatcher and her orphans and immediate successors. Increasingly, with the dearth of as yet unaffected objects, yesterday's 'modernised' settings have become the objects of new rounds of modernisation. Rather than being conceived of as a one-off operation, 'modernisation' has turned into the 'permanent state' of social and political institutions, further eroding the value of duration, and the prudence of long-term thinking, and reinforcing the ambience of uncertainty, temporariness and until-further-noticeness on which capitalist markets are known to thrive.

This has been, arguably, the greatest service that Blair's state-management has rendered to the cause of Thatcher's neo-liberal revolution, and to the uncontested rule of the 'invisible hand' of the market ('invisible' because it eludes all efforts to watch, let alone direct and correct, its moves; and an unbeatable 'hand' that a poker player could only dream of). All their particular characteristics notwithstanding, the successive bouts of modernisation have made the invisible hand yet more invisible, putting it ever more securely beyond the reach of the available instruments of political intervention. Paradoxically, the overall effect of the 'active government's' activity has therefore been a gradual yet relentless shrinking of the political realm, through the 'subsidiarising' of ever new political functions to non-political market forces. And as the deregulation and privatisation of the economy has proceeded at full speed, as nominally state assets have one by one been released from political supervision, as personal taxation for collective needs has stayed frozen, thereby impoverishing the collectively-managed resources required for such needs to be met – the all-explaining and all-excusing incantation 'there is no alternative' (also a Margaret Thatcher legacy) has turned unstoppably (more correctly, *has been* turned) into a self-fulfilling prophecy.

The process has been thoroughly explored and its direction thoroughly documented, so there is little point in restating once more what is (or has had every chance to become, if given attention) public knowledge. What has been left somewhat off the focus of attention however (while deserving all the public attention it could muster) is the contribution of every single measure of the Thatcher/Blair programme to the *progressive decomposition and crumbling of social bonds and communal cohesion* – precisely the assets which could enable Britain to face, confront and tackle the old and new, past and future, challenges of on-going globalisation.

ERODED HUMAN BONDS, WILTED SOLIDARITY

The above mentioned assets, which for the last thirty years have been consistently eroded and impoverished in Britain, have been prudently preserved in Sweden and other Nordic countries, where they are now deployed successfully to resist and withstand potentially destructive and incapacitating pressures. As Robert Taylor recently found out:

> today Sweden alongside neighbouring Denmark, Norway and Finland remains an affluent and equitable society with a high standard of living for the overwhelming majority of its citizens ... Under the often paternalistic direction of a rational and enlightened state, Sweden led the way in the conscious formation of what were genuinely social democratic societies. This admirable development reflected a conscious and deliberate government strategy to translate the abstract concept of social citizenship into a practical reality (Taylor, 2005).

Contrary to what one would expect, given British 'third way' derision of their continental neighbours' predilection for a meticulously regulated labour market, high taxes and high-powered trade unions (all mortal sins in the neo-liberal bible), post-Blair Britain will have to take off from a position sorely handicapped in comparison to many other European countries. In an oft-told Irish joke, a passer-by asked by a driver 'how can I get from here to Dublin' answers 'if I wished to drive to Dublin, I wouldn't start from here'. The plight of Britain is anything but a joke, and yet one is tempted to follow the example of the Irish passer-by, and answer in the same way the question about how to get from where we are now to some British version of a truly social-democratic society – one like Sweden, with its flourishing economy managing to obey the principles of social justice and sustain social solidarity, with its universal principles of common provision offered to all citizens irrespective of their income, its progressive redistributive taxation and its all-embracing national insurance system and high and steady economic growth: it would be much better to start from elsewhere. Blair's years have made the starting point singularly unfit for the task. Alas, post-Blair Britain has no choice but to start from the point to which the long years of Thatcherism – in its original and Blairist forms – has brought the country.

Among many bright ideas for which Margaret Thatcher will be remembered was her discovery of the non-existence of society ... 'There is no such thing as "society" ... There are only individuals and families' – she said. But Tony Blair may well yet be remembered for making that figment of Thatcher's imagination into a fairly precise description of the real world, as seen from the *inside* of its inhabitants' experience.

True, a Britain pulverised into solitary individuals and (crumbling) families could not be built without Thatcher having first thoroughly cleared the building site. It could not be built without her successes in incapacitating the self-defence associations of those who need defence; in stripping the incapacitated of most of the resources they could use to recover collectively the strength they don't have individually; in severely curtailing both the 'self' and 'government' bits in the practice of local self-governments; in making expressions of disinterested solidarity into punishable crimes; in 'deregulating' factory and office staffs (once greenhouses of social solidarity) into aggregates of mutually suspicious competitors, in the style of 'each man for himself and devil takes the hindmost' (or 'Big Brother' style); or in finishing the job of transforming the universal entitlements of proud citizens (through the humiliating 'means test' procedure and the war against 'welfare spongers') into the stigma of the excluded accused of living 'at the taxpayer's expense'. But Thatcher's innovations have not only survived the years of Blair's prime-ministership by and large intact, but have emerged from them reinforced, and more than ever immune to political intervention.

Equally, many of Thatcher's innovations in the language of politics have survived and emerged reinforced – today, as much as twenty years ago, this language speaks of individuals and their families as subjects of duties and objects of legitimate concern, while referring to 'communities' mostly as sites where the problems given up on by society need to be dumped (as with the mentally disabled who need to be transferred from state-run medical care, or the unemployed, under-educated and prospectless youngsters who need to be kept away from mischief).

And as more and more water has flowed under the bridges, the world before the Thatcherite revolution has been all but been forgotten by older people, and has never been experienced by the young. To those who have forgotten or never tasted life in that other world, it seems, indeed, that there is no alternative to the present one ... Or rather, any alternative has become all but unimaginable.

DISMANTLING THE SOCIAL STATE
More than anything else, the 'welfare state' (which I prefer to call the *social* state, a name that moves the emphasis from material gains to the principle of their provision) is a kind of arrangement of human togetherness that resists the present-day 'neo-liberal' tendency to shift the task of fighting back against and resolving socially produced problems onto individual men and women. The social state does not expect individuals, with their admittedly inadequate skills and insufficient resources, to resolve all problems on their own, and seeks to protect its members from the morally devastating competitive 'war of all against all'.

A state is 'social' when it promotes the principle of communally endorsed, collective insurance against individual misfortune and its consequences. It is that principle – declared, set in operation and trusted as working – that lifts abstract 'society' to the level of felt-and-lived community; to use once more John Dunn's terms, it replaces (or at least attempts to mitigate) the mistrust and suspicion-generating 'order of egoism' with the confidence and solidarity-inspiring 'order of equality'. And it is the same principle which lifts members of society to the status of *citizens* – that is, makes them stake-holders in addition to being stock-holders; beneficiaries but also actors responsible for the benefits' creation and availability; individuals with acute interest in the common good, understood as the shared institutions that can be trusted to assure the solidity and reliability of a state-issued 'collective insurance policy'. The application of that principle may, and often does, protect men and women from the plague of *poverty*; most importantly, however, it stands a chance of becoming a source of solidarity, one able to recycle 'society' into a common, communal good, thanks to the defence it provides against the horror of *misery* – that is, the terror of being excluded, of falling or being pushed over board from the fast accelerating vehicle of progress, of being condemned to 'social redundancy' and otherwise designated as 'human waste'.

The 'social state' was, in its original inception, an arrangement aimed at serving precisely such purposes. Lord Beveridge, to whom we owe the blueprint for the post-war British 'welfare state', believed that his vision of a comprehensive, collectively endorsed insurance for *everyone* was the inevitable consequence and indispensable complement of the liberal idea of individual freedom, as well as an indispensable condition of *liberal democracy*. Franklin Delano Roosevelt's declaration of war on fear was based on the same assumption. Freedom of choice, after all, brings along with it uncounted and uncountable risks of failure; many people find such risks unbearable, fearing that they may exceed their personal ability to cope. For most people, freedom of choice will remain an elusive phantom and idle dream, unless the fear of defeat is mitigated by an insurance policy issued in the name of community, a policy they can trust and rely on in case of personal defeat or a blow of fate.

If freedom of choice is granted in theory but unattainable in practice, the pain of hopelessness will surely be topped with the humiliation of haplessness; the daily coping with life challenges is after all the workshop in which individuals' self-confidence, and self-esteem, is cast or melted. Without collective insurance, there is no stimulus for political engagement – and certainly not for participation in a democratic game of elections. No salvation is likely to arrive from a political state that is not, and refuses to be, a *social* state. Without social rights *for all*, a large and in all probability growing number of people will find their political rights useless and unworthy of attention. If political rights are necessary to set social rights in place, social rights are indispensable to keep political rights in operation. The two rights need each other for their survival; that survival can only be a joint achievement.

Historical records show that with every extension of suffrage societies moved a step further toward a comprehensive, fully-fledged social state, even if that final destination was not visualised in advance and needed many years, and several ever more ambitious parliamentary bills, for its contours to become visible. And it is easy to understand why that trend was overwhelming. As more categories of population were granted electoral rights, the 'median voter', around whose satisfaction political parties had to orient themselves in order to win the elections, moved to the relatively more deprived parts of the social spectrum. At some point, inevitably though rather unexpectedly, a seminal shift had to occur; the line was crossed that divided those who sought political rights in order to make sure that the personal rights they *already enjoyed* would be neither withdrawn nor interfered with, from those who needed political rights in order *to gain* personal rights that they did not yet possess and would have found inoperable if formally granted.

At that point, the stakes of the political game underwent a watershed-like change. From the task of adjusting the political institutions and procedures to the *already existing* social realities, democracy moved to the task of deploying political institutions and procedures so as to *reform* social realities. It moved, in other words, from political democracy towards *social* democracy – from the task of *conserving* the extant balance of social forces to that of *changing* it. The effect of crossing the threshold was the coming into being of an unfamiliar and heretofore unconfronted need to use political rights to *create* and *assure* personal rights, instead of merely confirming them and firming them up. Instead of *growing up from* the already formed 'civil society' yearning for a political shield, the body politic in its new form of a social state faced the task of *laying the foundations* of civil society in the parts of society where it had been thus far missing, and assisting its extension.

John Kenneth Galbraith was one of the first to note the early symptoms, indeed prodromal signs, of the abandonment of that task, the retreat from the effort it involved, and, soon after, the retreat from any intention of pursuing it (1993). He blamed the withdrawal of the politicians' favour from the welfare state on the new 'affluent majority' – made into a majority largely thanks to the generosity of the 'affirmative action' endemic to welfare provision, and now eager to burn the bridges behind it (together with their own past, since the past is now seen as 'politically incorrect', due to its failing of the neo-liberal test). The affluent are inclined to use their newly gained majority status to vote the underdog out of their rights to state-endorsed collective insurance (now re-named 'the abuse of taxpayers').

The formal, legally endorsed, transformation of membership of the democratic body politic, from being a privilege to being the universal endowment of its subjects, preceded the *passage to* the social state. The present-day *retreat from* the social state is being followed by an informal, matter-of-fact and legally unnoticed retraction of the exercise of political rights to the level preceding the universalisation of suffrage. Once more, the membership of the democratic body politic is on the way to becoming a privilege – *de facto* if not *de jure*.

RETREAT OF AND FROM POLITICS

The void created as citizens massively retreat from the extant political battlefields, and reincarnate as consumers, is filled (to the acclaim of some enthusiastic observers of new trends) by ostentatiously non-partisan and altogether un-political 'consumer activism' – which however engages an even smaller part of the electorate than the orthodox political parties manage to mobilise in the heat of election campaigns (the parties are no longer trusted to represent their voters' interests and so are fast falling out of public favour). Frank Furedi warns: 'Consumer activism thrives in the condition of apathy and social disengagement. Consumer activists regard their campaigns as a superior alternative to parliamentary democracy. Their attitude to political participation expresses a strong anti-democratic ethos'. It needs to be seen clearly that the consumerist critique of representative democracy is fundamentally an anti-democratic one. It is based on the premise that unelected individuals who possess a lofty moral purpose have a greater right to act on the public's behalf than politicians elected through an imperfect political process. Environmental campaigners, who derive their mandate from a self selected network of advocacy groups, represent a far narrower constituency than an elected politician. Judging by its record, the response of consumer activism to the genuine problem of democratic accountability is to avoid it altogether in favour of opting for interest group lobbying (Furedi, 2000).

'There is little doubt that the growth of consumer activism is bound up with the decline of traditional forms of political participation and social engagement': that is Furedi's verdict, based on his thoroughly documented study.

'Consumer activism' is a symptom of the growing disenchantment with politics. To quote Neal Lawson: 'as there is nothing else to fall back on, it is likely that people then give up on the whole notion of collectivism and therefore any sense of a democratic society and fall back on the market [and, let me add, their own consumer skills and activities] as the arbiter of provision' (Lawson, 2004: 18).

A recent survey, conducted at the start of the 2005 electoral campaign, suggested that, contrary to popular perception, the British public was not apathetic about politics. A report from the Electoral Commission and the Hansard Society found that 77 per cent of those polled by MORI 'were interested in national issues'. It also adds, however, that, this high level of basic interest should be set against the figure of only 27 per cent who feel that they actually have a say in the way the country is run.

One could surmise (and this was borne out by the elections that followed) that the actual number of people going to the electoral booths would fall somewhere between those two figures, and would land perhaps closer to the lower of the two. Many more people declare their interest in whatever has been endorsed in the press or on TV as a 'national issue' than consider it worth the effort of walking to a polling station in order to give their vote to one of the political parties on offer. Furthermore, in a society oversaturated with information, headlines mostly serve the cause of effacing from public memory the headlines of the day before; the issues which the headlines recast as 'of public interest' have only the life expectation of a butterfly, and only a meagre chance of surviving from the date of the opinion poll to the date of the election. Most importantly, these two things – an interest in national issues and participation in the extant democratic process – just don't come together in the minds of an increasing number of citizens. The second does not seem to be a relevant response to the first. Perhaps it is considered altogether politically irrelevant.

According to *The Guardian Student* website of 23 March 2004: 'three quarters (77 per cent) of first year university students are not interested in taking part in political protests ... while 67 per cent of freshers believe that student protest isn't effective and doesn't make any difference, according to the Lloyds TSB/Financial Mail on Sunday Student Panel'. The website quotes Jenny Little, editor of the student page in the *Financial Mail on Sunday*, who says: 'Students today must cope with a great deal – the pressure to get a good degree, the need to work part-time to support themselves and to get work experience to ensure that their CVs stand out from the crowd ... It's not surprising that politics falls to the bottom of the pile of priorities for this genera- tion, though, in real terms, it has never been more important.'

In a study dedicated to the phenomenon of political apathy, Tom Deluca suggests that apathy is not an issue in its own right, but 'more a clue about the others, about how free we are, how much power we really have, what we can fairly be held responsible for, whether we are being well served ... It implies a condition under which one suffers' (2005). Political apathy 'is a state of mind or a political fate brought about by forces, structures, institutions, or elite manipulation over which one has little control and perhaps little knowledge'. He explores all those factors in depth, to paint a realistic portrait of what he calls 'the second face of political apathy' (the 'first face' being, according to various political scientists, an expression of contentment with the exist- ing state of affairs, the exercise of right to free choice, or more generally a phenomenon 'good for democracy' for the reason of 'making mass democracy work' – as stated in the classic 1954 study by Bernard Berelson, Paul Lazarsfeld and William McPhee, later rehashed by Samuel Huntington, and obliquely opted for by Anthony Giddens when welcoming the advent of 'consumer activism').

And yet if one wants to decode in full the social realities to which rising political apathy provides a clue, and which it signals, one would need to look further than this 'second face' that, as Tom Deluca rightly claims, has been unduly neglected or only perfunctorily sketched by mainstream scholars of political science. One would need to recall the meaning of 'democracy' – that once made it the battle cry of the same deprived and suffering masses who today turn away from exercising their hard-won electoral rights.

DEMOCRACY IN TROUBLE

A 'social state' is the ultimate modern embodiment of the idea of community: that is, an institutional incarnation of community in the modern form of an abstract, imagined totality, woven of reciprocal dependence, commitment and solidarity. Social rights tie that imagined totality to the daily realities of its members, and found that imagined totality in the solid ground of life experience; these rights certify the veridity and realism of mutual trust, and of trust in the shared institu- tional network that endorses and validates collective solidarity. 'Belonging' in the form laboriously put together and upheld by a democracy committed to T.H. Marshall's 'trinity of rights' for all, translates as trust in the benefits of human solidarity, and in the institutions that arise out of that solidarity and promise to serve it and assure its reliability.

More than anything else, the present retreat of the state from the endorsement of social rights signals the falling apart of a community in its modern, 'imagined' yet institutionally safeguarded incarnation. More generally, it signals the new frailty of human bonds. 'Freedom from', deprived of the company and co-operation of 'freedom in' and 'freedom through' the state, is increasingly presented as self-sustained and standing on its own feet; or as capable of finding all the support it may eventually need outside the realm of politics and certainly outside the domain of specifically political institutions.

Much like two centuries ago – a time well before the bold attempt to rebuild a 'lost community' in its updated modern form – the abdication of the state from exercising its (but presumed-to-be, or hoped-to-become communal) authority is nowadays proclaimed to be its most desirable virtue. 'Deregulation' – as that on-going, keenly recommended and widely praised abdication is now called – is coupled with 'privatisation' – the transfer of a growing volume of once politically (and so democratically) performed functions away from politics, and thus from a democratic supervision and guidance; and together they rebound on the receiving end as 'individualisation' – the dismantling or loosening of webs of interpersonal and group networks of obligation, commitment and solidarity, and a growing self-referentiality in individual life pursuits.

Elected authorities are no longer charged with the task of integrating the disparate and all too often conflicting and potentially antagonistic interests of free-roaming individuals; they are not expected to connect, but to disconnect – to separate and keep apart. By design or by default, they are busy paving the way for the 'order of egoism' and dismantling the socio-political conditions under which a solidarity-promoting 'order of equality' could take roots and thrive. The unanticipated consequence of this (or perhaps anticipated, given the proliferation of 'focus groups' invented to deputise for the constituencies as guides to policies?) is a massive exodus from politics by those who feel expropriated from the stake-holder's right to shape the policies that affect them (or were born too late to understand the meaning of this phrase, let alone claim and practice what it once implied).

FROM SOCIAL STATE TO PERSONAL SAFETY STATE?
Under such circumstances, an alternative legitimisation of state authority and another formula for the benefits of dutiful citizenship is

urgently needed; and it is currently being sought in terms of the state's protection against dangers to *personal safety*. The spectre of the misery caused by social degradation, against which the *social* state swore to insure its citizens, is being replaced by one calling attention to dangers to the body and to possessions – the threats of a paedophile let loose, a serial killer, an obtrusive beggar, mugger, stalker, prowler, poisoner, terrorist. Or, better yet, all such threats rolled into one, in the figure of the illegal immigrant, against whom the security state (or more precisely: the *personal safety* state) promises to defend its subjects tooth and nail.

In October 2004 BBC2 broadcast *The Power of Nightmares: The Rise of the Politics of Fear* (see Beckett, 2004). Adam Curtis, its writer and producer, pointed out that though global terrorism is an all-too-real danger likely to be continually reproduced inside the 'no-man's land' of the global wilderness, a good deal, if not most of, the officially estimated terrorist threat 'is a fantasy that has been exaggerated and distorted by politicians': 'It is a dark illusion that has spread unques-tioned through governments around the world, the security services, and the international media'. It is not too difficult to trace the reasons for the rapid and spectacular career of this illusion: 'In an age when all the grand ideas have lost credibility, fear of a phantom enemy is all the politicians have left to maintain their power'.

Numerous signals of the shift in state-power legitimisation to that of the personal safety state could be spotted well before 11 September – even if the shock of the falling Manhattan towers, reproduced in slow motion and for months on end on millions of TV screens, was needed for the public to absorb the news, and for politicians to re-harness popular existential anxieties to the new political formula. It is not coin-cidence that (according to Hugues Lagrange (2003)) there were comparatively few signs of a public concern with rising criminality during the post-war years he describes as the 'glorious thirty'; spectac-ular 'safety panics' and loud alarms about rising criminality (coupled with ostentatiously tough responses by government, and rapidly rising prison populations – 'substitution of a prison state for the social state') started to occur from the middle 1960s onwards in countries which had the least developed social services (like Spain, Portugal or Greece), and in the countries where social provision started to be drastically reduced (like the United States and Great Britain). No research conducted before 2000 showed any correlation between the severity of penal policy and the volume of criminal offences, though most studies did discover a strong correlation between 'incarceration push' and falling proportions of 'market-independent social provision'. All in all, the new focus on crime and on dangers threatening the bodily safety of individuals and their property has been shown beyond reasonable doubt to be intimately related to 'sentiments of vulnerability', and to follow closely the pace of economic deregulation, and the related substitution of individual self-responsibility for social solidarity.

The triumphant 'order of egoism', with its paraphernalia of individualism, fading human bonds and wilting solidarity, is but one side of a coin whose other side bears the stamp of globalisation. In its present, purely negative form, globalisation is a parasitic and predatory process, feeding on the potency sucked out of the bodies of nation states and their subjects. As observed by Jacques Attali a while ago, the nations organised into states are forfeiting their influence on the general run of affairs, and abandoning to global (anonymous) forces all means of directing the destiny of the world or resisting the many forms that fears may assume. Society is no longer protected by the state; it is now exposed to the rapacity of forces it does not control, and no longer has any intention, hope or even dream, of recapturing and subduing.

It is for this reason that state governments, struggling day in and day out to weather current storms, stumble from one ad-hoc crisis-management campaign and one set of emergency measures to another, dreaming of not much more than staying in power after the next election, but otherwise devoid of farsighted programmes or ambitions, not to mention visions of any radical resolution to the nation's recurrent problems. 'Open' and increasingly defenceless, the nation state is losing its might, as it simultaneously evaporates into global space (together with its political acumen and dexterity), and 'subsidiarises' to individual men and women. Any power to act that is left in the hands of the state and its organs is dwindling gradually to a volume sufficient perhaps to furnish a large-size police precinct. The reduced state can hardly manage to be much more than a personal safety state.

Few people, however, would be ready to claim for their own *personal* choices the kind of irresistible authority that once emanated from the *socially* enforced order – and if they do make such a claim, there is but a meagre chance that it will be accepted and respected by others. The social setting for the actions of contemporary men and women is now reminiscent of a theatre of perpetual war, in which innumerable *reconnaissance* battles are launched and fought daily; and these battles tend to be aimed not at promoting a consistent (let alone universal) code of behaviour, but at testing the limits to individual choices, and assessing the amount of ground that could be gained by the determined deployment of the right weapons. Once a deficit of legitimacy becomes the feature of all bids and claims, actions undertaken in their name and for their sake (once upon a time perceived as the proper expressions of an unquestionable, immutable and irresistible order of things) tend to be recast as acts of violence; that is, as specimens of *il*legitimate coercion. A widespread impression of a fast rising volume of violence results: another prolific source of fears.

Such fears are scattered and diffused over the whole spectrum of life pursuits. Their sources stay hidden and stoutly refuse mapping. If only we could focus our apprehensions, and any actions intended to mitigate the pain they cause, on an object that it was possible to *locate* and so, hopefully, would be amenable to *control*! As long as we fail to do that, we are doomed to grope in the dark.

Perhaps clinging to well-lit places is a less harrowing choice, even if it proves pointless in the end. Unable to slow down the mind-boggling pace of change, let alone to predict and determine its direction, we focus therefore on things which we can – or believe that we can, or are assured that we can – influence: we try to calculate and minimise the risks of falling victim to the uncounted and uncountable dangers that the opaque world and its uncertain future holds in store. We are engrossed in spying out 'the seven signs of cancer', or 'the five symptoms of depression', or in exorcising the spectre of high blood pressure and high cholesterol level, stress or obesity, or in spying out youngsters with olive skin, shifty eyes and bulky rucksacks. In other words, we seek *substitute* targets on which to unload the surplus existential fear that has been barred its natural outlets; we find such makeshift targets in taking elaborate precaution against inhaling someone else's cigarette smoke, or ingesting fatty food or 'bad' bacteria (while avidly swilling the liquids promising to contain the 'good' ones); we guard against exposure to sun, or unprotected sex, and strive to keep the neighbourhood stranger-free. Those of us who can afford it, fortify ourselves against dangers visible or invisible, present or anticipated, known or as yet unfamiliar, scattered but ubiquitous, through detoxicating the interiors of our bodies and homes, locking ourselves behind walls, stuffing the approaches to our living quarters with TV cameras, hiring armed guards, driving armoured vehicles or taking martial arts classes. Those of us who can't afford all this sink into depression, or seek oblivion in drugs, or a malefactor who could be blamed for their misery.

AFTER ALL THAT – WHERE TO START?

To quote John Dunn once more – 'individuals can, and conspicuously do, shape their own lives in very different terms. But it is difficult (and possibly flatly impossible) for them to override the main structuring principle of the form within which they live' (2005). More to the point, as Karl Marx observed long time ago – people make their history, but not under conditions of their choice.

Under conditions which they did not choose, but in which they found themselves at the end of Blair's rule, 'individuals' must first reintegrate themselves as 'people' before they earnestly set out to renegotiate, and change, 'the main structuring principle of the form within which they live'. Pondering the words of the Swedish Social Democratic Programme of 2004 would be a good point to start:

> Everyone is fragile at some point in time. We need each other. We live our lives in the here and now, together with others, caught up in the midst of change. We will all be richer if all of us are allowed to participate and nobody is left out. We will all be stronger if there is security for everybody and not only for a few.

Just as the carrying power of a bridge is measured by the strength of the weakest pillar, and grows as it is strengthened, the confidence and resourcefulness of a society is measured by the security and resourcefulness of its weakest sections, and grows as they grow. Social justice and economic efficiency need not be at loggerheads; nor do fidelity to socialist values and the ability to modernise swiftly, which can be achieved with little or no damage to social cohesion and solidarity. On the contrary, as the social democratic practice of our Nordic neighbours has demonstrated, 'the pursuit of a more socially cohesive society is the necessary precondition for modernisation by consent' (Taylor, 2005: 32). Though this is a kind of truth that is hard to perceive in the dusk of the Blairist era, this is the truth nevertheless.

There is more than one response to the pressures of globalisation and globalised competition. The excuse that 'there is no alternative' was the biggest and most odious political lie of the late twentieth century. It depends on the post-Blair generation whether or not the twenty-first century will go down in history as the time of calling its bluff.

REFERENCES

Beckett, A. (2004), 'The Making of the Terror Myth', *The Guardian*, 15 October.

Deluca, T. (2005), *Two Forms of Political Apathy*, Philadelphia: Temple University Press.

Dunn, J. (2005), *Setting the people free: The Story of Democracy*, London: Atlantic Books.

Furedi, F. (2000), 'It's just a failure of nerve', *New Statesman*, 12 January.

Galbraith, J. K. (1993), *The Culture of Contentment*, Harmondsworth: Penguin.

Lagrange, H. (2003), *Demandes de sécurité*, Paris: La Seuil.

Lawson, N. (2004), *Dare More Democracy*, London: Compass.

Taylor, R. (2005), *Sweden's new social democratic model*, London: Compass.

Labour, Britishness and concepts of 'nation' and 'state'

Gerry Hassan

INTRODUCTION

The Labour Party for most of its history has not thought very much about the concepts of 'nation', 'state' and Britishness. It has tended to assume these as a given and unproblematic.

Labour has never mounted a plausible and persuasive counter-story of what the UK and idea of 'Britain' means. Instead, it has adopted a narrative of the British nation and state which has been shaped by the dominant forces of British history, and thus by views which were established long before Labour ever came into existence.

In the arena of territorial politics and the composition of the UK, Labour has articulated Britishness and state power as an indivisible part of its progressive credo, despite strong decentralist traditions at its inception. It has bought into a conventional British and Westminster model of politics, based on parliamentary sovereignty, centralism and a misunderstanding of the nature of the UK.

The terminology used in these debates – nation, state, nation-state, national identity, nationalism – are all contested, not fixed. The idea of a nation is founded on an 'imagined community', with a sense of belonging, history, continuity and connection to the past, and even 'the dead nation', giving it an almost transcendent power (Anderson, 1983). Nations and states can rise and fall, while nations and states do not need to be co-terminous. There has historically been a difference between the German 'nation' and 'state'. A nation can exist without a state: the Poles pre-1918 were subjugated under three Imperial empires; the Kurds today. Mainstream Labour has traditionally given little thought to such matters and this has weakened its approach on questions of nation.

This chapter will explore Labour's attitudes to different elements of the UK nation, state and ideas of territoriality. While not attempting a comprehensive overview it will examine the experience of constitutional reform, the post-9/11 environment, and the nature of the British relationship with the US. It will conclude by assessing the ambiguities, confusions and consequences inherent in many of the debates on the nature of the UK.

THE LABOUR NATION: LABOUR AND BRITISHNESS

Labour has throughout its history been a very British party – a party of British sensibilities, the British polity and identities. But although Labour is profoundly British, it has had an ambivalent relationship with the idea of a 'British nation' – which has long been seen by many as synonymous with Tory ideas of Empire and reactionaryism. Labour's counter-story about 'the nation' has been about 'the people': 'The Labour nation was to be sustained by the social democratic state': full employment, redistribution, social justice (Aughey, 2001: 90).

Historically Labour has been the party of the outsiders of British society: the working classes, the industrial cities, Scotland, Wales and the North of England. It was often the party of the respectable, organised outsiders: those who came together and had a sense of voice and power, but who were clearly not insiders of the British state. These disenfranchised parts of Britain gave Labour much of its sense of itself. In particular, the importance of Scotland and Wales was central to Labour identity. The party had deep roots in the two nations, stretching back beyond its birth into Gladstonian radicalism, but given voice by Keir Hardie and John Wheatley in Scotland, and Nye Bevan in Wales. Significant elements of Labour's mythology came from and converged in Scotland and Wales: the combination of heavy industry, the importance of the coalfields, the rising power of the unions, and a suspicion of Westminster tradition.

The interweaving of Labour's story and Britishness can be seen in the crucial moment of the summer of 1940. Part of the British establishment came close to considering a peace deal with Hitler, and one major factor preventing this was the Labour Party. After the fall of Chamberlain, Labour entered the Churchill War Coalition, and contributed to the forging of the wartime domestic progressive consensus which changed British society, and in the process changed Labour. This was the point where Labour came in from the cold, and stopped entirely being a party of outsiders. Instead, it became a party of the British state.

Anthony Barnett's powerful polemic about the Falklands war coined 'Churchillism' to denote the long-term consensus which came out of this alignment. The British political classes became committed to a set of national myths in 1940 centred on 'an island people, the cruel seas, a British defeat, Anglo-Saxon democracy challenged by a dictator' (1982: 48). This lineage ran from the fall of France to the Falklands, and was based on the idea of the UK standing against aggression. It is not an accident that arguments surrounding those twin disasters of post-war foreign policy, Suez and Iraq, were frequently framed by invoking the ghosts of 1930s appeasement and the need to stand up to dictators. 'Churchillism' was also the crucial point where the British dependent relationship with the US was woven into the fabric of its outlook. This meant that Britain could exert influence far beyond its economic or military reach through its history and ties with the US. 'Churchillism' gave support to the idea of the UK as a bridge between the US and Europe: 'the Blair Bridge Project', in Garton Ash's words, with an 'unambiguous commitment to the United States, ambiguous commitment to Europe' (Garton Ash, 2004: 41).

British political debate has been informed by the experience of what Andrew Gamble has penetratingly called the idea of England as a 'world island' which led to the development of a multinational Great Britain and subsequently 'a much wider Greater Britain'. Making a distinction between England and Britain, Gamble – drawing on Churchill's idea of the three circles of Britain – identifies four circles of England: the British Union, British Empire, Anglo-America and Europe, which overlap (Gamble, 2003: 15, 30). These are not just national, but transnational political spaces which influence and affect the notion of what the UK is. These four circles express different identities which sometimes overlap and are sometimes exclusive, with each having a particular centre of power and politics: Westminster/Whitehall, London, Washington and Brussels. And each of the four has contributed specific doctrines to British politics and the state: the Crown in Parliament, the open seas naval doctrine of the Royal Navy, the world liberal capitalist order, and European integration.

Labour has from the defining point of 1940 seen the British nation as a champion of progressive values at home and abroad. The role of the Commonwealth has been important here in providing a non-imperial alternative to Tory ideas of Empire, but it is also true that supposedly radical policies such as unilateral nuclear disarmament have been presented as allowing Britain to act as a moral force for good in the world.

Even counter-stories to Labour's mainstream, from left-wing accounts such as that of Tony Benn at the height of his influence, are shaped by Labour's myth and folklore. Benn stressed that democratic socialism was a 'home grown British product which has been slowly fashioned over the centuries': 'Its roots are deep in our history and have been nourished by the Bible, the teachings of Christ, the Peasants' Revolts, the Levellers, Tom Paine, the Chartists, Robert Owen, the Webbs and Bernard Shaw who were Fabians, and occasionally by Marxists, Liberals and radicals ...' (Benn, 1979: 146). On one level, Benn was trying, by emphasising the British antecedents to his politics, to neutralise attacks by his opponents that there was something profoundly alien and unBritish in Bennism. However, this argument, in its search for respectability, comes close to a Whig benign view of British history, whereby those without power slowly accrue it without any drastic change and upheaval (Jones and Keating, 1985). The Bennite view of progress is not that different, fundamentally, from the evolutionary argument of T.H. Marshall's concept of citizenship, with the idea being, in this left version, that it eventually leads to the democratisation of the state. It is also, revealingly, a very English account of the British political radical tradition, and one in which the English are synonymous with the British.

If we move to the present day, we can see that the present generation of Labour leaders like to wax lyrical about what Britishness is, but they have remained conspicuously silent on the nature of the British state. Gordon Brown, in particular, has attempted to develop a set of ideas about 'progressive Britishness' – to challenge Tory notions, to make sense of the UK post-devolution, and to take on the Scottish nationalists. In more recent years, this has become interwoven with his campaign to become prime minister, and trying to creatively answer the issue of a Scottish based prime minister in an asymmetrical union.

Brown has tried to articulate a set of values about Britishness which are not shaped by the Empire, the military and religion, but instead by institutions such as the NHS and BBC and the liberal, inclusive values they contain. Brown argues that the old Tory idea of nation is ill-suited to the new and old nationalities that now make up the melting pot of the UK. He appeals to a progressive Britishness, centred on 'talking about the qualities of a people, of the collective experience they have shared over time' (quoted in Richards, 1999). One of the problems with such a project, however, is that it is so inclusive that it is near to being meaningless.

LABOUR AND THE BRITISH STATE: CHALLENGES FROM WITHIN AND WITHOUT

British Labour has for long articulated a very conservative view of the British state – a seamless view of political, economic and social rights slowly being accumulated by the people. Labour has uncritically taken the Whig view of British history, and wrapped its own history and advance around it, interweaving the two in 'The Forward March of Labour', which shaped the party's view of its history to the high point of the 1950s and beyond.

A particularly important strand in Labour's view of the state has been Fabianism, which stressed the neutrality of the British state, its basic fairness and adaptability to progressive ends and the impartiality of the administrative classes. Fabianism was intrinsically an elite ideology – centred on the importance of experts and technocrats – formed at the end of Victorian Liberal Britain – but its assumptions found sustenance in mainstream Labour reformism.

The coalescing of Labour's rise as a party of government and power and the use of the state in 1940-45 and in the 1945 Attlee government gave Fabian centralism a vital impetus as Labour, post-1945, turned its back on its decentralist, anti-state strands. Instead, Labour became incorporated in, and a party of, the Westminster system; a party which believed in the politics of the centralised state, the idea of mandate and parliamentary sovereignty. For all its roots in the periphery, Labour turned against Scottish devolution under Attlee and Gaitskell's leadership (Keating and Bleiman, 1979). The power of the British state was where progress and the politics of redistribution lay.

In the 1960s and 1970s Britain went into a period of economic decline, and social democracy began its long crisis; this was also the time when the British state started to unravel. It is no accident that the challenge to the British state was both internal, driven by the challenge of Scottish and Welsh nationalism, and external, in the growing instability in the world economy from the 1970s on.

It is more than coincidence that the junking of Wilson's National Plan in 1966-67 – and with it the Croslandite dreams of economic growth, faith in planning and greater equality – happened at the same time as the challenge by the SNP and Plaid Cymru to Labour's hegemony in Wales and Scotland. Their respective victories at Carmarthen in 1966 and Hamilton in 1967 changed British politics in ways unimaginable today; Hamilton happened sixteen days before Wilson finally bowed to the inevitable and the pound was humiliatingly devalued. This period saw the idea of 'the Labour nation' under threat from within and without, and was the beginning of the end of post-war British social democracy.

Labour's response to the challenge from the Scots and Welsh was painful. First they tried to punt it into the long grass, through the typical Wilson device of a Royal Commission (the Kilbrandon

Commission). But this did little to stem the tide and the internal and external challenges to the state fused again in an even more potent challenge in 1973-74. The second wave of Scottish nationalism corresponded exactly with the world economic shock of the same period. UK Labour responded with an embarrassing U-turn – in the Scottish case telling Scottish Labour to adopt a pro-devolution position: from 1974 until the end of the Thatcher-Major era, Labour tried to have the best of both worlds. They sought to preserve the Westminster politics of parliamentary sovereignty, while at the same time satisfying Scottish and Welsh demands for greater autonomy. Labour had to be seen in Scotland and Wales as answering national demands for greater democracy, but at the same time it wanted to be seen as maintaining its belief in the British state, and not threatening the territorial integrity of the UK.

This led Labour to insist until 1997 that its devolution proposals did not need to involve addressing the over-representation of Scottish MPs, or issues like the territorial secretaries of state. However, when Labour brought in devolution after the 1997 election, in a bold move it announced it would cut the number of Scottish MPs from 72 to 59, though retaining the territorial ministers and departments. At the same time, the White Paper on Scottish devolution states, in Diceyian terms: 'Scotland will remain an integral part of the United Kingdom, and the Queen will continue to be Head of State of the United Kingdom. The UK Parliament is and will remain sovereign' (Scottish Office, 1997, x).[1] Thus Labour continued to try to combine both devolution and Westminster sovereignty.

Labour's response to the internal challenges to the British state and social democracy have been characterised by a lack of élan and a lot of pain, but it has been possible to observe, since the 1970s, some kind of relationship back to older Labour traditions of decentralism and localism. Labour's reaction to the external challenges it faced was less sure footed, and had no previous traditions to draw upon to justify. These external challenges have shaken every assumption in the party about economic growth, the role of government and the state, and redistribution, and created the conditions for both Thatcherism and Blairism. This, ultimately, has been a much more bruising road.

LABOUR AND TERRITORIAL POLITICS: WHY THE UK HAS NEVER BEEN A UNITARY STATE

The United Kingdom is understood in conventional political discourse as a unitary state. The British state, its political classes, Labour itself, all share this belief. A unitary state, however, is a polity based on a degree of centralism, uniformity and very little local and regional differentiation. The United Kingdom is not and never has been a unitary state. It is actually a union state – a polity which is neither a unitary state nor a federal state, but a state which has significantly different arrangements across different parts of its territory.

The fact that the UK is not a unitary state is hinted at by its title: United Kingdom of Great Britain and Northern Ireland, and is even more underlined by the fact that it came into being by a Treaty of Union between England and Scotland, which preserved Scottish institutions, distinctiveness and autonomy. The UK has developed in a way which has accommodated, rather than abolished, these differences, for example in the Union of 1707, and the Government of Ireland Act of 1920, which created the Northern Irish statelet and instituted home rule; subsequently, Labour's post-1997 reforms have established democratic bodies in Scotland and Wales and reinstituted Northern Irish home rule. None of these arrangements would be possible in a unitary state.

However, where the unitary state does exist is in the mindset of the UK government – at its very centre. The UK political establishment – the Cabinet, leaderships of the main parties, the senior civil service, the Westminster media – understand and act as if the UK was a unitary state. They see the politics of Westminster as all-powerful and important, and understand the politics of the UK through the prism of the centre. For example, the Thatcher-Major administrations' imposition of unpopular policies on Scotland – seen at its worst with the poll tax – was only possible because they adhered to a rigid, dogmatic belief in the supremacy of a unitary politics.

This approach continues to this day, and can be seen in Labour's limited understanding of constitutional reform. Labour's reforms have tried to emphasise that the politics of the old state – of parliamentary sovereignty – remain unchanged; the politics of the centre have remained the same, and in many ways have actually got worse. The new devolved institutions in Scotland, Wales and Northern Ireland are little understood by the centre. The confusion which occurred in the botched cabinet reshuffle of June 2003, which created the Department for Constitutional Affairs (DCA), was a revealing episode. There was an initial confusion at the heart of government about whether the Scotland and Wales territorial departments had in fact been abolished or not – before it became clear that they had become part of the DCA. The above example illustrates the centre's lack of grasp or understanding about the constitutional fabric of the UK, both in devolved areas and in the centre itself.

The whole programme of constitutional reform carried with it much hope and rhetoric pre-1997, but Labour never fully embraced this, and implemented the programme half-heartedly and with caution. There is a strong case to be argued that Labour has not yet enacted a programme of constitutional change – for all the flights of fantasy in the early days – because such a programme would involve changing the nature of the centre, its understanding of what it has done, and the relationships it has with any new institutions (Hassan, 2003). The centre remains at its core unreformed – not just in the sense of the failure to implement proportional representation and elect a second chamber – but in the deeper sense that it clings on to the idea of parliamentary sovereignty, and has not changed its idea of itself. The senior leadership of Labour remain supporters of a unitary state politics, and, for all the problems they have faced in recent years, have faced very little challenge in this area.

LABOUR, THE REVOLUTION THAT NEVER HAPPENED AND THE 'WAR ON TERROR'

Labour's constitutional reform programme saw a flurry of bills in the first term, with twenty bills passed. This seemed a very British revolution at the time, with a degree of muddle and lack of an over-arching design – 'a revolution of sleepwalkers' according to Marquand (1999). Many commentators saw this in the early days as potentially far-reaching, however: 'a turning point' according to Barnett which was the beginning of the end of the 1688 ancien regime (1997). However, in the second term, any sense of impetus was lost. Constitutional fatigue set in, and proportional representation for the Commons, Lords reform, and English regional devolution were abandoned or stillborn. Furthermore, the government has appeared to backtrack on some of its earlier commitments, for example with the Human Rights Act and the Freedom of Information Act.

This has left us with the Westminster model remaining at the centre of the British state and polity. Norton argues that the Westminster model 'has been modified, perhaps vandalised, but it has not been destroyed' (quoted in Morrison, 2001: 509-10). A crucial question to be asked here is why Labour has supported a Westminster model of politics that has aided Conservative dominance in the twentieth century, and which, as Marquand says, is 'a constitutional system permeated with monarchical values' (1997: 44). One reason for this is that the Westminster model was in fact surprisingly inclusive and accommodating to the rise of Labour and collectivism from the 1920s to the 1950s. Successive Labour leaderships have thus been persuaded to see the constitution as the means to aiding a very British road to socialism, something that was not considered possible in many continental European countries. The British constitution's very flexibility, as well as its concentration of power, could be utilised for progressive ends. As two academics point out: 'Labour politicians have been conditioned as much as Conservatives by the Westminster model' (Richards and Smith, 2001: 44).

The Blair government has enacted a half-hearted constitutional reform programme while going out of its way to protect and preserve the Westminster model. It has done this because of the partisan advantages to the governing party of its fusion of the executive and the legislative, and the central nexus of political power built on parliamentary sovereignty and ministerial responsibility. According to Morrison, 'the core of the British political system of elective dictatorship has remained intact' (2001: 501).

The government's constitutional programme is hedged about with ministerial opt-outs, exemptions and reserved powers. The Freedom of Information Act retains a ministerial veto over the release of information. The Human Rights Act does not allow the courts to strike down legislation or compel the government to amend it. (All the courts can do is issue a 'declaration of incompatibility', with Parliament under no obligation to alter legislation, and allowed to judge the constitutionality of its own actions.)[2] The Independent Judicial Appointments Commission does not appoint judges, but instead makes mere recommendations to the Secretary of State for Constitutional Affairs, who makes the final decision. Labour's plans for a Supreme Court are much less radical than in other countries; they explicitly protect the idea of parliamentary sovereignty, and the court will not have the capacity to strike down legislation.

The government's retreat from constitutional reform has been compounded by the impact of the 'war on terror'. Its response to the threat of terrorism has been the introduction of legislation that has fundamentally altered the relationship between government and citizen. When Labour began its constitutional reforms, some commentators hoped that we were seeing the emergence of a new constitutional settlement – an increasingly codified set of arrangements – where legislation such as the Human Rights Act would be close to fundamental law. Sadly, this has not happened. Under the auspices of the 'war on terror' Labour has driven a horse and carriage through its own proposals.

This has led to serious conflict with the judiciary. In December 2004 the Law Lords decided that Part 4 of the Anti-Terrorism, Crime and

Security Act 2001, which allowed the detention without charge of non-British terror suspects, contravened the European Convention on Human Rights. This was an historic verdict, with the Law Lords unapologetically standing up to the powers of the Crown. According to Adam Tomkins, the verdict was 'a much-belated judicial awakening' to ensure respect for the rule of law (Blom-Cooper, 2005: 235). The government responded to this with the Prevention of Terrorism Act 2005, which introduced control orders to replace detention orders. But this was found by the High Court in April 2006 to be incompatible with the right to a fair trial.

The consequences of all this are profound. The Human Rights Act, drawn up to restrict the powers of the executive and catch up with the rest of Europe, was eventually drawn up in a restrictive manner, preserving the principle of parliamentary sovereignty. Subsequently, due to the shift in the priorities of the political classes from constitutional reform to anti-terrorist measures, restrictions have been placed on human rights and the HRA has not been given any opportunity to bed down, or become entrenched in the political arrangements of the country. Instead, it has been comprehensively diluted and destroyed by the actions of the Blair government. No administration which takes human rights seriously could have acted the way the Blair government has on 'the war on terror' and asylum and immigration (not to mention its acquiescence in Guantanamo Bay, rendition flights and so much more).

THE UNDEMOCRATIC CENTRE

Tony Blair's period as prime minister has seen an unprecedented degree of re-organisation at the centre. Downing Street has been endlessly expanded; it was fundamentally re-organised in 2001 and is currently divided into three directorates: policy, government relations and communications. These are resourced by civil servants, special advisers, consultants and secondments from the private sector. Anthony Seldon, writing in 2004, commented that Downing Street had 'seen seven years of almost Maoist "permanent revolution", with a bewildering number of changes of design to little effect' (Seldon, 2004: 343).

Blair's reworked centre, combined with Brown's hyper-assertive Treasury, has led to an executive of British government with a huge concentration of power. Gone are the old-fashioned centre-left critiques of prime ministerial patronage, or any ideas about the limits of the Treasury's view of the economy and government. Instead, we have an 'increasingly co-ordinated and coherent and increasingly proactive and performance driven' centre (Burch and Holliday, 2004:

24), driving forward a contentious agenda of choice, competition, marketisation and defining people as consumers.

This has become known as 'the McKinsey state', characterised by 'the new entrepreneurs of the state', whether it be businessmen seconded from the private sector or civil servants with entrepreneurial drive (Leys, 2006). The former can be seen, for example, in the figure of Lord Birt, ex-Director General of the BBC, who became a Downing Street adviser, and was paid £100,000 per annum by McKinsey. Business people were brought in to handle such commissions as funding of the NHS (Derek Wanless, ex-CEO Nat West) or the future of stakeholder pensions (Ron Sandler). However, more serious has been the influence of the 'Big Five' accounting firms – Arthur Andersen Consulting, Pricewaterhouse Coopers (PwC), Ernst and Young, KPMG and Deloitte – who have gained massively out of government policies, particularly in relation to PFI/PPP and the marketisation of the public sector (Craig and Brooks, 2006).

This penetration of the innermost workings of British governments by accountants and consultants has weakened a coherent civil service ethos. Previous Labour governments used to be paranoid about the monopoly of advice from civil servants and the narrow class base of senior personnel. Today we have moved far from that. Andrew Turnbull, Cabinet Secretary 2002-2005, observes that the civil service 'no longer claim[s] a monopoly over policy advice'. The new, wider, policy community includes ideas from 'think-tanks, consultancies, government abroad, special advisers, and frontline practitioners' (Turnbull, 2005). This is the same Andrew Turnbull who became, upon leaving the civil service, a Senior Adviser at Booz Allen Hamilton, and Director of Frontier Economics, an economic and regulatory consultancy.

Christopher Foster, in his magisterial critique of the deformed nature of British government, poses that the transformative change of recent years has not been the measures of constitutional reform, but the Blairite-Brownite concentration of powers in the centre. He characterises this as: 'the decline in the authority of many ministers, the undermining of the constitutional position and consequent effectiveness of the civil service, the fragmentation of government and the public sector into a mess of bodies with complex but ill-defined relations between them, and the ramifying of a system of government which ... is less interested in delivering results than managing news.' This has happened alongside the end of 'collegiate, effective Cabinet government' and its replacement by an omnipotent centre supported and resourced by an unelected political class (Foster, 2005: 252).

This has aided the rise of an informal, loosely arranged way of government working at the centre: 'government by sofa' and 'Tony's denocracy'. Thus, during the war in Iraq, the real discussions and decisions took place in an ad hoc War Cabinet, which circumvented existing cabinet and ministerial committees (Butler, 2004: 147-8). In contrast, the Falklands conflict of 1982 was run by a formal War Cabinet, which had the status of a ministerial subcommittee of the Cabinet, which received regular reports.

This decline of Cabinet government has been matched by the perception in Blair that every decision actually stops with him. This leads to a hyperactive government, driven not by results or what works but by being seen to be doing things, and news management. An example of this is the foot and mouth crisis in 2001. The government responded to this by creating the climate of a national emergency, bringing in the army, and postponing local elections. A similar foot and mouth outbreak in 1967 merits not one mention in the major biographies of Wilson, and is only briefly mentioned in Crossman's diaries (1977)[3]: a sign of too much government belief in 'high politics' then, perhaps, and over-concentration on 'low politics' today.

In a 2005 interview in the *New Yorker* Blair stated that the job of prime minister 'is utterly relentless': 'You are dealing with a multiplicity of issues the whole time. And the decision making process stops with you. That's an amazing thing – when every decision stops with you' (*New Yorker*, 2 May 2005). Such a sense of omnipotence was also evident in Blair's comment that, 'I have been involved as British Prime Minister in three conflicts involving regime change. Milosevic. The Taliban. And Sierra Leone' (Seldon, 2004: 571).

New Labour's idea of modernisation rested heavily on Tony Blair – his personal integrity and missionary zeal – along with individual ministers stressing their incorruptibility. This very narrow, personalised modernisation succumbed to the wear and tear of office, and combined with unprecedented centralism, led directly to Tony Blair's cash for honours scandal in the dying days of his administration. This was a scandal of epic proportions which went to the heart of British government, and some of Blair's key advisers; it illustrated the lack of proper boundaries between governing party and affairs of state.

NEW LABOUR, THE BRITISH POLITICAL CLASSES AND ATLANTICISM

The British state has consistently had reservations about the European Union project, ideas of political integration and shared sovereignty. At the same time, the British political classes have displayed a relatively uncritical view of Britain's relationship with the United States. The same fanatical Eurosceptics who obsess about the threat to British democracy and way of life from Brussels bureaucrats tend to ignore completely the way in which American national and security interests have shaped large parts of British government policy (see Redwood, 1999).

New Labour's election in 1997 saw very little mention or thought put into foreign policy. The party's election manifesto barely touched on the subject, but the party had aspirations to be more pro-European than the Conservatives, and ultimately, to be at the heart of the European project, while remaining committed to Atlanticism. New Labour in 1997 saw both of these approaches anchored in progressive values: modernising the sclerotic European economies with a trans-continental 'third way' while being in alliance with Clinton's New Democrats. It was to prove very different in both areas.

His early experiences of military conflict, his belief in the power of it to do good, and his ability to persuade President Clinton, all contributed to Blair's seeing himself as a world statesman. With the attacks of 9/11, the stage was set for him to take Britain into previously uncharted waters, driven by a combination of his capacity to see the world in black and white terms, and an over-estimation of the power of his persuasion and influence with American Presidents. Blair's identification with President Bush and the 'war on terror' led to the short, sharp intervention in Afghanistan and then the open sore of Iraq. Blair's leverage over the US was revealed as minor however: the war was not sanctioned by the United Nations and thus violated the five criteria he had carefully laid out in a 1999 speech on intervention in Chicago (Blair, 1999).

Post-Iraq war, things did not get better. Iraq was caught in a fractious civil war, the US and UK became bogged down in Afghanistan and Iraq, while the pursuit of a comprehensive Middle East peace settlement between Israel and the Palestinians barely figured in American priorities. Instead, we witnessed Guantanamo Bay, Abu Ghraid prison, rendition flights, and American-British support for Israeli indiscriminate attacks on Lebanon. This has led Seldon to conclude that the Americans seemed to listen to Blair 'only when his suit matched what they wanted to wear anyway' (Seldon, 2004: 624).

The Labour and Conservative leaderships colluded in a new Atlanticist consensus post-9/11 which most of the British public did not support and felt nervous about. In such controversies as the Iraq war and the 2006 Israeli invasion of Lebanon, the two main parties worked to prevent any public debate or criticism of America. The experience of 9/11 and afterwards 'reaffirmed the vice-like grip of Atlanticism on Britain's identity' (Dunne, 2004: 908).

The nature of the American-British relationship has proven to be a destabilising force in the world. From the time of the catastrophe of Suez, the British have attempted never to have a major public difference in foreign policy with the Americans; the French on the other hand have taken the opposite approach, withdrawing from the military command of NATO and throwing themselves fully into the Franco-German alliance in the EU. Despite differences at the time of Vietnam between Johnston and Wilson, and during the Falklands war between Reagan and Thatcher, no major British political figures have been prepared to question what Britain gains strategically from this alliance.

The American-British 'special relationship' may have served a purpose in the Second World War, but it now harms Britain's standing in the world, damages our democratic institutions, and is one of the major causes of our diffidence towards the EU. The nature of American foreign and military power is seldom examined by British politicians. America has for the last thirty years, post-Vietnam, been heading in the opposite direction from the politics of a negotiated international order. It has been moving from the politics of war as a policy of last resort, to one of intervening as a policy of first resort. This is not just about the ideological politics of the Bush administration, which will be ameliorated by a future Democrat President. It is spread across the US political spectrum. For example the US fought six wars during the Cold War ranging from Korea and Vietnam to invading Grenada; since then it has fought nine – from Iraq twice, to Afghanistan, Kosovo, Somalia – the latter two under Clinton's watch (Bacevich, 2005: 229).

Blair has merely pushed his commitment to Atlanticism to the point where it has become a controversial issue; the deeper problem is the nature of US power and Atlanticism rather than the mistakes and misrepresentations of Blair and company. These deeper questions are not part of public debate in Britain, or of the considerations of the Labour and Conservative leaderships, who are fanatically committed to upholding the Atlanticist cause for a variety of historical, cultural and economic reasons, including the cross-fertilisation of British and American political and security elites.

THE CHANGING NATURE OF THE UK AND PROGRESSIVE POLITICS

The basic character of the United Kingdom still causes huge problems of understanding for politicians, the media and the policy class. The misunderstanding of the UK as a unitary state is but one example. Another is the constant confusion between 'nation' and 'state': basic political concepts. The UK is a 'state' – a coming together of England, Scotland, Wales and part of Ireland – but it has never been a 'nation'. Scotland was a 'stateless nation' after 1707, while the UK is a 'nationless state'.

The fluidities and flexibility of what has been meant by Britishness historically is important to remember in the light of contemporary debates about the nature of Britishness which tap into all sorts of anxieties and fears about the modern world and change. The consideration of such ideas as citizenship tests for nationality is indicative of a shift from this previous flexible, negotiated attitude, to one more codified and demanding. This change can be seen in the shift in mood from Mark Leonard's *Britain™*, published in the afterglow of 1997, to David Goodhart's *Progressive Nationalism*, which came out nine years later, responding to the fears around 'the war on terror' and anxieties over asylum, immigration and race. Leonard's idealistic, slightly gauche pamphlet is filled with the air of innocence, and a belief anything is possible. He recognised that 200 years previously Britain had invented an identity 'which proved enormously successful', which could be achieved again as long as we recognised it would 'be a slow burn, not a quick fix' (1997). This mean 'regalvanising excitement around Britain's core values' and 'finding a better way of linking pride in the past with confidence in the future'. Leonard was trying to articulate a more inclusive Britishness after Thatcher's abrasive English nationalism, but it is revealing that his account is a rather narrow, urban English perspective, where Scotland, Wales and Northern Ireland are barely mentioned. He concedes this when he states 'Britishness has never been an equal arrangement' (1997: 72).

It is a long distance from Leonard to Goodhart. The latter's argument is shaped by a host of mainstream worries about asylum, race, immigration and security, which the Blair government has happily conflated into one, to justify punitive, populist measures. Goodhart states that the erosion of class as a basis for solidarity means that the left has to find another notion of community to locate its politics, and that this should be the nation-state and an 'inclusive, progressive, civic British nationalism'. He takes the view that the scale of immigration to Britain is undermining popular support for the welfare state, as people see outsiders getting benefits – but there is no hard evidence for this and he provides none.

Goodhart gets hopelessly confused about the British 'nation' and 'state', writing, 'Britain is (technically) not a nation at all but a state', and then on the next page, 'If British national citizenship is to be made more attractive ...' (2006: 21, 22). These fundamental confusions could have been addressed by Goodhart being a bit more ambitious, and daring to sketch out the grounds of an English 'progressive nationalism', which seems to be implicitly what he is talking about in all but name; he also might have addressed the idea of renewing British statehood – in particular looking at the concepts of citizenship and rights, which for most of post-war Britain has emotionally held the Scots and Welsh in the Union. Instead, Goodhart wants to give credence to the Blair government's authoritarian instincts on benefits, ID cards and immigration, and is happy to get an endorsement from David Blunkett.

This kind of approach is evidence of the current crisis of the UK state, which faces a more significant threat in the early twenty-first century than it did even in the 1970s, in particular the external challenges arising from the growing international instability. The emotional and ideological glue that has held the UK together for 300 years has been slowly evaporating over the last few decades. There is now, as McLean and McMillan argue, no primordial Unionism left in the UK body politic – by which they mean a gut sense of Britishness. But there is still an instrumental Unionism – based on a careful calculation by Scots that they are better off in the Union.

The degree of internal challenge from moves to decentralise the state has appeared dormant in recent years, but it has not gone away with the establishment of devolved bodies in Scotland, Wales and Northern Ireland. Current financial arrangements, carried over from previous arrangements (known as the Barnett Formula) are significantly advantageous to Scotland, but to no one else. These arrangements have few friends left (namely the Labour part of the Scottish Executive and Gordon Brown), and are likely to be abolished – probably after Labour loses Westminster power. This will have consequences far beyond dry finances, because it will reveal the true level of attachment to the Union in various parts of the UK. When Barnett goes, the Scots will no longer have a utilitarian argument for union, and this will provide a major crossroads for the UK. As McLean and McMillan argue, 'A union state without unionism can survive for a long time. But not, perhaps forever' (2005: 256).

We are a long way from the demise of the United Kingdom now, but existing attitudes, and the failure of the Blair government to reform the British state in a democratic direction, make such an outcome more likely, not less. The last decade has witnessed 'the twilight of the Westminster model' (Norris, 2001). It has been first diluted and then defended, by a Blair government that barely seemed to understand the consequences of its actions.

New Labour's blinkered co-option into the new American imperialist project has aided this hollowing out of any democratic impulse. This can only be understood as part of the continuation of the mindset of 'Churchillism' with its belief in Britain as a world power and subordinate partner to the US – something that which Labour has played such a supportive, uncritical role in. When this is combined with an ahistorical approach to notions of Empire and imperialism, with Labour politicians such as Blair and Brown appearing to celebrate the British Empire, the omens were not encouraging for the evolution of a progressive, inclusive story about Britishness and its place in the world (see Porter, 2006). If the foreseeable future and next few decades look gloomy at a national and international level, then Labour's contribution, and that of wider progressives, must be to resist the orthodoxies of our age, and set out some challenging questions and answers about what Britain is and its role in the modern world.

NOTES

1. The Government of Ireland Act s. 75 put it much more bluntly, 'the supreme authority of the Parliament of the United Kingdom shall remain unaffected and undiminished over all persons, matters and things in Northern Ireland' (McLean and McMillan 2005, 1303).
2. Tony Blair, in his debate with Henry Porter in *The Observer* on the government's authoritarianism, is disingenuous when he states, 'The point about the Human Rights Act is that it does allow the courts to strike down the act of our "sovereign Parliament"' (Porter and Blair, 2006). The HRA allows for no such provision.
3. The 1967 foot and mouth crisis is mentioned four times in Crossman (1977: 581, 583, 590, 596). It warrants not a single mention in the Castle or Benn diaries of the same period.

REFERENCES

Anderson, B. (1983), *Imagined Communities: Reflections on the Origin and Spread of Nationalism*, London, Verso.

Aughey, A. (2001), *Nationalism, Devolution and the Challenge to the United Kingdom State*, London: Pluto.

Bacevich, A. (2005), *The New American Militarism: How Americans are Seduced by War*, Oxford: Oxford University Press.

Barnett, A. (1982), *Iron Brittania: How Parliament waged its Falklands War*, London: Allison and Busby.

Barnett, A. (1997), *This Time: Our Constitutional Revolution*, London: Vintage.

Benn, T. (1979), *Arguments for Socialism*, London: Jonathan Cape.

Blair, T. (1999), Doctrine of the International Community', Speech delivered in Chicago, 24 April.

Blair, T. (2005), 'Interview', *New Yorker*, 2 May 2005.

Blom-Cooper, L. (2005), 'Government and Judiciary', in Seldon, A. and Kavanagh, D. (eds), *The Blair Effect 2001-5*, Oxford: Oxford University Press, 233-55.

Burch, M. and Holliday, I. (2004), 'The Blair Government and the Core Executive', *Government and Opposition*, Vol. 39 No. 1, 1-21.

Butler, R. (2004), *Review of Intelligence on Weapons of Mass Destruction*, London: The Stationery Office, HC 898.

Craig, D. and Brooks, R. (2006), *Plundering the Public Sector: How New Labour are letting consultants run off with £70 billion of our money*, London: Constable.

Crossman, R. (1977), *The Diaries of a Cabinet Minister: Volume Two: Lord President of the Council and Leader of the House of Commons 1966-68*, London: Jonathan Cape.

Dunne, T. (2004), 'When the shooting starts: Atlanticism in British Security Strategy', *International Affairs*, Vol. 80 No. 5, 893-909.

Foster, C. (2005), *British Government in Crisis*, Oxford: Hart Publishing.

Gamble, A. (2003), *Between Europe and America: The Future of British Politics*, Basingstoke: Palgrave Macmillan.

Garton Ash, T. (2004), *Free World: Why a crisis of the West reveals the opportunity of our time*, London: Allen Lane.

Goodhart, D. (2006), *Progressive Nationalism: Citizenship and the Left*, London: Demos.

Hassan, G. (2003), 'Talking about Devolution: A Decade of Constitutional Wish-Fulfilment', *Renewal: The Journal of Labour Politics*, 46-53.

Jones, B. and Keating, M. (1985), *Labour and the British State*, Oxford: Oxford University Press.

Keating, M. and Bleiman, D. (1979), *Labour and Scottish Nationalism*, Basingstoke: Macmillan.

Leonard, M. (1997), *Britain™*, London: Demos.

Leys, C. (2006), 'The Cynical State', in Panitch, L. and Leys, C. (eds), *The Socialist Register 2006*, London, Merlin, http://socialistregister.com/sample/1

McLean, I. and McMillan, A. (2005), *State of the Union: Unionism and the Alternatives in the United Kingdom since 1707*, Oxford: Oxford University Press.

Marquand, D. (1997), *The New Reckoning*, Cambridge: Polity.

Marquand, D. (1999), 'Populism or Pluralism?: New Labour and the Constitution', University College London, Misheon Lecture.

Morrison, J. (2001), *Reforming Britain: New Labour, New Constitution?*, London: Reuters.

Norris, P. (2001), 'The Twilight of Westminster?: Electoral Reform and its Consequences', *Political Studies*, Vol. 49 No. 5, 877-900.

Porter, B. (2006), *Empire and Superempire: Britain, America and the World*, London: Yale University Press.

Porter, H. and Blair, T. (2006), 'Britain's Liberties: The Great Debate', *The Observer*, 23 April.

Redwood, J. (1999), *The Death of Britain?: The UK's Constitutional Crisis*, Basingstoke: Macmillan.

Richards, D. and Smith, M. J. (2001), 'New Labour, the constitution and reforming the state', in Ludlam, S. and Smith, M. J. (eds), *New Labour in Government*, Basingstoke: Palgrave Macmillan, 145-66.

Richards, S. (1999), 'The NS Interview: Gordon Brown', *New Statesman*, 19 April.

Scottish Office (1997), *Scotland's Parliament*, London: The Scottish Office, Cm. 3658.

Seldon, A. (2004), *Blair*, London: Free Press.

Turnbull, A. (2005), Professionalising Public Management in An Era of Choice, www.cabinetoffice.gov.uk/about_the_cabinet_office/speeches/turnbull/html/index.asp

Learning to let go: The potential of a self-creating society

Tom Bentley

It is my belief, after a century in which, to tackle social injustice, the state has had to take power to ensure social progress, that to tackle the social injustices that still remain the state will have to give power away.

Gordon Brown (2000)

We start with an instinctive desire to put more trust in civil society and in the individual, rather than in the bureaucratic apparatus of the state.

David Cameron (2006)

Politics is both a contest of ideas and a struggle for power. Both forms of competition exist simultaneously in any political system. For any political project to succeed over time, it has to win on both fronts, and to show how power can be used to translate ideas into everyday reality.

Ideas and power come together in institutions. Institutions mediate between individual people and collective identities like nations, faiths and political movements. They also structure and order the activities which underpin everyday life, and which politics needs to govern and regulate. These include firms, families, public services, voluntary organisations, and so on. Creating, destroying and shaping institutions is the most important means through which political decision-making influences the development of wider societies.

This chapter argues that the left, in the twenty-first century, must embrace a new set of institutional means to achieve its ends of creating common goods. The result of wealth, freedom and information in today's societies is an ever-growing level of social and organisational complexity, which threatens to invalidate and undermine collective action, through the state, to create the shared goods which individuals need to thrive.

The growth of diversity and complexity does not reduce the need for these shared goods, or for public responses to collective risk and threat. But it does demand new ways of creating them and making them legitimate. Not only is the range of human and social *need* more diverse, but people's attachment to the collective institutional identities on which left-wing politics has been founded is much weaker. As a result, collective action and the uses of public institutional power need to be legitimised in new ways, so that people are prepared to respect the compromises and sacrifices that public rules demand, and so that they play a part in generating the shared goods and the organisational solutions that meet those human needs on an everyday level.

New Labour's record in meeting these challenges is mixed. Its political strategy has been brilliantly successful in marginalising the right and re-centring the policy agenda, making it possible to increase spending on public services, redistribute income and pursue long-term objectives such as ending child poverty. But its success in translating its 'balanced' agenda into sustained, long lasting institutional success is much weaker, and its approach to implementation has often been fragmented and incoherent. This lack of translation is one reason for the widespread questioning of Tony Blair's legacy.

In fact, while New Labour adjusted its attitudes towards open markets, it has been much more unreconstructed in its approach to using institutional power; often relying on a technocratic, over-centralised Fabianism which stretches far back into the history of the left.

One of the main challenges facing the centre-left after Blair is to fashion an approach to the use of institutional power which makes better connections between means and ends; which is more successful in achieving its specific outcomes and objectives; which creates democratic legitimacy rather than squandering it; and which works on a practical level amid the diverse, flexible, information-rich and anti-deferential conditions of twenty-first century society.

To renew successfully, the left must set out and dominate a political agenda in which wellbeing and quality of life become far more prominent, and in which the investment and guarantees of the state are dedicated more coherently to building institutions which can successfully meet human need through various forms of self-governance, rather than being directly owned, managed or controlled by government. This terrain – the empowerment of citizens to participate in collective governance without direct control – should be understood as an evolution of democracy into the twenty-first century, and as a central competitive battleground for the next generation of politics.

As well as setting out the argument and the record, this chapter sketches what such an approach might mean for policy, governance and institutional strategy.

THE LEFT'S MORAL PURPOSE

At the core of the left's identity is an assertion of the value of common goods; the proposition that good societies rely on shared forms of value which require collective action, including through the state, to ensure that they are created and distributed properly. That does not preclude a concern for personal freedom; but it includes an assertion that the enjoyment of freedom, for everybody, requires a society to be capable of creating and replenishing collective goods which make individual freedoms meaningful. Such goods come in many forms; often they are discussed in the abstract terms of equality, solidarity and community, but most people experience them in more concrete, tangible forms than this, for example by supporting the idea of a National Health Service or believing that all children should have the same chances to succeed in education, or campaigning to protect and enjoy the natural environment.

The staggering political success of New Labour in the mid-1990s rested partly on the public resonance of this proposition – that after the victory of markets, a rebalancing of British politics was needed to reinstate the value of shared goods. In the short term, it was represented by the promises to overcome 'sleaze' and to revitalise public services. This, combined with a carefully cultivated air of balance, pragmatism and common sense, proved a devastatingly successful political formula, so much so that the Conservatives have now found in David Cameron a leader who will create a centre-right version of it.

The need for common goods, protected and created by public action, is as great as ever. From security to public health, climate change to parenting, we are surrounded in modern societies by risks and needs which emphasise our interdependence with other people and other societies. Our ability to thrive as individuals is still bound up with our access to resources, many of which require public investment, regulation and provision, and many more of which depend on the respect, forbearance and choices of our fellow citizens.

For most of its history over two centuries, the left's moral purpose has been expressed by translating social movements into institutional power through the state – minimum standards of employment and service, legal rights, universal services like pensions and healthcare, schools, universities and libraries.

To have a long-term impact, such institutions must become embedded in society in ways which permanently change the social and economic context, and acquire a legitimacy, or level of public acceptance and attachment, which makes them impossible to reverse.

But the formulation which crafted a dominant political narrative in the 1990s has not been translated so successfully into institutional applications. Where Blair and his government have struggled consistently is in turning stated priorities into outcomes which are seen to have changed everyday reality for the better.

THE POWER OF INSTITUTIONS

Institutions embody ideas and values. When they succeed, they acquire a status which allows them to recreate themselves over time – to adapt continuously to changing circumstances, while seeking to preserve their underlying values. Successful large institutions in any sector – the BBC, the NHS, trade unions, companies like Philips and BP, follow this principle. But smaller, more local institutions also work this way – family firms, social clubs, libraries and schools, and so on. Their formal function and controls determine aspects of what they do, and set some limits on what they cannot do. But their ongoing evolution and adaptation – the way that they recreate themselves over time, and therefore the impact they have on the people in and around them – is influenced by myriad other factors, including their culture, their specific surroundings, their membership and so on. The formal rules determining their function, accountabilities, are one set of influences among many.

Historically for the left, political success has meant establishing institutional control over greater swathes of the economy and society, in order to pursue or create collective goods. This has been a given for revolutionary socialism, social democracy, Keynesian economics and social liberalism, albeit with very different implications and methods. This is why the great symbolic reverses for the left in the late twentieth century involved 'rolling back the frontiers of the state' through privatisation and tax cutting, even where the rolling back was more rhetorical than substantive

New Labour accommodated a market economy and celebrated personal freedom. But the legacy of campaigning to achieve social justice through institutional control means that the centre left still relies too heavily on particular *forms* of command and control in political organisation and the administration of the state, and has lazily associated them with egalitarianism and solidarity. There are real dilemmas and trade-offs involved in giving up the central power to direct and redistribute. But, even among modernisers, these forms of power have become too much of a 'default' mode.

To achieve more successful long-term strategies, the left after Blair must do a better job of connecting means and ends, and of using the direct power of Parliament and the state to create forms of institutional settlement which will outlive them. There are successes from the last decade; their lessons need to be incorporated into a fresh governing philosophy – an approach to power which combines values and principles with analysis of the wider environment, its opportunities and constraints.

THE RECORD

In fact, New Labour's record in embedding change in institutions includes some major successes. Most striking, at least from an historical perspective, is constitutional reform in Scotland, Wales, Northern Ireland and London. It is equally striking, though, that creating new representative political institutions has not led to very different approaches to governing; of course there are differences in political inflexion and the diversity is likely to grow over time. But one weakness of New Labour's approach has been its inability to combine representative and constitutional governance with the administrative state – procurement, regulation, service organisation and so on.

It is true there is a vast landscape of reformed and restructured institutions left behind by New Labour's decade in power, ranging from restructured regulators in communications and financial services to integrated local children's services and merged Inland Revenue and Customs services. But this is part of the point – the perpetual churn of review and restructuring which tends to accompany modern government, especially in hyperactive administrative cultures like Britain's, has not produced a permanent imprint which proportionately reflects either the political values of the reformers, or the time, money and energy spent.

Beyond devolution, there are other big successes such as the introduction of a minimum wage and the incorporation of human rights into UK law. It is telling that one of the most successful single policy decisions of the whole period has been the transfer of interest rate decisions to the Bank of England; a classic example of how a key idea – the long-term goal of stable inflation – becomes embedded and accepted through institutional means.

But in public services, social policy, and many areas of economic governance, the government has struggled to translate its objectives into coherent, legitimate, institutional strategies. Much of the approach to public service reform has sought to increase the control of central institutions through target-setting and regulation, even where money and 'flexibility' has been moved closer to the professional and the service user. The classic illustrations of this approach are still the highly prescriptive strategies used to improve literacy, numeracy and GCSE performance in education, and to reduce hospital waiting times. These approaches have evolved, of course, just as the Treasury-set Public Service Agreements have become more sophisticated over time. But overall, institutional power is still far more concentrated at the centre than it needs to be, and than the rhetoric of devolution and empowerment would have suggested.

Every political project uses tools inherited from its predecessors to pursue its own specific objectives. It is not surprising, then, that the methods of New Public Management which emerged during the 1990s were adopted and then refined with such zeal. It also fits with New Labour's use of the Private Finance Initiative and Public Private Partnerships to fund and manage public investment in infrastructure, from the London Underground to new schools and hospitals.

While direct ownership and managerial control may have passed from the state, it has often been transferred into other forms of control: primarily the attempt to exercise control through contract and regulation.

Local government, likewise, has been placed in a highly ambiguous position, granted new strategic duties and powers, but subject to new performance measures and forms of central intervention, and forced to share power with new regional and local institutions such as Learning and Skills Councils and Local Strategic Partnerships. Furthermore, alongside the narrative of 'invest and reform', focused on performance and delivery, there has been a parallel process of restructuring and reorganisation which is mainly administrative, prompted by the need for 'efficiency' and 'modernisation', through programmes like electronic government and the Gershon efficiency review.

In practice, the impact of these twin narratives has been closely intertwined; many specific gains, but combined with disruption, uncertainty and fragmentation. Sue Goss's chapter in this book describes many of the problems of this governance framework with great clarity. My point is that these struggles are a failure to embed; to make the use of public resource and the setting of public rules part of a range of public institutions which the public actually recognises and accepts.

THE NEXT STEP?

Amid these struggles, there has been a range of efforts to generate a more devolved, community-focused and participatory approach to governance; from Sure Start and the New Deal for Communities to foundation hospitals and the growing emphasis on preventative and community-based health care. Both Treasury and Home Office have made persistent attempts to encourage the involvement of voluntary organisations in public services and civic problem-solving, and the DfES still runs the Millennium Volunteers programme for young people, initiated by David Blunkett. Lottery funding has been channelled towards community organisations and infrastructure. But these programmes often look like small fry in comparison to the mainstream larger scale approaches to governance and service provision used in the public or private sectors.

There is little sign that the new infrastructure of regulation, procurement and implementation is able to offer the forms of responsiveness or local legitimacy that such approaches have been seeking, even when their political champions are passionately committed to creating them.

In almost every area of government and governance, it is possible to find a similar pattern of ambivalence; bold aspirations for better services and outcomes, willingness to invest, but lack of clarity about how to translate objectives into institutional patterns which simultaneously support the creation of public goods and meet the differentiated needs of a more diverse, vocal and mobile population. One major political question is whether the seeds that have been sown over the last decade – of a new, more community focused, collaborative approach to governance – can be harvested and scaled up quickly enough to become part of the left's next repertoire. This very practical difficulty is partly explained by a much deeper conflict.

THE CHALLENGE OF LETTING GO

In the late twentieth century, a profound victory took place in the battle of ideas, when the combination of capitalism and open societies won the cold war. When such shifts in politics occur, they seem definitive and decisive. But the forces which prompted the shift will create new challenges to the models of governance which are left standing. For example, one reason for the collapse of Soviet state socialism was the impossibility of controlling people's movement and ideas in an era of free, long distance electronic communication. But the advent of digital communication networks, and the social, economic and cultural changes associated with these spreading technologies, create deep and direct challenges to all inherited forms of governance; to post-war models of social democracy, to more recent forms of neo-liberalism such as the New Public Management and to other, non-western models of nation state governance.

Thatcherism was a specific, time-limited project. But its triumph reflected a deeper set of forces, some of which have been unleashed by progressive gains like universal education and the advance of social and human rights. The demand for personal freedom and individual recognition, combined with growing wealth, communication and mobility, *continues* to reshape the context in which politics operates. Thatcherism did not create these forces; it harnessed and amplified them.

In this setting, the greatest obstacle to the centre left's pursuit of common goods is not persuading people of their value, but finding practical ways to create them that are compatible with the diversity, flexibility and anti-deferential attitudes characteristic of our age.

In 2002 I argued that:

> the most difficult and pressing challenge facing the left today is the reconciliation of radical diversity and respect for personal autonomy with the need for institutional authority which can enforce common rules for the greater good.

This tension plays itself out in various specific ways. First, and perhaps most obvious, is a consequence of *social complexity*. As traditional forms of class identity break down and other forms of diversity grow, people's sense of solidarity towards one another comes into question. This tension is, of course, reflected in the ongoing debate over personal taxation, but income tax is just one crude measure of solidarity. More dramatic, and potentially even more difficult for the left is the critique levelled by David Goodhart, that a society which becomes 'too diverse' and seeks to treat all forms of diversity equally will lose the foundations of solidarity, and therefore undermine its ability to defend redistribution through institutions like the welfare state, shared local services and a general sense of social trust (Goodhart, 2004).

Second, a more fluid and mobile society is one which creates and demands more *technical* complexity. This means that the practice of enforcing shared rules designed to protect or create common goods becomes more difficult, and that when government struggles to do it successfully, people's support for such goods is threatened again. Two examples stand out which also point to the importance of institutions and what they represent. The Child Support Agency has come to symbolise everything that is unpopular about modern welfare policy. Its whole function – establishing fair parental contributions, usually by absent fathers, and then enforcing their payment – reflects the way that family life has become more complex. But its slow, intrusive, complex and largely ineffective organisational methods have made it loathed by its users and pilloried by the press. Tax Credits is an example of the same kind of difficulty. A policy designed to redistribute, and to integrate the administration of work, benefits and taxation, has been undermined by the ways in which the system needed to work in order to claw back its own overpayments, outraging users and campaigners and undermining the credibility of the whole policy.

The final, and perhaps most important, dimension of the challenge is declining political attachment and participation. Since 2001, when general election turnout fell dramatically in the UK, this issue has become closer to the political mainstream. Since the 2005 general election it has started to become a political priority, partly because the main parties are recognising how much they could be threatened by the loss of legitimacy that flows from low turnout. For Labour to realise that it was elected by only 36 per cent of a 61 per cent turnout – that is, by only around 22 per cent of the adult population – was sobering, to say the least. Again these changes have deep roots in changing patterns of attachment and identity, changing social values and a different set of attitudes to institutions like political parties. It is not automatically a bad thing to be more distanced from these political identities, but it begs the question of how politics can legitimately meet common needs and common challenges in their absence.

This tension, I suggested, would undermine the ability of the centre-left to use 'command and control' to achieve its objectives, whether in economic governance, social authoritarianism, or even political communication and management. As we have seen, there are two main reasons for this, which reinforce each other. Firstly, organisational solutions based on command and control are simply not effective; they do not produce outcomes which reflect the full range of circumstances, needs and preferences. Secondly, partly because of this, but also because of people's unwillingness to be told what to do by government, such solutions lose legitimacy. And the longer this goes on, the more the scope for government action is reduced because of the scorn and contempt that citizens feel for politicians.

LEARNING TO LET GO: BUILDING A NEW APPROACH TO SELF-GOVERNANCE

The greatest challenge for politics in the early twenty-first century is to build institutions which meet the public challenges of our age – for security, wealth, environmental sustainability, wellbeing – and work under the conditions of social and economic diversity that have emerged around us.

To succeed, centre-left politics must be able to shape the *context* in which people and government make choices, and not just seek to intervene to influence or control specific choices when it is politically viable. Otherwise, what is considered viable is continuously reduced by the changing context – the scope for democratic and collective choice shrinks and withers.

The problem is that the combination of representative democracy – in which professionals are elected to take political decisions on behalf of the public – with the regulatory state – in which governments seek to influence the behaviour of other institutions by setting rules and creating institutions to enforce them – cannot achieve the level of flexibility needed to govern complex processes of social and economic production, *and* the legitimacy demanded by a public who want a greater say in decisions affecting their lives.

What should be the response?

First and most basic, the centre left must recognise that supporting people to create their own wellbeing, individually and together, is the goal of progressive politics. This should lead relentlessly to a focus on what boosts and blights wellbeing, and to new tests for the effectiveness of policies, policy interventions, and institutions.

Second, this means an approach to politics and policy built around the need for institutions which create shared goods through *distributed* and *decentralised* means. This does not mean that everything must or can be decentralised, but that institutional and policy design must take open, distributed systems as a given feature of the world it is trying to influence.

Third, the left's approach to governance should be one of much greater institutional pluralism – recognising and supporting a wider range of institutional forms and legitimacy in all sectors, and seeking policy designs which involve those organisations in creating common goods, because of the way that they engage people in doing the same.

The rest of this chapter focuses on the practical and political implications of such an approach. The list of long-term challenges for government and public policy is unlikely to vary much over the next decade. They will be serious priorities whoever is in power:

- pensions and work in an ageing society
- skills, productivity and economic innovation
- health and social care, especially given demographic change
- science and technology; investment, regulation, entrepreneurship
- cities; infrastructure, economic growth and social cohesion
- education, including the expansion of childcare and higher education

- security, from combating terrorism to community policing
- climate change and energy supply
- poverty and economic inequality

Each area requires major, long-term policy decisions and investments by government. But it is equally striking how success in any of these areas depends on the distributed actions of millions of individual people, mediated by organisations and institutional rules. In each area, persuading and empowering people to take everyday decisions which somehow contribute to a larger goal is a fundamental part of achieving long-term progress; in making the population healthier and making retirement affordable; in reducing child poverty and lifting productivity growth; in raising educational attainment and creating a culture of lifelong learning; in enabling different ethnic and social groups to live successfully together in densely populated cities.

In all these areas, individuals are free to choose how they will participate; but their choices will play a small part in generating an aggregate outcome. And in turn, the state of that aggregate – the cost of pensions, rate of smoking-related heart disease, rate of enterprise creation, carbon emissions, and so on – will influence the quality of the environment and the infrastructure – the common resources – on which each individual will draw in living their own life. The challenge for politics is to fashion governance regimes – sets of rules, in other words – which establish the priorities, set the boundaries of permissible behaviour, and maximise the ability of autonomous people and organisations to contribute to the creation of these common goods.

The question is not just whether the left will take them seriously, spend money on them or develop ambitious policies; it is whether it can develop an approach to tackling them which intertwines means and ends, so that the institutions through which the policies are applied acquire their own legitimacy, and their own capacity for recreation and renewal.

Where could it do this? First, central government can, and should, devolve real political and administrative power closer to local communities. The signs are that Gordon Brown is ready to embrace the emerging narrative of constitutional reform which includes local and neighbourhood government, described by Geoff Mulgan as 'double devolution'.[1] This would involve the slimming down of central government, as outlined by Sue Goss, to focus on strategic and regulatory decisions, and (in my view) on promoting the flow of innovation and knowledge between other units of government.

Second, the left could invest far greater thought and energy in learning *how* institutional learning and adaptation actually occurs, at ground level, in order to influence it more effectively without seeking to restructure or control from the centre. Even in market-driven sectors, the flow of innovation is not solely created by profit-driven competition, but through many other aspects of organisational design, location, culture and so on. If Jake Chapman's characterisation of public services as complex adaptive systems was the starting point for developing reform strategies, it would lead to a very different set of methods for improving social outcomes.

Third, the left needs to embrace far more seriously the rhetoric of civil society, civic entrepreneurship and local self-organisation, and seek to translate it into institutional strategies for every sector; this does not just mean finding additional funding for civic organisations, but becoming far more serious about enabling a wider range of organisations to take part in the provision of statutory or publicly funded services; exploring a range of new governance forms, like co-operatives, mutual and shared ownership, in the process.

Fourth, the large-scale institutional designs – of regulation, procurement, accountability and budgeting – need to reflect the contributions that organisations make to supporting people's autonomy and wellbeing: organisational qualities like transparency, interactivity, responsiveness to users, and the level of contribution to social outcomes – and not simply standardised outputs. Measuring and incentivising such qualities is very difficult, but it is not impossible – all governance regimes reflect values and ideas in their categories. The growing debate on 'public value' is the most promising way to embed them in institutional systems.

Fifth, the left needs to focus on the crucial importance of everyday institutions – schools, clinics, workplaces, local public spaces, clubs, museums and so on to act as 'civic intermediaries' rather than simply as providers of a single, functional, professionalised service. One example of this is the introduction of extended school hours in every school by 2010. This can be interpreted simply as an extension of a traditional service to meet new levels of demand; but the intermediate space before and after the core school day represents a huge opportunity to grow new relationships and experiment with new uses of a familiar institution.

Sixth, and perhaps most important, the left needs to champion direct and deliberative democracy; not just by creating new rights of consultation and encouraging the use of citizens juries, panels and so on, but by seeking to integrate the decision-making power of citizens into the everyday workings of this wider spread of institutions. In other words, democracy may evolve not by giving direct decision-making power to millions of people issue by issue, but by enabling people to exercise voice and collective choice through more diffuse, mediated channels of smaller scale institutional participation in settings much closer to their everyday lives.

Most long-term changes in governance are evolutionary; they appear before the political project which makes them an everyday reality. The UK's first privatisation, for example, was carried out by a Labour government. The embryonic elements of a new approach to democratic governance have already formed; it is an approach that could bring together the distributed efforts of millions of individuals into the shared production of various common goods, as well as meeting increasingly personalised needs. The question is whether these elements can be picked up and made into common sense by a reforming, social democratic left, or whether they will be incorporated into the revival of a socially liberal conservatism.

NOTES

1. For more details on 'double devolution', see the Young Foundation's neighbourhoods project at: www.youngfoundation.org.uk

REFERENCES

Bentley, T. (2002), 'Letting Go: Complexity, Individualism and the Left', *Renewal*, Vol. 10 No. 1.

Brown, G. (2000), 'Civil Society in Modern Britain', 17th Arnold Goodman Charity Lecture.

Cameron, D. (2006), 'Modern Conservatism, speech at Demos, 30 January, at www.conservatives.com/tile.do?def=news.story.page&obj_id=127560

Goodhart, D. (2004), 'Too Diverse?', *Prospect*, February.

Re-imagining the public realm

Sue Goss

What has always differentiated a social democratic perspective from that of conventional liberals or liberal conservatives is an understanding of the role the state can play in supporting and creating the conditions for a successful civil society; what Kinnock referred to as the 'enabling state'. It is that concept of the state neither as nanny nor as policeman, but as the expression of the collective will of the people, powerful enough to challenge and defeat the vested interests of the rich and economically powerful, which we are in danger of losing.

To secure its electoral future, Labour needs to consolidate public support for public values. Public services are precious, not simply because they meet consumer needs but because they offer something outside the consumer experience. We need to develop collectivist habits because they contribute to our health and well-being. A resilient, self-confident social democracy has a public realm in which market values and market relationships don't apply.

By re-imagining the public realm not as a marketplace, or as a centralised machine for delivering ministerial targets, but as a sophisti-cated network of collective provision, responsive to local communities, Labour could begin to recreate the complex social fabric that we will need to create a tolerant, creative and energetic social infrastructure on our small islands.

THE BLAIR LEGACY

The New Labour government in 1997 planned to invest in public services, and at the same time to modernise them – concerned that the middle classes might exit old-fashioned and dilapidated public services, leaving the poor behind in residual services which taxpayers would then be reluctant to support. The solution was to extend choice and improve delivery.

Yet, after eight years of government, problems with public services remain at the top of New Labour's agenda. In a poll in *The Guardian* published in September 2005, 65 per cent felt that Labour was putting too much emphasis on the private sector, and 62 per cent of the public believed that the additional billions had made no difference to the quality of services. Even those who have experienced better services explain it through what is now called the 'I'm lucky' syndrome – assuming that their individual experience is not typical.

We have seen new investment in schools and hospitals, and the recruitment and training of teachers, doctors, nurses and police officers, but outside policing, health and education, public service spending has climbed back only to the levels at the tail end of the Major government. Even where the investment has been substantial, after so many years of decay it has been expected to do everything at once – repair and replace old and dilapidated buildings, recruit, train and retain more staff, increase throughput, increase productivity, fund new services and modernise delivery. Some has been swallowed up in serial restructurings and reorganisations, some has lagged because of recruitment difficulties, some has been spent on new computer systems and new initiatives such as NHS direct. Over the past decade, expectations have continued to rise, and the public sector has had to keep up with the accelerating potential of new technology.

THE PROBLEM WITH DELIVERY

For all the talk of modernisation, assumptions about how government makes things happen have been curiously outdated, relying on targets and tight civil service control of the delivery process, seeing government as a centralised machine resembling the giant private corporations of the 1960s. The government has tried to create a 'delivery machine' that could guarantee ministerial promises on service improvement and simultaneously deliver choice in key services such as health and education.

The effects are brilliantly documented in Jake Chapman's chapter in this book; local priorities are distorted by national targets; outcomes are agreed which are neither resourced or properly understood; local innovation is stifled; and an inspection and compliance culture reduces delivery to its lowest common denominator. One local authority has estimated that it costs them between one and two million pounds a year to comply with government requirements to develop strategies and plans! The fastest expansions of staff numbers have often been furthest away from delivery, and yet the most creative parts of the public sector are in the localities, where ideas can be tested and lessons learnt. Local authorities face recruitment problems in key areas, including top managers, youth workers, social workers, planners, finance officers. Attempts to reduce resource use at the centre fail to see that bureaucracy cannot be reduced by using the very systems that caused the bureaucracy in the first place. The culture of micro-management will micro-manage cultural change – leading to a sort of policy gridlock. Chapman and other systems theorists like Seddon point to more radical approaches to improvement, used by Toyota and others, that rely on accurate feedback and the relationship between front-line workers and customers to drive improvement (Seddon, 2003).

While there are pockets of heroic innovation, much of Whitehall remains old-fashioned, serving ministers rather than the public. Work is still about the production of paper rather than the changing of practice; and complex social problems are split up into a myriad of isolated 'policy tasks' which are addressed separately by different teams, who find it hard, in the Whitehall culture, to work collaboratively.

THE PROBLEM WITH CHOICE

The 'big idea' of Labour's third term is choice; but public sector choice is not simple. We want choice on the one hand, and we want to avoid wasting tax-payers' money on the other. Any choice-based system has to have surplus capacity; otherwise those at the end of the queue have no choices. That surplus capacity will always mean empty places or empty beds somewhere – funded by taxpayers. The 'efficiency' pressures to manage choice out of the system are at least as strong as those to manage it in.

John Clarke's interesting research shows that the public understands that choice is a far more complex idea than either old Labour or New Labour recognise (Clarke, 2005). He has found that people don't identify themselves as 'consumers' of public services, and see little fit between their understanding of a consumer and the relationships that characterise public services. People are mildly 'pro-choice' in abstraction, but this is tempered by anxieties about the consequences for inequality, and by a wider ambivalence. Even when being offered a personal service that we like, we will always ask questions about it as taxpayers and as citizens – 'what does this cost?', 'Is it fair?'. As citizens, we want to influence the impact of public services on society as well as on ourselves. We worry that private sector values might be inimical to values of equality and fairness, and corrosive of social cohesion. We are concerned that if rich consumers are able to insulate themselves from the experiences of the poor, our society becomes segregated. Already we begin to see that choices made about schools, separating rich and poor,

Christian and Muslim, Protestant and Catholic, impact on our communities. Probed on reasons for choice, the public is more likely to talk about access to high quality services for all. Choice is a weak proxy for 'greater control, an aspiration to define one's own needs and a desire to shape outcomes, process and relationships'.

While New Labour accepts limits to choice, excluding 'core functions of the state' such as defence and foreign policy, and 'public goods' such as safe streets and air quality, these are often treated as if they are 'economic givens' (Goodman, 2005). History teaches us, however, that 'public goods' are not fixed economic categories, but have been won by the political campaigns of the past century. Extended by nineteenth century reformers to include water, gas, electricity, telephones, public parks – and again in the second half of the twentieth century to include health, clean air, river quality, national parks, comprehensive education, universities, theatres, concert halls – public goods are once again under attack: as gated communities reduce a sense of collective safety; as playing fields, libraries, post-offices and allotments disappear. There have been a few, brave, attempts to extend public goods into new areas, for example the right to roam, but by and large New Labour has been content to accept the neo-liberal view that public goods are what's left over when the market has provided everything else.

The past nine years, then, have been characterised by a relatively old-fashioned view of the state as a 'car to be driven', in Harold Wilson's famous phrase; with a centralist, target-driven approach to service improvement and a preoccupation with structural change and competition as the main vehicles for change. Choice has been a mantra, but in reality there has been little attention paid to customer views and needs; indeed, as decision-making moves away from localities, the relationships between service user and provider becomes ever more distant.

FROM PUBLIC SECTOR TO PUBLIC REALM

When David Cameron says that 'there is such a thing as society, it just isn't the same as the state', he is redefining a core difference between conservatives and social democrats. Conservatives are suspicious of government; they see it as able to challenge privilege and power. They instinctively prefer small, and less powerful state organisations, and, where possible, private provision. Social democrats, on the other hand, have always championed collective action; wanting to ensure that government has sufficient power and leverage to take on the most powerful private individuals and companies in the interest of public good.

Public services were a central part of Labour's rethink after the defeat of 1979. It was widely recognised that during the 1960s and 1970s, state provision had failed, not only middle-class, but also working-class people; and indeed, as Clarke points out, much of the campaigning against unresponsive state provision came from feminists, tenants associations and disability activists attempting to wrest some autonomy and control from arrogant professionals (Clarke, 2005: 52). Social democrats began to accept some of the dangerous tendencies of state provision to 'decay' over time, to bureaucratise, to become producer driven, and to centralise. The concept of an 'enabling state' was coined, which would have built into it constant counter-pressures: a vigorous pluralism, a recognition of the need for strong independent institutions in civil society, accountability that was close-up and personal, services that were responsive to user needs. Now that a mixed economy has become a core part of public service provision, systemic counter-pressures are also needed to counteract new potential sources of public service 'decay' – pressures from within the market to put profit ahead of consumer and public interests.

Instead of an out-dated picture of a 'public sector' consisting of large publicly owned service providers, we need to recognise instead the 'public realm' – areas of our lives in which we have legitimate collective interests as citizens, and where social and community values should prevail. In these areas, provision will continue to be from a mixture of public, private and voluntary organisations – but the orchestration and commissioning of provision must be directly accountable to the people, and must be governed by values that protect the public.

THE CHARACTERISTICS OF A STRONG PUBLIC REALM

All public services need to be responsive to their users, building in constant feedback and dialogue. As Brendan Martin has argued recently, there are many examples, both in the UK and abroad, of public services that manage to be highly responsive outside a market context. These are likely to have good feedback systems, and pressure within the service to constantly improve the service to customers; to be accountable to local people, and close enough for them to feel ownership; and to build a close relationship between providers and service users at the front line, with enough autonomy for local managers to respond to local needs.

In the fast moving entrepreneurial world, the concept of choice is already considered to be dated. To paraphrase: 'we don't want choice, we want what we want'. Barry Schwartz in *The Paradox of Choice* argues that too much choice is disabling (Schwartz, 2003). Consumers are becoming tired of choice in the sense of major global conglomerates adding vast numbers of petty differences to their mass-produced products. We want instead to have something tailored especially to our needs – the private sector is beginning to think about 'co-creating' products. Ironically, of course, this is far harder to achieve through market mechanisms than within the public and voluntary sectors. Instead of offering limited choice, the public sector could concentrate on co-design. We now have the potential to use technology, pooled budgets, integrated services and partnerships to tailor services to individual or neighbourhood needs, planned in consultation with users or groups of users, just as the middle classes plan a designer long-haul holiday or use a wardrobe advisor. To achieve this we need not only flexible individualised delivery systems, but also flexible professionals – the 'reflexive practitioners' that Donald Schon talked about (1983). A pre-requisite for modern public services is that professionals are taught from the beginning to challenge and question their own expertise in the light of the experience and knowledge of service users, and to build reciprocal and equal relationships with users.

Many of the things we want as citizens – places for kids to go, safe streets, cohesive, safe communities, less waste, less congestion – can't be achieved by a smart government delivery machine. We don't know, as a society, how to achieve these outcomes. There is only fledgling evidence about what works. In order to achieve these things we have resources at our disposal not limited to those we can buy in the market place, resources that include collective action, moral pressure, tolerance, compassion, charitable efforts, reciprocal support. But these resources cannot be commanded by the centre. Nor can they be bought in the marketplace. The state is not remotely like a supermarket, offering consumer choice; it has to engage in dialogue with citizens, individually and collectively, about how best the investment of state resources can support the resources of the public. To access them, citizens need to be treated not as passive consumers but as 'activist-providers' playing a role in achieving social outcomes alongside government – and 'co-designing' services that use public resources to maximum effect. As Mark Moore has argued (1995), by accounting for public sector activity as if it was simply comparable to commercial activity, we both distort the reality of resources being used, and fail to optimise collective resources.

It is that combination, of individually crafted services and integrated delivery systems, that should replace current departmental silos. There is space, within those solutions, for public, private, not-for-profit and voluntary providers all to play a role – but there is a need for strong enough governance to hold the ring, and to legitimate the trade-offs that are being made. As citizens it doesn't help us to hold each power-less agency to account; we need to be able to hold the 'whole system' to account for the balancing decisions being made.

The state is not always right. It is essential to any democracy to have a vibrant civil society, strong enough to challenge and promote alternatives to state action or provision where necessary. A govern-ment interested in optimising the resources available to the public realm would recognise trades unions, universities, third sector, volun-tary and community based organisations as having their own legitimacy and accountability outside the state; and their own reasons for action and knowledge about what might work. They would be treated as a resource, and as valuable and knowledgeable partners in their own right. Voluntary, community and 'third sector' organisa-tions attracted attention in the early years of the first New Labour government, but are often now disadvantaged by government policies that favour the private sector. Voluntary organisations – crucial allies in creating a vibrant civil society – tend to be treated simply as cheap providers, commissioned and controlled as if they were simply agents of government.

The private sector is a valuable source of new thinking, innovation and competitive challenge, but it is helpful to differentiate between those private organisations which can make a distinct contribution of specialist expertise from a base of shared goals, and the run-of-the-mill companies for whom there is always an uneasy compromise between achieving profit and meeting social needs. A preoccupation with large conventional capitalist companies rather than with social businesses and values-led companies impoverishes the pool of potential institu-tions that could be developed to provide public services.

Markets, however immature, which rely on public funding, must operate in the public good. Markets in the public realm are not like private markets, since public money and government conditions distort outcomes, and providers are highly protected from market risk. Government has a role in designing the conditions for entrants to the market; in planning supply and skill-mix; in the inspection and regula-tion of quality; the prevention of abuse; the public assurance of public values such as equity and justice; and holding the private sector accountable for their actions.

Crucially, in the public realm we need to have a clear public under-standing of the obligations to be expected of private sector organisations. What are the provisions for recovery when private sector organisations fail? Is it acceptable for all risk to be transferred to the state? The absence of trust in public agencies, combined with an 'in principle' belief in the efficacy of the market, has led to the over-regulation of the public sector, while the accountabilities of the private sector go unexplored.

REASSERTING PUBLIC VALUES

Public values define the role and boundaries of the public realm, and enable us to design an effective modern social architecture without losing sight of the reasons for doing so. As Robin Cook wrote, 'the good society is defined not by its pass rate on performance indicators but by the values that shape it' (Cook, 2003: 342).

It is because private sector values can be inimical to values of equality and fairness, and corrosive of social cohesion, that the public realm must have within it the power to control and constrain the private sector; it is because the drives of self-interest, accumulation of profit and competition are at odds with social values of sharing, mutuality and collaboration that we need social spaces in which non-market values prevail. Fairness is not simply an irritating preoccupation of old Labour backbenchers, standing in the way of progress. Fair societies are open, where citizens share broadly comparable life experiences, enjoy better health, suffer less crime and benefit from wider opportunities.

Public values are important, since they mark out a terrain for human life which values collective endeavour, and ensures that the well-being of others is not harmed by our actions. It is within the public realm, for example, that our children will learn to constrain and contextualise the values learnt in capitalism – greed and instant gratification. Collective endeavour is not simply a second best to private consumption. Through taking part in a march, a charity run, a vigil, a youth parliament, a trades union, a school concert – we satisfy a basic human need for expression as part of a group, a collective. Not only is there such a thing as society, but it is a rich diverse place, full of encounters with the unexpected and opportunities to learn from others.

The work on social capital by David Halpern (1998) and others showed that what began to be called 'weak' social capital was by far the most important in offering people access to opportunities beyond their own lives. Strong social capital bound communities tightly, tribally, but could sometimes turn them in on themselves. It was the looser linkages provided by tenants associations, community groups, parish councils, consultation meetings, parents evenings, citizen juries, school governors – that offered people a chance to meet others and access networks beyond their own.

As our lives become increasingly dominated by capitalist relation-ships and commodification, the public realm is needed to take back social space in which we learn to share, to work and act together, to protect the weak, and to act as guardians of our social wealth for future generations. Public parks, public libraries, schools, concert halls, theatres, swimming pools, are some of the few social spaces where people from all social classes can come together – where people are not defined, segmented and targeted, based on age or income. While insti-tutions need to be modernised, collectivist values cannot simply be dismissed as old fashioned. Young people brought up as 'uber-consumers' may not choose collective solutions now, but the government is fighting with every authoritarian weapon it can against the social consequences of a shrinking and impoverished public realm.

The public realm creates the conditions for effective democracy. These are neither inevitable nor certain – indeed in the US we begin to see the conditions for democracy close to breakdown; as society consolidates into two opposing blocks without the conditions neces-sary for dialogue or compromise. This must not happen here. Government has a role in ensuring that all voices can be heard, ensur-ing equal access to decision makers, providing an infrastructure that enables disadvantaged groups to negotiate inclusion. Government has to secure equity and justice, both through the ways that public servants treat people, and through the design of appropriate 'governance spaces', that enable communities to come together, understand each other's needs and negotiate solutions.

Public values, therefore, have to govern moments of tension and conflict; to enable civil society to negotiate and compromise. A cohe-sive society is one in which everyone can show each other tolerance and respect. Values of civility, reciprocity and mutuality cannot be upheld by making speeches and setting rules; they require an example to be set through the behaviour of political and community leaders. To nourish and support deliberation and dialogue as forms of governance would require a change in the way that politicians behave – ceasing to 'tell' and 'spin' and learning to listen, disclose and have meaningful conversations.

Ways have to be found to make the public realm relevant to young people. The debate about public values will need to be conducted in modern ways, more creative and energising than the sombre public meeting and the dull committee. To engage properly, government would have to move away from its current sterile approach of opinion polling followed by speech making. Instead of trading on the unexamined opinions sparked by the *Daily Mail*, it could engage in a grown-up debate with the British people about the values that should underpin social action. New technology offers opportunities to share information and decision making on a far more exciting scale than ever before. The potential to use public service broadcasting for deliberation at local and national level, the scope for exchange on the internet, the opportunities already being developed at local level to engage with communities in serious, long-term dialogue, offer the prospect of new sorts of accountabilities and new sorts of conversation between communities and their representatives.

A RE-IMAGINED PUBLIC REALM
A re-imagined public realm would be upside down, or rather inside out, with the locality at the centre; a small enabling infrastructure at regional level; and Whitehall at the periphery – three mutually support-ive and interacting sites of governance of equal value; the contribution of all three areas would be valued, and the importance of subsidiarity recognised. Localities would negotiate with the centre the way they intended to achieve nationally prescribed goals and standards, and would try to win support and resources for local priorities.

Instead of rigid government structures organised and reorganised from the centre, we would see a more fluid, open network of provision – welcoming the private sector as creative partners, alongside other voluntary, third sector, not-for profit and public sector providers. User-centred services tailored to individual needs and choices would sometimes involve markets and sometimes involve direct provision; there would be confidence that public assets were still held by the people and markets still managed in the interests of citizens and consumers.

It is at local level that government can cope with complexity. The complex social outcomes that public agencies are trying to achieve are the results of multiple interacting streams of causality. It takes equiva-lently complex thinking and the critical mass of several linked interventions to make a difference. It is really only at local level that government can be successfully 'joined up' – where the complexity clears to reveal a place, a neighbourhood, an estate. Communities can only be engaged at a locality level. It is there that dialogue can take place and 'decision-making' spaces be designed to bring different communities together, since the design of such arrangements requires local knowledge of the history and the geography. While some issues affect a town or a city, or key groups of consumers, some services can be designed at the level of a neighbourhood a village, a street, an estate.

New technology makes it possible to replace the old stodgy town halls with networks of governance, capable of moving from the delivery of a few standard services to orchestrating the resources of a place. The community leadership role expected of a democratically elected council should be a strong rather than a weak one. Local government should have the leverage to make things happen on behalf of local citizens.

Local authorities can no longer achieve this alone. Local Strategic Partnerships offer scope to integrate a local service network, and create the leverage necessary to make things happen. Of course partnerships are hampered by political, organisational and geographical rivalries, and their work is made harder by the mixed messages and conflicting pressures exerted by the centre. Nevertheless, where partnerships can be made to work, they create the potential for localities, 'as a whole system', to negotiate directly with government and other powerful interests. The alternative, which seems now ridiculously unlikely, would be to return powers directly to the local authority. Either way we need to think through the systems of accountability and public engagement.

At regional level, what would then be needed would simply be a fluid network of powerful enablers (accountable either to a regional electorate or to the centre); these would be small, tight and strategic in focus, undistracted by detailed process control; they would operate across government silos, promoting enterprise and innovation, and capable of funding and sponsoring major experimental projects (for example long-term transport projects); they would support innovation and the sharing of expertise, creating a strong evidence base around the regional economy; they would be able to evidence resource choices within the region, holding onto strong public service values, looking across the public and private agencies in each region and managing larger regional markets.

This would leave a far smaller civil service at the centre. Instead of vast central departments, all that would be needed would be highly skilled strategic thinkers; and a handful of experienced policy specialists, many of whom might be seconded from outside. Liberated from the fiction of delivery, civil servants could concentrate on what they do best; creating the framework of legislation, policy, finance and sanctions to secure government goals in a way that accords with a fluid, innovative mixed market. The work process of the civil service could shift to highly focused, multi-disciplinary policy teams, organised around each of the government's key policy goals and knowledge management and innovation teams, responsible for R&D and bringing together thinkers and experts from the field to test out radical ideas. These could be supported by a serious long-term research capability, based in universities, protected from short-term ministerial preoccupations.

With smaller cross-boundary policy teams, duplication would reduce and collective memory and experience would build. Government advice could increasingly come directly from academics, practitioners, community leaders and professionals. Instead of cumbersome guidance, a network of conversations between the centre, regions and localities would transmit learning about what was happening on the ground. The centre would still want to check for value for money; there would still have to be consequences for poor performance; and a process such as CPA should continue. But more transparent, shared access to data could lead to collaborative discussions of problems in delivery; challenge and dialogue could replace rigid process control. Inspection services are due to be streamlined. What's left should be seen as clearly independent of government and accountable to the public; able to comment fearlessly on, and investigate the effectiveness of, all levels of government in the public interest.

If the civil service ceased to be a separate and protected organisation – if we created a common entry level for local, regional and central government – with equivalent prestige given to running a great city as to running a government department – we could change the invisible hierarchy between localities and the centre. We could begin to see a single public service system, with stronger linkages between different areas of public service, encouraging people to move between sectors. Government would need to think about long-term workforce planning across public services, offering retraining to young civil servants to move across into other fields – as youth workers, social workers, finance officers, planning officers. The era of targets could be succeeded by constant, real time performance improvement, driven at the front line instead of at the centre; with open access to performance data for the public as well as government, and performance being subject to regular challenge dialogues between agencies and their stakeholders, exploring how well public money is being spent, and how successfully outcomes are being achieved.

A LAST CHANCE?

In the next government, we know that additional resources for the public sector will begin to dry up. And yet public services still need investment. A critical 'last chance' therefore exists; we might be able to release the people and money bound up currently in what John Seddon would call 'waste activity' (Seddon, 2003) at all levels of government to enable us to continue to expand provision at the front line.

The actions needed require government to act on a large scale, and with a sense of courage and a consistency of purpose which could be sustained for a decade. Labour needs a new infrastructure for government, and a new way of thinking about the public realm.

REFERENCES

Clarke, J. (2005), 'The People's choice? New Labour and public service reform', *Renewal*, Vol 13 No 4, 52-59.

Cook, R. (2003), *The Point of Departure*, London: Simon and Schuster.

Seddon, J. (2003), *Freedom from Command and Control*, London: Vanguard Press.

Goodman, H. (2005), 'Choice and voice in service reform', *Renewal*, Vol 13 No 4, 59-65.

Halpern, D. (1998), 'Social Capital, exclusion and the quality of life; towards a causal model and policy implications', unpublished paper *Nexus* conference.

Moore, M. H. (1995), *Creating*, Cambridge, Mass: Harvard University Press.

Schon, D. A. (1983), *The Reflexive Practitioner*, New York: Basic Books.

Schwartz, B. (2003), *The Paradox of Choice*, New York: Harper Collins.

Living in the machine: New Labour and public services

Jake Chapman

Since the 1990s it has become clear that many public services in the UK are failing to meet the expectations of the public. That failure has two primary causes. The first is a growing sophistication and higher aspirations amongst the general public. The second is the steady reduction in expenditure and investment in public services throughout the 1980s. A commitment to correct this failure, especially in education and health care, was one important factor in the dramatic support New Labour received from the electorate in 1997. So demonstrating an improvement in core public services is a key requirement if New Labour is to retain its electoral support.

There is no doubt that much has been accomplished since 1997, with many important indicators showing substantial improvement. However, the improvements are not yet sufficient to close the gap between public expectations and the services provided. There is a sense that the improvement does not justify the enormous increase in expenditure and investment. And many of those involved in public service provision, from ministers, through policy-makers and senior managers, to 'frontline' staff, express a sense of frustration. At every level individuals feel trapped in a system that prevents them from making significant improvements – and at every level people blame those above or below them for the difficulties they experience. So what is the truth? Are the managers incompetent? Are the policies formulated by Whitehall impossibly out of touch? Are the frontline staff wedded to old ways and resistant to modernising at all costs? Is there too much or too little management? Where has all the money and investment gone? Or is the core problem that we, the public, are simply unwilling to pay enough tax to fund the level of services that would satisfy us?

In this chapter I will use concepts and ideas from the field of systems to generate a different perspective on what is happening. Systems ideas have been around since the end of World War Two and they have been used in all areas of human activity. Some of the concepts have entered everyday language, for example feedback, but by and large the public sector has only engaged with systems ideas at the local level, for example in the design of hospital IT systems. The use of systems in business was widely promoted by Peter Senge's books (see Senge, 1990). A brief history and introduction to systems thinking relevant to the public sector was published by Demos (Chapman, 2002). This chapter develops that analysis further and sets out to explain why modernising public services has proved so much more problematic than politicians and policy-makers had anticipated – and without spoiling the plot I can say now that it has nothing to do with blaming managers, frontline staff or anyone else.

To the uninitiated the problem of improving public services does not appear to be difficult. The previous lack of capital investment, in buildings and equipment, can be made up over a period of years. Annual expenditure can be increased to provide more police, teachers, doctors and nurses and where necessary the organisations can be modernised. New Public Management (NPM) had already introduced the notion that what mattered was performance, as measured by outputs and outcomes, so this could be developed further to ensure that the increases in public expenditure would provide the required results. And broadly this is what the New Labour government set out to do.

They went quite a lot further than NPM in developing measures of performance, and recast the whole budget process in terms of Public Service Agreements (PSAs). These agreements allocated funds over a three-year period in return for improvements in specific performance measures – the targets. Although NPM had made use of performance measures and audits, departments continued to focus on their annual budget – their *input*. The design of the PSA process, incorporating longer budget cycles and linking funding to outcomes, was expected to force departments to modernise and focus more on the *outputs* – the services provided to the public. This has been a significant shift and may be one of the important legacies of the New Labour government.

The use of targets to drive improvement served other purposes. Governments and ministers are under pressure to show improvement within their period of office – otherwise they are open to the accusation of having accomplished nothing tangible. By setting targets for public services the politicians achieved two potentially useful goals.

First the targets communicated to the policy-makers, managers and organisations involved in providing public services exactly what the priorities were – and what was expected by way of improved performance. Second, by making these targets public the politicians could claim that they were making the process of improvement transparent and making themselves directly accountable. These are significant benefits.

There is another, more subtle, benefit to politicians in the use of targets. By declaring an improvement target publicly the politician can, to some degree, gain credit before any real improvement is in place. 'We are going to cut waiting lists (or crime or truancy or illiteracy) by X per cent' makes it clear that this government and this minister mean business, they are actually setting out to make a difference – and on a performance measure that is known to matter to the public. Clearly there is a risk that the target may not be met, but with luck by then the minister will have changed, the focus of public attention will have shifted and a new target will be capturing the headlines. In the meantime the target creates or reinforces an image of a politician determined to provide the improvements that the public seeks.

THE LIMITS OF TARGETS

This approach to improving and modernising public services seems obvious. And the use of targets suits both the modernising agenda and other political goals. It is an obvious and compelling logic. The reason why it appears so compelling is because it fits with the way that our culture teaches us to think about organisations and the provision of goods and services. However, from a systems perspective there are a number of ways in which targets can distort and disrupt the *system*. There are five important distortions.

The first is that targets encourage everyone in an organisation to 'face the wrong way' – they are all seeking to satisfy the requirements placed on them by their superior rather than focusing on the needs and requirements of their subordinates or clients or customers. This is not a trivial issue, as indicated by the following commentary on a National Audit Office report:

> Last week's report by the National Audit Office on the NHS rightly highlighted how health delivery is disastrously subverted by waiting list targets. The NAO found that to avoid being fined for over-long waiting lists, 20 per cent of consultants 'frequently' ignored clinical priorities in their operations lists, performing simple routine procedures rather than complicated ones in order to make their numbers (Caulkin, 2001).

The second distortion introduced by the use of targets is that the target usurps the more general goal or purpose of the system. Here is an education example that illustrates the issue. Schools are assessed on the number of students scoring A, B or C grades in GCSE examinations. Teachers have responded to this target by focusing most of their effort on students that they expect to score C or D. The A and B students are certainly going to count towards their target and therefore do not need attention. And the lower grade students cannot be brought up to the C grade no matter how much time the teacher invests in them. So teachers concentrate on the borderline cases. This is a severe distortion of the teacher's educative role towards all the students and an inevitable consequence of imposing such a target.

The third distortion is more subtle because it involves manipulating the data on which the target is based. It is a well-known phenomenon that as soon as there is a consequence (either positive or negative) upon some data then the agents involved will seek to manipulate the data to their advantage. This is technically referred to as 'gaming'. For example I recently had my wallet stolen whilst travelling home from London. When I contacted the police to report the theft I was passed from one agency to another. The police in Taunton (where I live) said it was a matter for London, the police in London passed me to the Transport Police, who said they could only help if I knew that the crime had occurred on the train. I did not know where the crime had occurred, so I started around the loop once more. Finally someone explained that no one wanted to accept this crime report because it would certainly add to their 'unsolved crime' statistics: the person who explained this was gracious enough to save me further telephone calls and accept the report.

The fourth distortion is one that the so-called 'frontline staff' – the teachers, doctors police and nurses – have vociferously complained about. It is the loss of productive time that is involved in collecting all the data required to demonstrate compliance (or not) with the target. Provision of management data is always a chore, but the very large number of targets being enforced within the public services has created a significant burden that represents a serious loss of productive effort. Here is one account that puts the loss at more than 50 per cent!

The Guardian [May 22nd 2003] reported how a man running a Drug Action Team – whose purpose is to deal with the drug problem – quit because he could no longer stand the waste and bureaucracy. His work was dictated to by 44 different funding streams, each with its own detailed guidance and micro targets from the centre. Each required a detailed business plan and quarterly reports back to the centre. He was obliged to sign endless service agreements with every local provider, who had their own micro targets and were obliged to send quarterly reports back to him so he could collate them and pass them back to the centre. He was to follow nine planning grids with 82 objectives. The funding was always announced too late for planning and then handed over too late to be spent and finally spent for spending's sake to prevent it being reclaimed by the centre. Staff were hired and trained and then suddenly sacked when funding or targets were switched by the centre (or they just quit because they couldn't stand it any more). He estimated he and his staff spent only 40 per cent of their time organising services for drug users – the rest of their time was consumed by producing paper plans and paper reports for Whitehall. Talking about the government, he said: 'They don't know very much about drugs but they do know about management and monitoring and data collection. So that's what they do (Seddon, 2003).

The fifth distortion that targets create is that they frequently fail to distinguish variation in people's requirements or differences in context. This disregard for variation can force people into bizarre behaviour. One that struck me recently was the difficulty people have making appointments at the local doctor's surgery. The problems in my area started with the introduction of a target to see 80 per cent of patients within 24 hours of them contacting the surgery. The reason this has added to many people's difficulties is that this is a rural area and people try to make their visits to the doctor coincide with other trips into town – usually a few days ahead. The receptionists at the surgery are refusing to make these appointments because they break the target – which was supposed to make doctor's surgery appointments more responsive!

These distortions and unintended consequences of targets seem obvious once they are pointed out. And there are literally hundreds of examples across the entire spectrum of public services. Why is it that such a simple and compelling logic of how to improve public services should produce such bizarre effects? Is it that the targets being set are too crude? Or are the managers and staff deliberately undermining them?

THE MACHINE MEN
Earlier I pointed out that the logic used to support the modernising agenda and use of targets was compelling in part because it matched the way that we have been taught to think about organisations. If you engage with a civil servant or politician about the improvement of

public services you will find that they will talk in a language that represents the organisations involved as if they were machines. 'The levers of power', 'stepping up a gear' 'changing direction', 'driving through change', 'the machinery of government' are some of the most common examples.

> The ubiquity of the machine metaphor was the legacy that the military bequeathed to governments and then to manufacturing ... Well oiled, efficient and measurable, the ideal machine had a clear purpose or function which it carried out perfectly. Everything could in principle be conceived as a closed system, consisting of cogs and wheels, instructions and commands, with a boss or government at the top, pulling the requisite levers and engineering the desired effects ...
>
> These machine images have had a profound influence on how we think ... They influenced ideas of organisation to such an extent that many organisations were built deliberately as machines, and so long as their environments remained stable, these machine bureaucracies proved extremely effective in marshalling resources and energies to particular ends. But the environment for machine-like things has gone into decline (Mulgan, 1998: 150-1).

This mechanistic thinking underpins scientific management and the use of performance measures and targets. It works very well when the issues involved are complicated but not complex. Things that are complicated can have many parts and many interactions, but they remain essentially predictable and controllable. This is in contrast to issues that are *complex*; they are inherently unpredictable and uncontrollable. The unpredictability and uncontrollability arises because within the context of the issue there are a large number of *autonomous* agents or agencies that are communicating and influencing each other. Many of the technical advances in the late twentieth century made communication much easier and cheaper. This, coupled with the erosion of shared values and the rise of individualism, has meant that most large organisations have become complex rather than complicated. From a systems perspective it is more appropriate to view an organisation as a complex system than as a machine.

The network of organisations and agencies involved in providing public services is amazingly complex – and becomes more complex each year, with additional legislation, new European directives, new risks to be accommodated, new targets to be met or passed on. And at every level the people involved experience a high level of frustration – which they attribute to those either above them or below them. Senior politicians are certain that professionals are resisting change because they have a cushy position. Managers are certain that politicians are out of touch – and the people they are managing are out to prove them wrong. Professionals and other frontline staff feel mistrusted, see politicians and managers as completely out of touch and object to having to spend ever more time undertaking tasks that do not benefit the people they are serving. Yet in my own experience everyone I have worked with and interviewed is *doing their best*. Indeed I have been impressed by the level of commitment and ingenuity, as well as the intelligence and desire to serve, shown by everyone involved – including politicians, senior civil servants, policy-makers, senior managers, agency managers and professionals. *But no amount of good intention can correct flaws built into the way that they all think about what needs to be done.*

The differences in approach and perceptions between the mechanistic and the systemic are important because they condition the policies that are formulated and the decisions made by managers. The argument I am making is not about the way that the organisations providing public services operate, though that may be inadequate in various ways. What I am arguing is that by thinking about, and treating an organisation, as if it were a machine – when it is actually more like a complex system – then the policies and decisions made will fail. And they will fail in predictable ways, as explained in *System Failure* (2002). The outcomes will be an increasing number of unintended consequences, the alienation of professional staff (who will feel instrumentalised and mistrusted) and a loss in overall system capacity (due in part to additional administration loads but also due to people becoming disheartened). Examples of these characteristic failures are everywhere within the public services – and as government and management try to enforce more targets so these disabling outcomes will increase. If you look back over the examples of perverse outcomes from the use of targets, you can see these three ingredients at work. In the examples I gave everyone involved – the teachers, police, surgeons and so on – were behaving completely rationally within the context created by the mechanistic policy – but it was not what was intended by the policy-maker.

When confronted with a situation in which public services being provided are inadequate or failing to meet expectations, most observers and those involved want to be told what to *do* differently. My argument is different. I am claiming that before changing what is done it is critical to change the way the situation is *thought* about. Without a shift in thinking, all prescriptions of what to do will create the same failure – and this is the point that has eluded politicians, managers and commentators alike.

One of the innovations introduced by New Labour has been 'delivery units', the most powerful being the Prime Minister's Delivery Unit (PMDU). These have been established to 'drive through change' and ensure that modernisation and better public services are 'delivered'. Now it is quite feasible to deliver many things – such as food – which are the object of a one-sided relationship: i.e. they are consumed. But it is nonsense to talk about delivering public services or modernisation. Not only is it a semantic nonsense; the associated conceptualisation and assumptions are precisely the problem that needs to be addressed.

The point is that if something is delivered to me then I am a passive recipient. I may have had to choose what it was I wanted, and I certainly have to pay for it – but I do not have any hand in its production. So this conceptualisation of 'delivering public services' conceives of the public as passive recipients whose only function is to choose the particular service flavour they require.

But it is obvious that you cannot 'deliver' education or health, nor even modernisation. These outcomes are *co-produced* by the recipient and the service provider. For an individual to be educated they have to choose a subject and educational provider – *and* they have to be motivated, sufficiently able, and willing to devote sufficient time for the desired outcome to be achieved. Similarly if I want to improve my health then I have to be willing to make changes to what I eat, how much I exercise, whether I smoke or drink – as well as receive advice and medication from medical practitioners. To describe or think about these processes in terms of delivery denies the significance of the interactive and co-productive aspects of what is occurring. And it is this denial of the interaction and co-production that is a major contributor to the sense of dissatisfaction. And the denial is built into the language used and the way of thinking. So reform, modernisation and change must, in my view, start by changing the language and the way of thinking about what is occurring.

One feature of public services that has emerged, as it has become clear that increased investment and expenditure do not resolve the issues, is the need for 'personalised services' (Leadbeater, 2004). It has been recognised that as the public have become more sophisticated and more diverse, in culture, backgrounds and goals, so the services they require vary significantly. But the mechanistic language still persists: personalised services still have to be 'delivered' and are contrasted to 'one size fits all' – all of which is still conceptualising public services as a product received by a passive consumer.

What difference would it make if public services were regarded as being co-produced by a complex interaction between citizens and professional service providers? One of the immediate issues would be the need to devolve a great deal more decision-making – about the nature of what is provided and the processes involved – to the professional interacting with citizens seeking improvement in some aspect of their lives. Another consequence could be the expansion of what public services actually facilitate. For example the health service could radically transform and become fully engaged with helping people to take preventative measures, use the full spectrum of medical and alternative health treatments and improve their lifestyle – rather than simply engaging with people when they are seriously ill. Whilst it is focused on reducing waiting list times and ensuring 80 per cent of appointment enquiries are satisfied within 24 hours the health service cannot begin to engage with such an agenda, even though countless studies have shown prevention to be far more efficient and effective than treatment.

So, ironically, the New Labour focus on improving public services and its emphasis on delivery and targets has become the major obstacle to radical improvement and modernisation of public services! The problem is not one of finance or commitment, or good intentions; it is down to the way the issues are conceptualised and how that mode of thinking then fashions policy and management decisions.

It is not accidental that mechanistic thinking has such a grip on the way all branches of government think about and conceptualise the world. Anyone who wishes to change the world requires a model or conceptualisation that makes it plausible that they could be sufficiently influential – that they could exert sufficient control over events and organisations to make a difference. At the heart of the mechanical world view is the presumption that control is possible and that if you can control causes you can have predictable effects. It is this promise of predictability and control that lures all politicians into the same fallacy. You don't have to believe that they are power-mad control freaks (though they may well be). Anyone who wishes to change the world in some way has to presume that they will have the ability to influence or control events and organisations. This presumption is also built into the notion of ministerial responsibility – the minister can only be held responsible if she is regarded as being in control. Even though memoirs and anecdotes from countless ministers have pointed out that what they actually control is precious little, the myth is retained, because it provides the basis of government by ministers.

This presumption of control and ability to change is not peculiar to politicians, it is endemic in our culture. There will be many readers of this chapter who dismiss it as 'too theoretical', because I am not laying out a prescription to do X, Y and Z. The whole point of a systemic way of thinking about complex problems is that it is actually a fallacy to think that such prescriptions have any validity. There are two core reasons for this.

The first is that the complexity of the real situation is such that no-one, no matter how clever or experienced, will be able to predict the outcomes of specified actions. The system really is unpredictable and uncontrollable – no matter how many people think otherwise.

The second core reason for prescriptions being invalid from a systemic perspective is that they fail to accommodate the many different perspectives, values and goals of the different participants and stakeholders. Systems practice is deeply pluralist – by which I mean it deliberately seeks to surface and accommodate differences in value and perspective. It is only in this way that the agents and agencies involved can be committed to a common improvement and share the knowledge and understanding that enables them to avoid unintended consequences. A systemic approach does not start from a prescribed policy or solution. It starts with a collaborative process with the aim of seeking agreement on what would constitute improvement and then learning, through experimentation and innovation, how best to achieve such change. So for me to come up with some sort of prescription would actually be directly contradictory to the approach I am recommending.

If a systemic approach is so obviously a better way to proceed, why is it not being adopted? In Chapter 9 of *System Failure* the main institutional obstacles to implementing such an approach are set out. However I have now come to the conclusion that these are not the most serious. Governments and the civil service are actually rather good at making institutional changes. What they are far less good at is changing the underlying culture, the way of thinking about government and policy.

Successive governments of different political persuasions, over the last two decades, have steadily developed a framework that is rooted in the mechanistic presumptions of predictability and control. Indeed both Thatcher and Blair have been widely regarded, and begrudgingly respected, as control freaks. The respect arises because everyone, the media, the electorate, the managers and civil servants expect and require the government to 'be in control'. Long live the machine metaphor!

REFERENCES

Caulkin, S. (2001), 'On target for destruction', *The Observer*, 5 August.

Chapman, J. (2002), *System Failure: why governments must learn to think differently*, London: Demos 2002 (available as free download from www.demos.co.uk).

Leadbeater, C. (2004), *Personalisation through Participation*, London: Demos.

Mulgan, G. (1998), *Connexity: Responsibility, Freedom, Business and Power in the New Century*, Vintage: London.

Seddon, J. (2003), *Freedom from Command and Control*, Buckingham: Vanguard Education Ltd.

Senge, P. (1990), *The Fifth Discipline: the art and practice of the learning organisation*, London: Random House.

Hard Labour? The future of work and the role of public policy

David Coats

Work consumes much of our adult lives. It is the place where we find satisfaction, friendship and even romance. Of course, while many of us would agree that we should work to live rather than live to work, nobody is indifferent about their employment. How we work, when we work and how long we work determine our overall quality of life and can affect our general health and life expectancy. There is a rich political vein to be mined here if only New Labour can find a language and a policy prospectus that offers a coherent vision of 'good work'.

Historically, social democrats have viewed work as a fully human activity that engages all our skills, talents, capabilities and emotions. What makes our position distinctive is that we do not believe that individuals surrender their rights as citizens when they cross their employer's threshold. Furthermore, we believe that the workplace is characterised by inequalities of power and that collective action is needed to redress these inequalities – hence our historic support for trade unionism.

One might reasonably say that New Labour has found it difficult to make practical sense of these principles. Indeed, there appear to be some profound contradictions in the government's approach. On the one hand legislation has been introduced that, in conventional terms, has made the labour market less 'flexible' – the National Minimum Wage (NMW), new rights for working parents and stronger protections against unfair dismissal – and on the other the government continues to obsess about 'burdens on business' and 'red tape'. Perhaps the confusion is rhetorical rather than practical; after all, the Warwick agreement contains commitments to further interventions in the labour market – but New Labour seems to have sacrificed policy coherence in the belief that everything possible must be done to retain the neutrality of 'the business vote'.

While the strategy may have worked for a while, the CBI is increasingly immune to the seductions of triangulation. Sir Digby Jones, and subsequently the new CBI Head Richard Lambert, have become much more critical of government policy, suggesting that the UK's prized 'flexible labour market' is under threat and that if nothing is done then 'China and India will eat our lunch'. Many on the left take a rather different view, believing that the government is committed to a neo-liberal policy of weak employment rights, feeble unions and a high degree of wage flexibility.

Both sides cannot be right and the truth lies somewhere between the extremes. Of course, the UK's labour market is more heavily regulated than in 1997; and New Labour has done things that no Conservative government would have contemplated. But the contrary argument contains more than a grain of truth too, in that the UK continues to have the second least regulated labour market in the developed world – only the USA scores higher on the OECD's 'flexibility' index.

In the meantime, however, work seems to have disappeared from the political agenda, even though researchers and journalists are now devoting more attention to the quality of working life than at any time in the recent past. There is a huge volume of material documenting the realities of 'overwork' and the persistence of low pay despite the success of the NMW (Bunting, 2004; Toynbee, 2003; Abrams, 2002). Similarly, there is an accumulating body of research which shows that, while most workers do not view their jobs as awful, they still express real dissatisfaction with some important features of the working environment, particularly pay and influence over decision-making (Kersley, 2005).

It would be a tragedy if a prolonged period of Labour government made no significant impact on the world of work beyond the introduction of the minimum wage and the new rights for working parents – both of which would be left to wither on the vine by David Cameron's soft-focus conservatism. What is needed is a more determined effort to create 'a progressive consensus in the workplace' that can survive a change of government. Labour must devise an approach that both speaks directly to the concerns of the majority of people at work *and* secures the support of better employers. The strategic objective must be to put labour market policy beyond the reach of a Conservative assault for the foreseeable future.

YOUR FLEXIBLE FRIEND?

The continued emphasis on labour market flexibility has been a source of real irritation for many on the left. Ministerial speeches sometimes leave one with the impression that there was no change of government in 1997 and that New Labour has continued to follow the Conservative route map. Nevertheless, there are two senses in which this is manifestly untrue. First, New Labour has, albeit tentatively, reintroduced full employment as an objective of public policy. Second, since 1997 the government has consistently evinced a profound concern for those at the rough end of the labour market – hence the NMW, the expansion of tax credits and the new commitments in Warwick.

What the government has not done with any conviction is to unpack the rhetoric of 'flexibility' and identify those elements of policy which explain the UK's good employment performance and those which are irrelevant. It might be objected that this is a rather unfair criticism, not least because HM Treasury (HMT) published a comprehensive review of labour market flexibility in 2003, to coincide with their assessment of the five tests for membership of the single currency. But HMT's presentation of the argument is rather orthodox, and it is easy to read some of the comments as an explicit endorsement of a neo-liberal approach to labour market policy. For example:

> The UK system of industrial relations appears conducive to wage flexibility. The decentralised and uncoordinated nature of collective bargaining means that relative wages can adjust to the conditions across industries, sectors and regions. The decline in collective bargaining over the past two decades also supports aggregate wage flexibility (HMT, 2003: 77, para 4.72).

This may require some decoding for those unfamiliar with HMT's lapidary drafting. Essentially the argument is that wage flexibility is an essential component of labour market flexibility, allowing wages to adjust to economic shocks. Falling union membership has made the UK labour market more flexible, which could lead one to conclude that HMT believe that weak unions are a rather good thing – at least so far as wage formation is concerned.

Other aspects of the analysis cast more doubt on the overall 'flexibility' thesis. For example, it is often argued by business lobbyists that employment protection legislation (EPL) is a burden on business that increases costs and leads to rising unemployment. HMT offer a more sanguine assessment: 'The net impact of EPL on employment and unemployment is ... uncertain. Evidence suggests the impact is small and/or ambiguous or that there is only a general relationship, which can break down when other explanatory factors are taken into account' (HMT, 2003: 72, para 4.52). Decoded, this means that analysts cannot be sure that tighter employment laws lead to higher unemployment.

A further important element of flexibility concerns the operation of the benefit system. At one time it was suggested that low benefits, time limited entitlements and rigorous job search requirements were all essential if the unemployed were to be incentivised to find work. In other words, high benefits tend to increase unemployment, so benefits should therefore be kept at the lowest possible level consistent with protecting people against destitution. This was the justification for the introduction of the Job Seekers' Allowance by the previous Conservative government – and Labour has done little since 1997 to increase benefit levels, which remain amongst the lowest in the EU 15.

HMT's own analysis offers a rather different perspective:

> Despite high replacement rates (high benefits), some continental European economies have managed to maintain work incentives and sustain high rates of employment. Empirical evidence suggests that the way in which the benefit system is administered is just as important as the level of financial support; most notably, the eligibility period and eligibility requirements (HMT 2003: 66, para 4.19).

It appears therefore that HMT have accepted that the true story is slightly more complex than the conventional wisdom. But these very useful arguments, which point in the direction of a wider range of policy options, rarely find their way into the public conversation. All that one hears from government ministers is that 'Europe' is sclerotic and needs a hefty dose of 'structural reform' before unemployment can fall. What fails to be mentioned (or at least reported) is that some states in the EU15 have enjoyed employment performance either as good as the UK's or slightly better. Denmark, Sweden, Austria, the Netherlands (until relatively recently) and Portugal have all managed to keep unemployment low with more regulated labour markets. The first four countries all have higher unemployment benefits than the UK, the first three have much stronger unions and Portugal has amongst the strongest EPL in the EU 15. Holland, with similar levels of trade union membership to the UK but much higher levels of collective bargaining coverage, has the highest wage flexibility of all these countries.

The rather misleading nature of the conventional wisdom has now been recognised by the OECD, the institution that might reasonably claim authorship of the flexibility story. Their *Employment Outlook* for the last two years has reviewed the evidence and concluded that policy-makers have a range of choices available to them, all of which are consistent with strong employment performance. In particular, while their work in the early-mid 1990s suggested that the US model was infinitely superior to any European alternatives, the OECD now praise the Danish labour market model of 'flexicurity' – easy hire and fire rules, generous benefits, well-developed active labour market programmes (a Rolls-Royce version of the UK's New Deal), investment in reskilling – and, one might add, amongst the strongest unions in the world (OECD, 2004: 97).

We should note too that Danish workers express a high level of employment security despite the relative ease of hire and fire and somewhat shorter job tenures than in the UK. There are two possible explanations for this. First, high benefits mean that unemployment is a much less catastrophic experience in Denmark than in the UK. Second, the strength of Danish unions guarantees that individual workers have an opportunity to influence critical decisions in the workplace, which is very different from the situation here (see the discussion below). Rather curiously, HMT's index of labour market flexibility shows that Denmark has the second *least* flexible labour market in the EU (only Belgium is more 'inflexible') – which throws some doubt on the value of their approach to these questions (HMT, op. cit.: 78).

An obvious conclusion to draw is that there is no 'right way' to achieve high levels of employment. Certainly, there is no evidence to show that convergence on the model of 'flexibility' applied in the USA is a necessary response to globalisation – quite the contrary in fact, as David Howell and his colleagues have persuasively argued (2005). Their comprehensive review of employment performance across the developed world demonstrates the reality of the social and political choices that remain available to us. In particular they show quite conclusively that the early-mid 1990s OECD framework cannot explain differences in employment performance between countries – for example, the Netherlands had a more regulated labour market than Germany throughout the 1990s and consistently enjoyed *better* employment performance (Schettkat, 2005).

One can conclude that the UK could quite reasonably *choose* to have a more regulated labour market, higher benefits and stronger unions without threatening employment, although trade unions might need to reconsider their approach to wage bargaining to ensure that settlements take proper account of the wider macro-economic situation.

The task now is to create an environment where these issues can be discussed openly. As a first step the government should abandon the strategy of triangulation and explain with much greater clarity exactly what they believe is needed to sustain the UK's good employment performance. It is not the role of a Labour Chancellor to make Irwin

Steltzer or Richard Lambert happy. Shifting to new terrain is also a necessary response to the Cameron-led Conservative Party and will help either to highlight differences between government and opposition (with the Conservatives taking a rather orthodox view of the need for limited regulation and weak unions) or to forge a consensus where the nature of the disagreement between the parties is less significant than in the past. In either case Labour will be on strong ground and will have a powerful response to any Tory effort to revive the argument for deregulation and a weakening of employment rights.

WHAT'S GOING ON?

So much then for the case for labour market flexibility, but developing a persuasive story about the world of work demands that the government has a keen appreciation of the realities as they are experienced by most employees. In this context it is important to debunk the myths surrounding working life in Britain today.

For example, how often have we heard that 'jobs for life' have disappeared, or that in the future most people will work in small firms? Such 'trends' are said to be 'irresistible' and driven either by globalisation or by the more intensive application of ICT. The reality of course is that job tenures have scarcely changed in fifteen years and job change is no more frequent than in the past; temporary work is a rather small component of the UK labour market, and, while employment in medium-sized firms has increased somewhat, there has been no significant growth in employment in small firms. Guru-driven narratives about 'the end of work', 'portfolio work' and 'living on thin air' have all proved to be so much hot air, as has the story of the 'knowledge economy'.

While we may have more 'good jobs' than at any time in the recent past, we also seem to have more 'bad work'. This is perhaps the most profound change of the last two decades. The labour market now has the shape of an hourglass, with more 'MacJobs' in the knowledge economy, more 'McJobs' in low-pay, low-productivity, low-status service occupations and fewer jobs in the middle (Goos and Manning, 2003). This phenomenon can be detected in all developed countries, and wage inequality has increased everywhere as a result – even in a country like Sweden with a relatively narrow distribution of earnings.

A critic might say that there is no problem to be solved here. After all, work is better than worklessness. Nevertheless, we also know that a 'good job' is better than a 'bad job'. Low status employment can lead to worse health and lower life expectancy and can therefore contribute to a reduction in the life chances of the least advantaged (Marmot, 2004).

If we pay no attention to the quality of work at the rough end of the labour market we are abandoning a fundamental social democratic objective. 'Work first' may be the right approach, and necessary to deliver full employment. But we should not forget the 'fulfilling employment' side of the equation. For us work *is* a fully human activity rather than a purely economic transaction, and allowing the growth of bad jobs to continue unchecked is inconsistent with our notion of human flourishing.

Tackling the problems of low-wage labour markets might seem like a big enough challenge for any government, but alongside the phenomenon of labour market polarisation lies the evidence that there has been a general deterioration in the quality of working life for all groups. Robert Taylor (2002) argues persuasively that employee satisfaction since 1992 has declined on almost every dimension – with significant falls in happiness with pay, job prospects and training. Perhaps the most striking finding is the decline in satisfaction with working time, and an increase in the intensity of work. People say that they have more work to do and they have to work harder to do it.

These results are confirmed by the 2004 Workplace Employment Relations Survey (WERS), which shows that only a third of employees are satisfied with their pay and their involvement in decision-making. One in six are concerned about their employment security. WERS also reveals high levels of tension or stress: one in five employees say that their job makes them feel 'tense' all or most of the time and almost half say that their job makes them 'worried' all, most or some of the time (Kersley, 2005). Other research has shown a significant increase in the percentage of employees agreeing with the statements 'my job requires me to work very hard', 'my job involves working at high speed all or almost all of the time' and 'I work under a great deal of tension' (Green, 2003). Work intensification is a well-documented phenomenon.

Of course, it was not supposed to be like this. It was said that the irresistible emergence of the knowledge economy would lead to higher quality jobs. Rising skill levels would give employees more labour market power, and full employment combined with the NMW would improve the relative position of the lowest paid. All the evidence suggests that this rosy scenario will only materialise if government creates the right institutional environment. We cannot rely on technological change and market processes to generate quality employment for all. There is no invisible hand at work here.

Most importantly, we cannot be confident that all 'bad jobs' will disappear. It is difficult to imagine a world where burgers are no longer flipped, toilets cleaned or bedpans emptied. Placing a high value on knowledge work could exacerbate the problems of labour market polarisation. What happens to those people who, by virtue of their natural endowments, may find it difficult to find a secure place in a high-skill, high-productivity, high-performance workforce?

The challenge of course is to improve the quality of work in low-wage occupations and create ladders of opportunity so that *all* workers can develop their skills and careers. Government has responsibility to ensure that low-wage employment is not relentlessly awful, and that workers have the possibility of a transition to more rewarding occupations in the future.

This analysis runs counter to the view that our future prosperity depends *entirely* on the development of more 'high performance workplaces', where high skills and flexibility are combined with high rewards and high levels of job satisfaction. Indeed, there is very little evidence to suggest that more organisations in the UK are moving in the direction of the high performance model, which helps to explain the persistent productivity gap with other major developed economies.

Francis Green (2003) points out that one of the reasons for rising employee dissatisfaction is that the workforce is more highly skilled than at any time in the recent past, but an increasing proportion of employees are overqualified for the jobs that they do. Duncan Gallie notes that 'task discretion' has fallen over the last decade despite the ubiquitous rhetoric of 'empowerment' (Gaillie, 2004). We might say therefore that many organisations in the UK are over-controlled and under-managed. When presented with a more highly skilled workforce, too many employers simply lack the capacity fully to utilise these skills.

WHAT IS TO BE DONE?
At this point it would be helpful to clarify the government's somewhat incomplete story about work. Their narrative could be summarised as follows:

- Strong employment performance depends upon labour market flexibility. This means that there should be no further regulation of the labour market and no serious effort made to encourage the growth of stronger unions. Cost is all-important in an increasingly globalised world and heaping 'burdens on business' will make the UK poorer. Unless costs are kept low and the supply of skills improved then the UK will be unable to respond to 'globalisation' or 'the threat of India and China'.
- Our prosperity in the future depends on moving to a knowledge

intensive economy, but this demands little more than improvement in skill levels, more effective links between universities and industries and the use of instruments like the R&D tax credit to encourage innovation.

- It is vital to sustain the commitment to full employment, and the most important factor here is the maintenance of macro-economic stability to create the right environment for business investment. The operation of the fiscal rules still allows some scope for effective counter-cyclical policies. There is a case for the state to intervene through active labour market programmes, tax credits and the national minimum wage to get the unemployed back to work and 'make work pay'. Beyond this no further intervention is required.
- Government should help working parents and carers achieve proper work-life balance.

The limits of this approach should be clear. There is nothing here that addresses the phenomena of work intensification or declining job satisfaction. Too much faith is placed in the ability of unfettered markets to generate quality employment for all but the most disadvantaged – where the government believes that it has a legitimate role in correcting 'market failure'. One might also say that Labour has a touching belief that improvements in the supply of skills will automatically lead to an increase in the demand for skills, despite experience to the contrary. It is simply assumed that employers will be able to make the best possible use of human capital so that skills are fully utilised.

As we have seen, much of the evidence points in a rather different direction, suggesting that a new policy departure is needed. A cursory reading of ministerial speeches could lead one to the conclusion that this argument will be received unenthusiastically. But, as our analysis of 'flexibility' has shown, the government's approach is rather more complex than their rhetoric suggests. Certainly, the modest re-regulation of the labour market since 1997 is inconsistent with the 'pure' flexibility story; those who continue to believe that the government is in favour of labour market *deregulation* seem to have absorbed the pro-business spin and missed the pro-worker practical action. More specifically, it is difficult to see the agenda contained in the Warwick agreement as explicitly 'pro-business', even though these commitments may fall short of the expectations of some trade unions. If New Labour really were ideologically committed to neo-liberalism red in tooth and claw then Richard Lambert would be effusive in his praise rather than unrestrained in his criticism.

Perhaps the most important challenge for social democrats is to recognise the good things that the government has done *and* make the argument that we must recast the frame of reference for the discussion of labour market policy. Dumping the rhetoric of 'burdens on business' and 'red tape' is critical; otherwise the government will always be on the defensive when any enhancement of workers' rights is proposed. The terms of the debate remain those established during that long period of Conservative government from 1979-97. With the prospect of twelve or more years of Labour government, the time has come to redefine the limits of the national conversation. If the centre-left fails to take the initiative then the desire for a progressive consensus will remain an unfulfilled quest for the Holy Grail.

Returning to the theme discussed earlier, the left has always seen work as a fully human activity. Values of autonomy and control, the importance of industrial citizenship and the role of trade unions as a countervailing force to the power of employers were all features of thinking on the centre-left throughout the twentieth century. However, for most of Labour's history the quality of working life was *not* seen as a legitimate area for state intervention. Trade unions jealously guarded *their* autonomy and were resistant to the introduction of statutory employment rights – 'voluntarism' was the watchword in British industrial relations. Now the position is rather different. Labour has accepted that the state has a role in regulating the employment relationship, partly because trade unions have declined in power and influence but also because the unions were unable, through collective bargaining, to achieve socially desirable ends like gender pay equality. All this suggests that there is now a more powerful political imperative for Labour to give a clear account of 'good work', one which articulates the role of the state and is far more precise about the role of trade unions and voluntary action by employers.

The underpinning principle remains that articulated by Lord Wedderburn in his classic *The Worker and the Law*, first published in 1965:

> Most workers want nothing more of the law than it should leave them alone. A secure job is preferable to a claim to a redundancy payment; a grievance settled in the plant or the office is better than going to a court or an industrial tribunal (Wedderburn, 1986: 1).

This is not an argument for 'light touch' regulation, but a recognition that voluntary institutions for the resolution of disputes and effective high quality management are better for workers and employers than a progressive juridification of the labour market. In other words, government and employers have a clear choice; they can have more regulation or more negotiation. In the absence of effective vehicles for collective worker voice – like trade unions or works councils – dependency on the law will become a permanent feature of the UK's employment relations scene.

One could go further and say that Labour needs to adopt a persuasive account of the *objectives* of the employment relationship, so that we have an accurate political compass for the development of public policy. John Budd (2004) has suggested that this might be described quite simply, and that there are three principles that should underpin our thinking about 'good work'. First, *efficiency*, defined as the ability of employers to make the best possible use of human and physical capital to produce goods and services at a price that customers are wiling to pay. Second, *equity*, which emphasises the importance of fair treatment for people at work and fairness in distributional outcomes. Third, *voice*, which is another way of expressing the objective of industrial citizenship. People should have the right to speak truth to their employers both individually and collectively, and the rights to freedom of association and collective bargaining are therefore constitutive of what it means to live in a democracy.

Any attempt to give a practical account of how these principles should be applied will inevitably give rise to contested conceptions. Nevertheless, it is important to make the effort, and the following is offered as a vision that might secure wide support on the centre-left:

- Full employment – defined as the availability of jobs for all those who wish to work
- Fair pay (including equal pay for work of equal value)
- The absence of discrimination on the grounds of race, gender, sexuality, disability or age
- Secure and interesting jobs that employees find fulfilling, which contribute to the achievement of high performance and sustainable business success
- A style and ethos of management that is based on high levels of trust and recognises that managing people fairly and effectively is crucial to skilled work and high performance
- Choice, flexibility and control over working hours
- Autonomy and control over the pace of work and the working environment
- Statutory minimum standards to protect the most vulnerable workers against exploitation
- Voice for workers in the critical employer decisions that affect their futures

These objectives may look ambitious, but we might also reasonably say that they are a modest statement of the conditions that need to be met before we can argue with conviction that work is being treated as a fully human activity.

Labour's performance to date can be measured against both this vision and Budd's three principles. We might observe that there has been a more than adequate focus on *efficiency* (witness for example HMT's relentless attention to the UK's productivity problem), a patchy commitment to *equity* (beyond a concern for the most marginal and exploited) and an ambiguous approach to *voice* (with the government failing to articulate a clear role for trade unions in the economy and initially opposing the EU directive on information and consultation). This assessment, read alongside the evidence of declining job satisfaction discussed earlier, is highly suggestive of a new policy agenda, which could create 'a progressive consensus in the workplace' and sustain a durable settlement in the world of work.

For example, the government could draw on the experience of active labour market programmes in the Nordic countries and recognise that more carrot than stick is needed to get the excluded back into employment. This is particularly important in the context of Incapacity Benefit reform, where the evidence suggests that a largely coercive approach is unlikely to be successful.

The commitments to 'fair pay' and *equity* suggest that the time has come for a more determined assault on the gender pay gap. Government has already established the *Women and Work Commission* to undertake a fundamental review of the causes of unequal pay and make recommendations to close the gender gap. The enthusiastic implementation of these recommendations should be a priority.

Similarly, the principles of both *equity* and *efficiency* suggest that more should be done to improve the performance and productivity in low-wage sectors to reduce the reliance on low pay. The NMW is highly effective at setting a floor under wages but is not in itself an adequate incentive for employers fundamentally to change their business models.

Declining levels of job satisfaction are matched by declining trust in managers. The *Workers' Index*, published by MORI and the Work Foundation, shows that 27 per cent of employees have little faith in the leaders of their organisations and one in four report that they are not inspired by their line managers (MORI, 2005). In large measure this is a consequence of the accelerating pace of organisational change, the reduction in autonomy and control and the disappearance of institutions that give workers effective *voice*. This suggests that the government should give more priority to the effective implementation of the Information and Consultation Regulations (I&C) to fill the institutional gap left by the retreat of trade unionism. Furthermore, the case for I&C should be couched in terms of industrial citizenship rather than efficiency, consistent with the idea that workers need *voice* if work is to be seen as a fully human activity.

Finally, a durable consensus depends on the strength of the institutions on which it is built. Any settlement will remain vulnerable to a Conservative assault unless employers, trade unions and other stakeholders are committed to it. So far New Labour has been rather sceptical about 'social partnership' and the only successful institution created since 1997 is the Low Pay Commission. Once again, however, there are some signs that the position is changing. The Warwick commitments include proposals for new institutions that will encourage trade unions and employers to collaborate on problem solving activities – sectoral forums in low-pay sectors, the new compact on 'employment standards' in contracted-out public services, and the proposed 'standard of good employment practice'. Rapid progress is needed, which means that government and unions should focus their attention here rather than engage in a prolonged and futile dispute about the practicality of 'repealing all the anti-union laws'.

These are simply indications of how a new agenda might be constructed and are intended to give a flavour of the argument. Perhaps the most important point is that this 'new departure' for policy builds upon what the government has already done. It recognises the progress that has been made and seeks to identify problems that have, so far, been left untouched. The explicit intention is to create a framework for the renewal of Labour in government rather than construct an agenda around which the left can rally in opposition. While the argument here may be a critique of existing policy it is written from the standpoint that ministers remain open to influence and are in the market for popular ideas that address real problems in the world of work.

SOME FINAL REFLECTIONS

Even though the case made here may look persuasive to those with an interest in labour market issues, the language still seems rather technocratic and could lack resonance with the electorate. In part this is a failing that affects many of us on the centre-left. We may be very effective in identifying the problems, competent in devising policy solutions, but poor at describing both our diagnosis and prescription in terms that can be readily understood. Simply put, Labour needs to have a story about work that is more than a sound bite and less than an academic treatise. Finding a new and distinctive mode of expression is part of the process of renewal in government.

We must sound as if we are speaking *for* employees rather that *at* employees – reflecting the problems that people experience in their daily lives instead of threatening them with the challenges of 'globalisation', 'the rise of India and China' and the demands of the 'knowledge economy'. Our political task is not to terrify the electorate but to create an environment where workers both know that change is a constant *and* have confidence that they can influence the pace and direction of change. At the core of social democracy lies a belief in the possibility of human agency – that we are not victims of circumstance, helpless in the face of the awesome power of events. We must revive the idea that the direction we take as a nation can be determined by political choice. Applying this principle to the world of work means that we can choose to have higher quality jobs and more productive workplaces. It is primarily a matter of determination, imagination and political will.

REFERENCES

Abrams, F. (2002), *Breadline Britain: Living on the Minimum Wage*, London: Profile.

Budd, J. (2004), *Employment with a Human Face*, New York: Cornell University Press.

Bunting, M. (2004), *Willing Slaves*, London: Harper Collins.

Gallie, D., Felstead, A. and Green, F. (2004), 'Changing Patterns of Task Discretion in Britain', *Work, Employment and Society*, Vol. 18 No. 2, pp. 243-266.

Goos, M. and Manning, A. (2003), 'McJobs and MacJobs', in R. Dickens et al (ed.), *The Labour Market Under New Labour*, Basingstoke: Palgrave, 70-83.

Green, F. (2003), 'The Demands of Work', in Dickens (ed.), op. cit, 137-49.

HM Treasury (2003), *EMU and Labour Market Flexibility*, London: HM Treasury.

Howell, D. (ed.) (2005), *Fighting Unemployment: The Limits of Free Market Orthodoxy*, Oxford: Oxford University Press.

Kersley, B., Carmen, A., Forth, J., Bryson, A., Bewley, H., Dix, G. and Oxenbridge, S. (2005), *Inside the Workplace: First Findings from the 2004 Workplace Employment Relations Survey*, London: Department of Trade and Industry.

Marmot, M. (2004), *Status Syndrome*, London: Bloomsbury.

MORI and The Work Foundation (2005), *The Workers' Index*, London: MORI/The Work Foundation.

OECD ((2004), *Employment Protection Legislation and Labour Market Performance*, in *Employment Outlook*, Paris: OECD.

Schettkat, R. (2005), *Is Labour Market Regulation at the Root of European Unemployment?: The Case of Germany and the Netherlands*, in Howell (ed.), op. cit.

Taylor, R. (2002), *Britain's World of Work: Myths and Realities*, Swindon: Economic and Social Research Council.

Toynbee, P. (2003), *Hard Work: Life in Low Pay Britain*, London: Bloomsbury.

Wedderburn, K. (1986), *The Worker and the Law*, Andover: Sweet and Maxwell, 3rd edn.

The real egalitarianism? Social justice after Blair

Ruth Lister

Equality is pivotal to debates about New Labour's political philosophy. Such debates take place against a background of levels of inequality and poverty that are shamefully high in both post-war and international context. This chapter begins with a brief account of levels of inequality and poverty in the UK and of the impact of New Labour's policies. It then discusses how opportunity and inclusion displaced a concern with equality as such in New Labour's thinking on social justice. The chapter then makes the case for an egalitarian model of social justice and suggests some policy implications. It concludes by reflecting on the prospects for the debate on equality and social justice 'after Blair'. The chapter focuses primarily on the domestic dimension of inequality and social justice. However, the even starker inequalities in the global distribution of resources in an increasingly interdependent world mean that the social justice agenda must embrace the idea of global justice (see also Barry, 2005; Mepham, 2005).

INEQUALITY AND NEW LABOUR

The state of inequality
New Labour inherited levels of poverty and inequality that had soared during the Thatcher years. Official statistics show that the richest tenth of the population enjoy nearly three-tenths of total national income while the bottom tenth make do with just under one per cent (DWP, 2005). This compares with a fifth and four per cent respectively in 1979 (Hills, 2004, DWP, 2005). Wealth is even more unequally distributed, with the top one per cent owning 23 per cent and the top tenth 56 per cent of all marketable wealth in 2001 (Church, 2004; Hills, 2004). At

the other end of the scale, just over a fifth of the population, including over a quarter of all children, live in poverty (DWP, 2005).

The Blair (and Brown) government has committed itself to tackling child and pensioner poverty and has had some success, with 5.5 per cent and 8.2 per cent reductions in child and pensioner poverty respectively (Brewer et al. 2005). However, there has been a slight increase in poverty among childless adults of working age. During the first term inequality continued to rise and it was only in the second term that it started to fall again slightly. According to the Institute for Fiscal Studies 'the net effect of seven years of Labour government is to leave inequality effectively unchanged and at historically high levels' (Brewer et al., 2005: 11). Nevertheless the general consensus is that, without New Labour's tax-benefit policies, inequality would be even higher (Hills and Stewart, 2005; Sefton, 2005). Wealth inequality has widened significantly since the mid-1990s, probably reflecting the earlier increase in income inequality (Hills, 2004). Cutting across socio-economic inequalities are those associated with social divisions of gender, 'race' and disability.

From equality to opportunity and inclusion

A key move in the distancing of 'New' from 'Old' Labour was its rein-terpretation of the central value of equality. This was done in two ways. First, in the words of Anthony Giddens 'the new politics defines equal-ity as inclusion and inequality as exclusion' (1998: 102). The notion of inclusion/exclusion can be helpful, provided it is not used too narrowly to refer simply to inc/exclusion into/from paid work (Lister, 2004). However, it is not a substitute for equality. As deployed by New Labour, social inclusion can be characterised as a social geometry of a horizontal, dichotomous relationship of 'in' or 'out', which tends to ignore the inequalities in the labour market into which the 'excluded' are to be included.

This contrasts with a more egalitarian model, which foregrounds vertical, hierarchical relationships of inequality and polarisation throughout society. New Labour's approach to social ex/inclusion is also associated with a tendency to treat structural divisions, notably of 'gender' and 'race', as discrete social problems amenable to techno-cratic 'what works' solutions (Franklin, 2000; Lister, 2001). An 'inclusive political discourse' thereby results in 'the obfuscation of divisions and antagonisms' (Fairclough, 2000: 37).

Second, opportunity has replaced equality as a guiding principle. Two slightly different New Labour positions can be discerned here: the meritocratic and 'the new egalitarianism'. Both make a clear link between opportunity and responsibility. As Blair explained back in 1997, 'our contract with the people was about opportunity and responsibility going together' (1997). Likewise, the 'new egalitarianism ties rights to corresponding responsibilities' (Diamond and Giddens, 2005: 107).

The meritocratic model was epitomised by Blair's vision in his 2004 party conference speech: 'Not a society where all succeed equally ... but an opportunity society where all have an equal chance to succeed'. What is at issue is who gets the attractive, well-rewarded positions but not the level of those rewards. Prior to the 2005 Election, Alan Milburn spelt it out as 'an opportunity society where the chance to get on is extended from the privileged few to all who are prepared to work hard and play by the rules, so that Britain becomes a nation based on merit not class' (2005: 77).

The political attack on the meritocratic model has been led by Roy Hattersley in a series of articles. He dismissed the ladder metaphor typically used by meritocrats, pointing out that 'some children, because of the disadvantages with which they are born, are incapable of climbing ladders' (1999: 26). He quoted Tawney: 'opportunities to rise are not a substitute for a large measure of practical equality of income and social condition. The existence of such opportunities ... depends not only upon an open road but upon an equal start' (Tawney, 1931: 143). Hattersley also debated with Gordon Brown in *The Guardian* soon after New Labour came to power. Although less meritocratic than Blair in his language, Brown rejected 'equality of outcome as neither desirable nor feasible, imposing uniformity and stifling human potential' in favour of 'a view of equality of opportunity that is recurrent, lifelong and comprehensive' (Brown, 1997). In response, Hattersley pointed out that 'true diversity is only possible in a society which avoids great discrepancies in wealth and income' (Hattersley, 1997).

The meritocratic model can also be criticised on a number of other grounds: the narrow definition of merit upon which it rests (see also below); its tendency to exacerbate underlying inequality both directly through the 'winner takes all' tendency it fuels and indirectly through its legitimisation of socio-economic divisions; and for the fact that the economic inequality which underpins it undermines the very equality of opportunity and equal worth espoused by its proponents.

The last of these arguments has been put by some exponents of the other main version of New Labour's model of equality as opportunity and inclusion, in particular, Anthony Giddens. In one of his expositions of the third way, Giddens argued that 'the contemporary left needs to develop a dynamic, life-chances approach to equality, placing the prime stress upon equality of opportunity' (2000: 86). Giddens has promoted such ideas in the context of what he has dubbed a 'social investment state' in which the emphasis is on investment in human capital for future prosperity rather than on redistribution for greater equality in the present.

Despite Giddens's espousal of opportunity, he has acknowledged that a fully meritocratic society 'is likely to be highly unequal on the level of outcome. In such a social order the privileged are bound to be able to confer advantages on their children – thus destroying meritocracy' (1998: 102). More recently, in an essay with Patrick Diamond (former Special Adviser at No 10 Downing Street), he describes 'pure meritocracy' as 'incoherent because, without redistribution, one generation's successful individuals would become the next generation's embedded caste, hoarding the wealth they had accumulated' (Diamond and Giddens, 2005: 108).

The collection in which this essay appears, edited by Giddens and Diamond, marks a significant development in the equality debate within New Labour. The essay makes the 'case for a new egalitarianism'. Having established that the issue represents 'a primary source of division between traditionalists and modernisers on the centre left', Diamond and Giddens imply that the former's criticisms of the latter for 'having abandoned an effective commitment to equality and social justice ... rests on a series of simplifications' (2005: 100). In particular, they argue, 'the sharp contrast perceived by some between "equality of opportunity" and "equality of outcome" is misguided. The promotion of equality opportunity in fact requires greater material equality: it is impossible for individuals to achieve their full potential if social and economic starting-points are grossly unequal' (*ibid.*).

This is somewhat disingenuous, for it is exactly the argument that 'traditionalists' (such as myself) have put all along in response to 'modernisers' who have been withering in their criticisms of the case for 'equality of outcome'. Indeed, the quoted statement is clearly based on a very similar (in some places identical) passage in Ben Jackson and Paul Segal's Catalyst pamphlet (2004), which makes a cogent case for why the left should still be concerned with inequality as such and not just inequality of opportunity.

Another of the 'simplifications' that has been deployed by 'modernisers' to discredit the 'traditionalist' case has been to argue as if the latter were advocating literal, uniform, 'equality of outcome', as opposed to greatly reduced inequality of outcome. That myth is finally nailed by Ed Miliband (former adviser to the Chancellor and now

Labour MP) in another chapter in the Giddens and Diamond collection. He clarifies that 'nobody actually advocated a position of strict equality of outcome; in fact, the argument is better explained as being a debate between those who thought inequality of opportunity was the most pervasive source of injustice in our society, and those who saw inequality of outcome as more important' (2005: 47).

Diamond and Giddens position 'the new egalitarianism' firmly on the 'opportunity' side of this debate. They explain that the new egalitarianism 'focuses primarily on widening opportunities rather than traditional income redistribution – equality of outcome – *per se*' (2005: 107). Thus, while the new egalitarian modernisers and the more traditional egalitarians can now agree that equality of opportunity cannot be divorced from greater material equality, the debate, as identified by Miliband, continues. I will therefore now set out the case for an egalitarian model of social justice, which has equality rather than equality of opportunity as its prime concern.

AN EGALITARIAN MODEL OF SOCIAL JUSTICE

The case for equality

Greater material equality is critical to the achievement of many of the goals and values articulated by New Labour, including that of social justice. As Jackson and Segal put it: 'large economic inequalities matter because they are *unjust*: they prevent individuals from achieving their potential, and they signal that the lives of those who have been fortunate are worthy of greater attention and respect than the lives of those who have not been as lucky'. The reference to luck indicates that such wide inequalities 'cannot plausibly be defended, even as deserved rewards for varying talents' (2004: 21, 11, emphasis in original). Miliband likewise argues that unequal market outcomes, which reflect accidents of 'birth, circumstance or even talent ... cannot be considered to produce a just outcome'. Moreover, notwithstanding the role that effort plays, 'market outcomes have inevitably arbitrary effects which may bear no relation to individual "desert"'; and personal effort itself is supported by public investment (Miliband, 2005: 43).

As already discussed, equality of opportunity is central to New Labour's articulation of social justice and the modernising 'new egalitarians' accept that its achievement depends on greater equality of outcome. Inter-generational mobility is generally higher in more egalitarian societies (Esping-Andersen 2005). Both privilege and poverty undermine genuine equality of opportunity. The one gives those at the top of the ladder an unequal start while the other makes it difficult, if well nigh impossible, for some children to grasp the opportunities being offered to them through the education system. Furthermore, as Diamond and Giddens observe, 'the strategies of the affluent in gaining concentrated access to the best housing, health and education plainly affect the life chances of poorer groups' (2005: 112). Research for Shelter, for instance, indicates 'unprecedented and rising levels of housing inequality', which are increasingly determining 'a child's chances in life' (Shelter, 2004: 2).

This is one reason why the child poverty and social exclusion agenda cannot be divorced from wider inequality. Cross-national analysis suggests that both poverty and the persistence of poverty are related to a country's level of inequality (Esping-Andersen, 2002, 2005; Jackson and Segal, 2004). Moreover, the growing emphasis on material success and conspicuous consumption in a consumer culture makes poverty that much harder to bear, particularly for children and young people. According to the editor of *Tatler* there has been a 'seismic' change in the spending habits of the rich, with 'brash cash ... very much on show' (Greig, 2004). Anthony Sampson has likened today's prosperous British to the Edwardians a century earlier, 'with their luxury, complacency – and indifference to inequality' (2004). The difference today is that the media dangle the accoutrements of luxury in front of those who cannot afford them, creating a kind of negative trickle down effect.

Inequality conflicts with a number of New Labour's other ideals also. One of the propositions of the original Compass statement is that 'liberty demands equality' (Compass, 2003: 7; see also White, 2002). The positive 'freedom to' pursue one's life goals is constrained in an unequal society. As noted earlier, inequality prevents the flourishing of human diversity and potential. Closely connected is its damaging impact on health and wellbeing (Marmot, 2004; Burchardt, 2005; Wilkinson, 2005).

Inequality also weakens social solidarity and cohesion for it is corrosive of social relations (Wilkinson, 2005). Moreover, it undermines the bonds of equal and common citizenship. Wealth enables some people to segregate themselves in exclusive enclaves and exclude themselves from the common institutions of society – education, health and transport (Barry, 2002). They are thereby less likely to recognise the common citizenship of people living in poverty (or even that poverty exists) and their own responsibilities as citizens towards them. Yet New Labour's principle of 'rights and responsibilities' is not applied even-handedly to rich and poor.

Inequality is inimical to genuine equal political citizenship. As the

Compass statement warns, 'we cannot have equal democratic rights when the resources available to different groups and individuals are so unequal' (2003: 7). Inequalities of economic resources translate into inequalities of power. Anne Phillips makes the link between economic and political equality with reference to equal worth (a value frequently enunciated by Blair): 'political equality presumes that all individuals are, in some important respect, of equal worth' (Phillips, 1999: 79). She is referring to more than formal equality before the law, as some understand equal worth. In its thicker sense, the notion represents what David Miller terms 'social equality': a non-hierarchical pattern of social relationships 'in which people regard and treat one another as equals' (1999: 232). As Phillips argues, 'the disparity between rich and poor blocks the recognition of equal worth', thereby undermining democracy and equal political citizenship (1999: 80). She continues:

> A society that condones excesses of poverty in the midst of wealth, or arbitrarily rewards one skill with one hundred times the wages of another, is not recognizing its citizens as of equal human worth ... When the gap between rich and poor opens up too widely, it becomes meaningless to pretend that we have recognised all adults as equals (1999: 131).

This failure underlies one of the key links that Richard Wilkinson identifies between inequality and ill health: low social status and the psychosocial stresses that it creates. 'Social status differentials' he writes:

> have a huge impact on whether people feel valued ... or looked down on, ignored, treated as insignificant, disrespected, stigmatized, and humiliated. And one of the most powerful influences on how important social status differentials are in a society is the scale of income differentials (Wilkinson, 2005: 26).

This illustrates the connection between the distributive and recognition paradigms of social justice. According to Axel Honneth, the starting point for the latter is that 'the recognition of human dignity comprises a central principle of social justice' (2004: 352). An egalitarian model of social justice needs to incorporate the dimension of recognition. It must do so in relation both to inequalities associated with 'difference', with which the recognition paradigm is typically identified politically, and to those associated with social class, typically identified with the distributive paradigm.

Policy implications

This section does no more than sketch some possible policy directions for a more egalitarian social justice strategy. The primary goal is a more equal distribution of both disposable (post tax-benefit) and original income and of wealth. In other words, the real egalitarianism is concerned with how the income and wealth gap privileges those at the top and creates a gradient of advantage throughout society, as well how it denies opportunity and equal status to those at the bottom.

A more equitable distribution of disposable income requires redistribution through the tax-benefit system. One proposal on the tax side, which appears to divide 'new' from other egalitarians, is the introduction of a 50 per cent tax rate for those earning over £100,000 a year. Some dismiss the demand as a totem. In some ways it is – a totem of a commitment to a more equal society. It would, though, also do something to cap the massive increase in rewards enjoyed by the very highest paid in recent years and would skim off some of the 'fiscal cream' enjoyed by these 'fat cats' (Johnson and Lynch, 2005). Estimates vary as to how much revenue this would raise. Diamond and Giddens suggest £3.5 billion a year rather than the £5 billion sometimes claimed. Although they dismiss this as 'small beer', it is money that could make a real difference to the anti-poverty strategy.

A higher tax rate has been ruled out yet again for this Parliament. However, it is not the only fiscal measure available to redistribute resources from the highest paid. Others might also include the abolition of the ceiling on national insurance contributions and reduced opportunities for tax avoidance as well as more effective action against tax evasion (all of which Diamond and Giddens support). In addition, further reform of tax reliefs and allowances (particularly subsidies to private pensions) is needed so that they do not benefit higher rate taxpayers more than others. Reform of inheritance tax, possibly replacing it with a tax on all wealth transfers, is also vital in the face of the phenomenal rise in wealth inequalities (see, for instance, White, 2003).

On the benefits side, the priority is a proper review of the adequacy of social security benefits. Benefits should provide security and a standard of living consistent with human dignity, as acknowledged in various statements by the European Commission. The review must include benefits for working-age adults, which have been neglected. This has blunted the impact of the real and welcome improvement in support for children (see Women's Budget Group, 2005) and has contributed to the rise in poverty among childless working-age adults.

The tax-benefits system cannot, on its own, carry the full weight of the change needed to achieve a more equal income distribution. Here is

After Blair

another example of where a false dichotomy can all too easily be created between 'traditionalists' who emphasise *redistribution* and 'modernisers' who focus on the *initial distribution* of resources through promoting high levels of paid employment. Of course, access to paid work represents the most important route out of poverty for most (though not all) people of working age. More needs to be done to remove the barriers to paid employment faced, in particular, by women and by marginalised minority groups. In the case of women this includes designing policies, for example with respect to parental leave and working time, so as to encourage a more equitable gendered division of labour and time within the family (Lister, 2003; Andersson, 2005).

However, as is increasingly being acknowledged, it is not enough simply to increase the number of people in paid employment, if they get stuck in low paid jobs in poor conditions. On the one hand, this means measures to help people progress out of such jobs; on the other, it means further action to tackle low pay and poor conditions. Further improvements in the minimum wage are needed to tackle low pay, especially among women and minority ethnic groups. If the aim is a more egalitarian wages structure, there may be a case for linking the minimum wage to average wages at one end of the wages distribution and opening up debate around a maximum wage at the other. The case for the latter has been put by the Blairite journalist Martin Kettle (2003). He points out that the intellectual arguments for a maximum wage are similar to those for a minimum wage with regard to placing morally derived constraints on market inequalities.

More fundamentally still, we need a debate about the overall distribution of pay and the rewards attached to different kinds of work. Should the market be the only arbiter or should we not also be considering the contribution to society of different jobs? The low pay associated with certain kinds of work – notably care work – marks the lack of recognition of the value of this work (largely done by women) to society.

The recognition paradigm of social justice also raises issues concerning the delivery of benefits and services. Research for the Social Exclusion Unit found that service users at risk of social exclusion place great emphasis on being listened to and treated with respect (Woodfield et al., 2004). This is the other, all too often overlooked, side of Blair's 'respect' agenda. Being listened to and treated with respect are both dimensions of recognition and for many people the two go together (Commission on Poverty, Participation and Power 2000; Lister 2004). The Office of the Deputy Prime Minister has acknowledged that 'for social justice we must give everyone – and especially the deprived –

more of a say' (2005: 1.14). This raises much wider questions about democracy and equal political citizenship, which are also part of the social justice agenda (Pearce and Paxton, 2005).

CONCLUDING COMMENTS

This chapter has suggested that the creation of New Labour involved a narrowing of the terms of the debate around inequality and social justice. The more politically challenging goal of greater equality has been replaced by a weaker discourse of opportunity and inclusion. As espoused by Blair, this has meant the displacement of an egalitarian with a meritocratic model of social justice. The meritocratic goal of greater social mobility was promoted by a number of Ministers close to Blair before and after the 2005 election. Nevertheless, there are some signs that the debate might broaden again 'after Blair'. The 'new egalitarianism' espoused by leading figures in New Labour acknowledges that 'tackling inequality, not only poverty, matters if New Labour is to promote a fairer and more open society' (Giddens and Diamond, 2005: 1), even if its watchword is still opportunity rather than equality. The Fabian Commission on Life Chances and Child Poverty has placed equality squarely at the heart of the new life chances agenda (Fabian Commission, 2006). Since the 2005 election numerous media commentators have drawn attention to inequality and its damaging effects. Indeed, even the leading Conservative Oliver Letwin told the *Daily Telegraph* (23 December 2005) that 'of course, inequality matters. Of course, it should be an aim to narrow the gap between rich and poor', even if he made clear that that would not involve 'clobbering the rich'.

To argue that the 'new egalitarianism' might pave the way to a 'real egalitarianism' is perhaps therefore optimistic but not totally unrealistic. Much will depend on the wider constellation of political forces 'after Blair', discussed elsewhere in this volume. What is important at this stage is for the 'real egalitarians' to promote a coherent philosophy that can be translated into a compelling political message, which can in turn build public support for specific policies that will reduce inequalities. Without such a philosophy and political message, individual egalitarian policies will lack credibility and will all too easily be opposed.

In order to effect change, a coherent philosophy and policy agenda have to be backed up with the necessary political will. At present, New Labour appears to work on the assumption that an overt policy of closing the income and wealth gap through redistribution and wages policies would be electorally damaging. Thus, for instance, any proposal to raise the income tax rate on the highest earners is ruled out for fear that it could be attacked as 'penalizing success' (Diamond and Giddens, 2005: 112). This is despite the fact that, prior to the 2005 election, nearly three-quarters of the electorate supported a 50 per cent rate on incomes over £100,000 (*The Independent*, 12 April 2005). More generally, the government has preferred to redistribute by stealth rather than make the political case for a more equal society.

Yet the annual British Social Attitudes Survey has consistently found widespread antipathy towards high levels of inequality, particularly towards what are perceived as rewards that are too high at the top, even though the ratio of rewards is generally underestimated (Bromley 2003; Taylor-Gooby, 2005). The survey shows clear and continued majority support for the proposition that government has a responsibility to reduce the gap between high and low incomes. Admittedly, support for explicit redistribution from rich to poor is lower and falling and Peter Taylor-Gooby (2005) suggests that views on inequality are not strongly held. Nevertheless the findings, Catherine Bromley argues, imply 'strong public support for redistribution in practice, if not in word' even if there are some caveats, particularly as regards spending on welfare benefits (2003: 90). Perhaps when even a Labour government is uncomfortable with the 'r' word, the wider public comes to think that redistribution is a 'bad thing'. This could then weaken support for the further redistribution that is necessary to achieve greater equality.

A political strategy and vision which explicitly espouse a more equal society, building on the supportive elements of public attitudes and engaging with the less sympathetic elements, should thus be at the heart of Labour politics 'after Blair'. If, after three terms in office, Labour has not reduced inequality significantly, it will have squandered the political capital it built so successfully to gain power and failed to achieve its ideal of a more socially just society.

REFERENCES

Andersson, M. (2005), 'Why gender equality?', in A. Giddens and P. Diamond (eds), *The New Egalitarianism*, Cambridge: Polity.

Barry, B. (2002), 'Social exclusion, social isolation and the distribution of income', in J. Hills, J. Le Grand and D. Piachaud (eds), *Understanding Social Exclusion*, Oxford: Oxford University Press.

Barry, B. (2005), *Why Social Justice Matters*, Cambridge: Polity.

Blair, T. (1997), 'Why we must help those excluded from society', *The Independent*, 8 December.

Brewer, M., Goodman, A., Shaw, J. and Shephard, A. (2005), *Living Standards,*

Inequality and Poverty, 2005 Election Briefing Note No 9, London: Institute for Fiscal Studies.

Bromley, C. (2003), 'Has Britain become immune to inequality', in A. Park, J. Curtice, K. Thomson, C. Bromley and M. Phillips (eds), *British Social Attitudes: The 20th Report*, London: Sage.

Brown, G. (1997), 'Why Labour is still loyal to the poor', *The Guardian*, 2 August.

Burchardt, T. (2005), 'Just happiness? Subjective well-being and social policy', in N. Pearce and W. Paxton (eds), *Social Justice: Building a Fairer Britain*, London: Politico's.

Church, J. (2004), 'Income', in P. Babb, J. Martin and P. Haezewindt (eds), *Focus on Social Inequalities*, Office for National Statistics.

Commission on Poverty, Participation and Power (2000), *Listen Hear: the right to be heard*, Bristol: Policy Press.

Compass (2003), Statement, London: Compass.

Diamond, P. and Giddens, A. (2005), 'The new egalitarianism: economic inequality in the UK', in A. Giddens and P. Diamond, *op. cit.*

DWP (2005), *Households Below Average Income: An analysis of the income distribution from 1994/5 to 2003/04*, London: Department for Work and Pensions.

Esping-Andersen, G. (2002), *Why We Need a New Welfare State*, Oxford: Oxford University Press.

Esping-Andersen, G. (2005), 'Inequalities of incomes and opportunities', in A. Giddens and P. Diamond, *op. cit.*

Fabian Commission (2006), *Life Chances: the new politics of equality*, Report of the Commission on Life Chances and Child Poverty, London: Fabian Society.

Fairclough, N. (2000), *New Labour, New Language?*, London/New York: Routledge.

Franklin, J. (2002), 'After modernisation: gender, the third way and the new politics', in A. Coote (ed.), *New Gender Agenda*, London: IPPR with the Fabian Society and Fawcett Society.

Giddens, A. (1998), *The Third Way*, Cambridge: Polity.

Giddens, A. (2000), *The Third Way and its Critics*, Cambridge: Polity.

Greig, G. (2004), 'Welcome to the flashocracy', *The Observer*, 6 June.

Hattersley, R. (1997), 'Why Labour is wrong about income tax', *The Guardian*, 6 August.

Hattersley, R. (1999), 'Up and down the social ladder', *New Statesman*, 22 January: 25-7.

Hills, J. (2004), *Inequality and the State*, Oxford: Oxford University Press.

Hills, J. and Stewart, K. (2005), 'A tide turned but mountains yet to climb?', in J. Hills and K. Stewart (eds), *A More Equal Society?* Bristol: Policy Press.

Honneth, A. (2003), 'Redistribution as recognition: a response to Nancy Fraser', in N. Fraser and A. Honneth, *op. cit.*

Jackson, B. and Segal, P. (2004), *Why Inequality Matters*, London: Catalyst.

Johnson, P. and Lynch, F. (2004), 'Sponging off the poor', *The Guardian*, 10 March.

Jones, F. (2005), The effects of taxes and benefits on households income, 2003-04, *Economic Trends*, July, National Statistics Online .

Kettle, M. (2003), 'We have a minimum wage – now let's set a maximum', *The Guardian*, 21 May.

Lister, R. (2001), 'New Labour: a study in ambiguity from a position of ambivalence', *Critical Social Policy*, 21 (4): 425-447.

Lister, R. (2003), *Citizenship: Feminist Perspectives*, Basingstoke: Palgrave.

Lister, R. (2004), *Poverty*, Cambridge: Polity.

Lister, R. (2005), 'Recognition and voice: the challenge for social justice', ESRC seminar series on Social Justice and Public Policy, London School of Economics, 21 March, .

Marmot, M. (2004), *Status Syndrome*, London: Bloomsbury.

Mepham, D. (2005), 'Social justice in a shrinking world', in N. Pearce and W. Paxton, *op. cit.*

Milburn, A. (2005), 'Labour values', in Fabian Society, *Why Life Chances Matter*, London: Fabian Society.

Miliband, E. (2005), 'Does inequality matter?', in A. Giddens and P. Diamond, *op. cit.*

Miller, D. (1999), *Principles of Social Justice*, Cambridge, Mass./London: Harvard University Press.

ODPM (2005), *Sustainable Communities: People, Places and Prosperity*, London: Office of the Deputy Prime Minister.

Pearce, N. and Paxton, W. (eds) (2005), *Social Justice: Building a Fairer Britain*, London: Politico's.

Phillips, A. (2003), *Which Inequalities Matter?*, Cambridge: Polity.

Sampson, A. (2004), 'We are in danger of remembering the First World War but forgetting its lessons', *The Independent*, 7 August.

Shelter (2005), *Know Your Place: Housing wealth and inequality in Great Britain*, London: Shelter.

Sefton, T. (2005), 'Inequality and redistribution under New Labour', *Benefits* 13 (2): 109-114.

Simms, A. (2003), 'Now for a maximum wage', *The Guardian*, 6 August.

Tawney, R. H. (1931), *Equality*, London: Allen and Unwin.

Taylor-Gooby, P. (2005), 'Attitudes to social justice', in N. Pearce and W. Paxton, *op. cit.*

White, S. (2002), 'Must liberty and equality conflict?', *Renewal*, 10 (1): 27-38.

White, S. (2003), *The Civic Minimum*, Oxford: Oxford University Press.

Wilkinson, R. (2005), *The Impact of Inequality*, London/New York: Routledge.

Women's Budget Group (2005), *Women's and Children's Poverty: making the links*, London: WBG.

Woodfield, K., Graham, J., Mowlam, A., Dixon, J. (2004), *Making a Difference to Disadvantaged Families? Qualitative Case Studies*, London: Office of the Deputy Prime Minister.

Economics and neo-liberalism

Edward Fullbrook

Neo-liberalism is the ideology of our time. And of New Labour and Tony Blair. What happens after Blair becomes seriously interesting if we suppose that within the Labour Party neo-liberalism could be dethroned. Although this event hardly appears imminent, it could be brought forward if the nature and location of the breeding ground of the neo-liberal beast became public knowledge.

For a quarter of a century people to the left of what was once a staunchly right-wing position (too right-wing for the right-wing of the Labour Party) have been struggling against neo-liberalism with ever diminishing success. This failure has taken place despite much cogent analysis of the sociological and geopolitical forces fuelling the neo-liberal conquest. The working assumption has been that if neo-liberalism's books could be opened so that the world could under-stand who its real winners and losers were, and the extent of their winnings and losses, then citizens would see the light, politicians of good will would repent, and the political process would once again enter into a progressive era. *This essay breaks with that tradition.*

While I wholeheartedly agree that the analysis described above is a necessary condition for stopping neo-liberalism, I am less certain that it is by itself sufficient. Understanding the consequences of neo-liberalism is not enough. We must also understand where this intellectual poison comes from and the primary channel by which it continues to be injected into the body politic. It is only then that we can stop or reduce its flow.

Neo-liberalism's intellectual origins seem little known and poorly understood. Its abstract complexity, its improbable association of ideas, its institutional convolutions and its long period of gestation make its history difficult to grasp and comprehend. Yet understanding neo-liberalism's intellectual history reveals not only its hollow core, but also the academic power relations by which, with public funds, it is today implanted in successive generations of students. Western universities both gave arise to neo-liberalism and continue to be its primary pushers.

The neo-liberalism story begins not in the last century but in the 1870s, and not with political or economic ideas but with Newtonian physics. Nor did it initially arise out of political aspirations. Yet out of its distant, bizarre and unworldly origins it has, via the United States Air Force (that is not a misprint), and university economics departments, become the political ideology that today rules the UK, the US and most of the world.

There is, however, now a major cause for hope. Over the last few years a radical but apolitical reform movement in economics has mushroomed, which if successful will destroy neo-liberalism's intellectual powerbase. My essay concludes with a brief account of this surprise development and of how those seeking a post-neo-liberal Labour Party might both give and receive help from this movement.

NEO-LIBERALISM AND SCIENCE: THE PROBLEM OF PHYSICS ENVY

To understand neo-liberalism's pull one must first take on board the relation between ideology and science. One tends to think of ideology and science as polar opposites, but in our age the former is more often than not strategically linked to the latter. For over a century ideologies have emerged from science or from pursuits that claimed to be scientific – Marxism, social Darwinism, modern forms of racism and now neo-liberalism being examples. We can expect more in the future, not because science is ideologically prone, but because before ideas can function ideologically they must appear credible, so that ideologies are most likely to emerge from those domains whose authority is in the time and place the most uncontested. In our time, in the West, that domain is science. In the age of hereditary rule it was religion, hence the divine right of kings. But the ideology that spurred the American and French revolutions was grounded in political philosophy, it having usurped the authority of religion.

Before other disciplines concerned with human society had even begun to seriously put themselves forward as sciences, economics was touting itself as a science on a par or near par with physics. This conceit, which in the last century gradually pervaded most of the profession, originated in the 1870s with the founders of neo-classical economics. Today the neo-classical approach is often called 'mainstream economics', it being the only kind permitted in most university economics departments.

That a century after its invention neo-classical economics provided the intellectual rationale of an ideology, neo-liberalism, is pure accident. Its primary founders, Stanley Jevons and Leon Walras, were obsessed not with politics but with classical mechanics. They sought to associate themselves with the latter as the means of gaining recognition in the public eye as scientists. Although they were writing at a time when classical mechanics no longer figured as a major player on the frontiers of physics, in the popular imagination it was still king. Science was science, ran the common view, only to the extent that it mimicked the Newtonian model. So, wrote Jevons:

> all branches and divisions of economic science must be pervaded by certain general principles ['the general principles of mechanics']. It is to the investigation of such principles – to the tracing out of *the mechanics of self-interest and utility*, that this essay has been devoted. The establishment of such a theory is a necessary preliminary to any definite drafting of the superstructure of the aggregate science [emphasis added] (Jevons, 1970: 50).

This meant developing an economic model that had the same formal properties as Newton's model of the universe. Whether or not economies and their markets have the same formal properties as Newton's model was never an issue. Jevons, like Walras a few years later, had discovered the delusional and contagious delights of upside-down science. Whereas Newton, backed by a century of *empirical research*, had identified fundamental properties of the physical universe and then modelled them, Jevons and Walras set about *defining* a set of concepts that could be combined in a manner formally analogous to the physical relations modelled by classical mechanics. It is these ego-serving *a priori* concepts, which I will outline and which are hammered into the heads of undergraduates as if they were scientific truths, that today underpin neo-liberalism.

Mechanics is concerned with the *motions* of *bodies* and the *forces* that cause them. Its principles say that physical systems, consisting of bodies, forces and motions, tend toward *equilibrium*, this being when the sum of the *forces* acting on each body of the system is zero. Classical mechanics (unlike quantum mechanics) also constitutes a determinate model, meaning that if a change in one of the system's variables is supposed, then the end state of the system can always be predicted. In the mid-nineteenth century, before Darwin and modern physics, the property of determinacy was thought to be the hallmark of a truly scientific theory.

In neo-classical economics, 'bodies' translates into 'individuals' or 'agents'; 'motions' translates into 'exchange of goods'; 'forces' translates into 'desires' or 'preferences' which when summed become 'supply and demand'; 'mechanical equilibrium' becomes 'market equilibrium', this being when the difference between supply and demand is zero; and 'physical systems' translates as 'markets'. But that is only the beginning of the neo-classical fabrication. To make the model determinate it was necessary to define the terms 'exchange of goods', 'individuals' and 'preferences', and thereby 'markets' in bizarre ways. All exchanges were said to magically take place at the prices that equated demand and supply. There were no disjunctions arising from innovation and competition and no distortions from oligopoly and monopoly. This elimination of dynamics placed the focus entirely on when the market is in equilibrium, thereby ignoring actual market processes. Individuals were defined as atomistic, that is as having no social dimension, and as being one-dimensional, meaning that they have only one criteria, preference satisfaction, for making decisions. And the preferences of these non-social beings were defined as unchanging, completely independent of life experiences, including consumer ones.

Walras surpassed Jevons in both influence and self-delusion. In his *Elements of Pure Economics* (1874-77) he proclaimed: 'this pure theory of economics is a science which resembles the physico-mathematical sciences in every respect' (71). Despite the preposterousness of this assertion, Walras's theory and its modern offshoots do resemble physics in *one* respect, their mathematical formalism. Driven by physics envy, economics has increasingly shaped itself solely on the basis of its one resemblance to physics, with the consequence that much of its substance has vaporized in a formalist fog. If you doubt that this is really the situation, then here is how some winners of the economics 'Nobel Prize' see it:

... economics has become increasingly an arcane branch of mathematics rather than dealing with real economic problems (Friedman, 1999: 137).

Page after page of professional economic journals are filled with mathematical formulas ... Year after year economic theorists continue to produce scores of mathematical models and to explore in great detail their formal properties; and the econometricians fit algebraic functions of all possible shapes to essentially the same sets of data (Leontief, 1982: 104).

Existing economics is a theoretical [meaning mathematical] system which floats in the air and which bears little relation to what happens in the real world (Coase, 1999: 2).

How did the detachment of economics from reality come about? And what is its tie-in with neo-liberalism and New Labour?

NEO-CLASSICAL ECONOMICS

Nineteenth-century neo-classical economics is largely a late twentieth-century success story. It was not until the 1970s that in academia it became truly and ruthlessly hegemonic. The manner by which it won dominance helps explain its current political clout.

In the United States at the beginning of the last century, the emerging dominance of the neo-classical school was stalled by the institutionalists. Led by Thorstein Veblen, institutionalist economics analysed institutions as well as isolated and unchanging individuals, emphasised emergent social phenomena, argued that habit influenced economic choice more than rational calculation, rejected all forms of reductionism, and stressed the importance of knowledge in economic evolution. This approach steadily gained adherents in the years leading up to the First World War, and in 1917 one of its leaders, John R. Commons, was elected president of the American Economics Association.

For several decades neo-classical and institutional economics profitably co-existed in many economics departments. The profit fell to humankind, because each approach was capable of analysing and understanding aspects of economic systems that the other was not. This epistemological pluralism reflected the age. It directly paralleled the then emergent and much publicised new pluralism in physics, whereby quantum mechanics, premised on concepts that directly contradicted those of relativity theory, had been found capable of analysing and understanding fundamental aspects of physical systems that the other was not.

But the Great Depression destabilised these institutional arrangements. Neither the neo-classicals nor the institutionalists had a plausible explanation or a cure. In stepped John Maynard Keynes. He offered a new theoretical interpretation of capitalist economies, which both explained their collapse and pointed to practical measures that would – without interfering with their general principles – get them going again and keep them functioning smoothly. Given the dire straits of capitalism and the growing fear of revolution, not even neo-classical economists dared for long to keep Keynes's theory from being tried. When it was shown to work, that, at one level, ended the argument. Henceforth, in the basic management of the economy, all American presidents would be Keynesians, none daring to cut public expenditure when facing a recession. But at the theoretical level, which in the neo-

classical tradition means theory that is axiom-led rather than empiri-
cally-led (otherwise their axioms would have been abandoned long
ago), the argument had only just begun. In 1946 Keynes died and neo-
classical economists began their counterinsurgency. This time, with the
prodigality of the US Department of Defence behind them, they would
not be satisfied until most economics departments in the world had
been cleansed of economists who voiced non-neo-classical ideas.

Keynes, a mathematician turned economist, had said some rude
things about mathematical economists. Shocked by the way they
abused mathematics, especially when they applied them in meaningless
ways to unsuitable phenomena, he made no secret of his professional
contempt for their empty pretentiousness. But these economists were
soon to have their revenge. Led by Paul Samuelson in the US and John
Hicks in the UK, they set about mathematicising a part of Keynes's
theory. They left out all those bits that were inconsistent with the neo-
classical axioms, and their end product was a formalised version of
Keynes called 'Keynesianism' which soon became standard fare in
undergraduate courses. Even graduate students were discouraged from
reading the primary text. With this co-optation of Keynes's reputation
and with the real Keynes out of the way, and Veblen and all the other
free spirits forgotten, the road was now clear to establish a neo-classical tyranny. But it could never have happened on the scale that it did,
nor have given rise to such ideological virulence (and New Labour),
without the leadership and largesse of the Pentagon.

Following the Second World War, the United States increasingly
came to determine the shape of economics worldwide, while within the
United States the sources of influence became concentrated and
circumscribed to an absurd degree. This state of affairs, which persists
to the present day, was engineered in significant part by the US
Department of Defence, especially its Navy and Air Force (Bernstein,
2003). Beginning in the 1950s it lavishly funded university research in
mathematical economics. Military planners believed that game theory
and linear programming had potential use for national defence. And,
although it now seems ridiculous, they held out the same hope for
mathematical solutions of 'general equilibrium', the theoretical core of
neo-classical economics. The really big event, the one that would make
neo-liberalism the ideology of our time, came in 1965 when RAND,
the research and development wing of the US Air Force, created a
lavish fellowship programme for economics graduate students at the
Universities of California, Harvard, Stanford, Yale, Chicago, Columbia
and Princeton, and in addition provided post-doctoral funds for those
who best fitted the mould.

These seven economics departments, along with that of MIT – an institution long regarded by many as a branch of the Pentagon – have subsequently come to dominate economics globally to an astonishing extent. They control the three most prestigious economics journals, in which papers by their staff and PhDs predominate. Of the over 800 economists employed by the World Bank, a majority have been trained at one of the Big Eight. The International Monetary Fund is similarly provided, as are the other highly ranked economics departments in the US and in some cases in other countries. A glance through the 2003 edition of Penguin's *Dictionary of Economics* illustrates the accentuated continuation of this tiny all-powerful closed shop engineered by the United States Air Force. The dictionary has entries for 29 living economists. Of these, 26 – 89.7 per cent – are from the US, or have had all or the most important part of their careers there. Of the 26, 100 per cent have either taught at or received their PhD from one of the Big Eight.

Four years after the launch of the RAND programme, economics pulled off one of the greatest public relations coups of all time. The Central Bank of Sweden decided to mark its tercentenary by creating an award for economics. Rather than naming it in memory of Adam Smith or some other ancestral economist, it named it 'The Bank of Sweden Prize in Economics Sciences in Memory of Alfred Nobel', shrewdly anticipating that this unwieldy title would be shortened by journalists to the 'Nobel Prize in Economics'. To further the deception, the bank adopted nomination and selection procedures identical to those of the real Nobel prizes. It even arranged for it to be awarded at the same time as the Nobel prizes. Soon even people who know better couldn't help but refer to the Bank of Sweden Prize as a 'Nobel Prize'. The fraud has been so successful that not only is the general public deceived, but also, it is my impression, many economists honestly believe that what they call the 'Nobel Prize for Economics' is a Nobel Prize. Given human nature, it is not surprising that winners of the Bank of Sweden Prize have been disinclined to discourage this false belief. But in some cases the degree of their disinclination is noteworthy. For example the science historian Yves Gingras wrote:

Paul Samuelson (1970 winner) wrote about his 'Nobel coronation' – not his 'Bank of Sweden Coronation' – and filled his talk with references to Einstein (4 times) Bohr (2 times) and eight other winners of the (real) physics Nobel prize (not to mention, of course, Newton) plus a few other names as if he were part of this family (2002).

The effects of the RAND programme and the 'Nobel Prize' scam, in combination with the 'genetic' weakness of economics for self-delusion about its scientific status that dated from the time of Jevons and Walras, pushed economics over the precipice. Within a generation the 'dismal science' became the autistic science. Its storylines increasingly bore scant relevance to economic reality. More and more the pages of economics journals were given over to mathematical symbols that, unlike those of real science journals, have no empirical, real-world referents. Toeing the empty formalist line became virtually the only path to academic employment. Out of this enforced fantasy world emerged neo-liberalism in the real-life political world. It was another of those public relations hat tricks at which the economics profession is so shamelessly peerless. Given that it was impossible to escape its autism without de-formalising and thereby losing its treasured illusion that economists are kissing-cousins of physicists, *why not demand that the real world change so as to conform to the imaginary world of neo-classical economics.* This is how neo-liberalism came into being and continues to be.

ALL YOU NEED ARE MARKETS
In the neo-classical make-believe world everything works wondrously well. There is never any unemployment; markets of all kinds always clear instantly; everyone gets exactly what they deserve; market outcomes are invariably 'optimal'; everyone maximises their potential; and all citizens possess a crystal ball that infallibly foresees the future. In this axiomatic paradise (without messy things like social beings, institutions, history, culture and ethics) there is no government ownership, no regulation, no corporate accountability and no public bodies. Instead there are just 'markets'. For those who take the model literally, the solution to all human problems is to make the real world more like the neo-classical make-believe world. 'All you need are markets.' That is the central idea of neo-liberalism. This may be simple-minded, but as the Blair government has shown, it can be applied to virtually everything.

There is, however, a way out of this ideological prison. The problem is not neo-classical economics itself, but its monopoly position. Economic reality, like the natural world, is extremely complex, and requires examination from numerous points of view. Neo-classical economics is but one of those points, and one with a narrow sightline. When neo-classical analysis is offered and accepted not as a partial truth but as the whole truth, all the other economic knowledge that could be gained and that should be part of political debate and decision-making is excluded. Instead the political process takes place on the basis of a small fraction of the economic knowledge potentially available. *It is this enforced ignorance in matters economic that is the primary basis of neo-liberalism.*

In the summer of 2000 some economics students in France started a rebellion against this knowledge censorship as exemplified in their curriculum. In a petition they characterised economics as an 'autistic science' and proclaimed their desire 'to escape from imaginary worlds'. The state of affairs that their petition describes characterises the teaching of economics in most of the world's universities today, including Britain's. Its first paragraph is worth quoting because, although intended to be apolitical, it identifies the fountainhead of neo-liberalism:

> Most of us have chosen to study economics so as to acquire a deep understanding of the economic phenomena with which the citizens of today are confronted. But the teaching that is offered, that is to say for the most part neo-classical theory or approaches derived from it, does not generally answer this expectation. Indeed, even when the theory legitimately detaches itself from contingencies in the first instance, it rarely carries out the necessary return to the facts. The empirical side (historical facts, functioning of institutions, study of the behaviours and strategies of the agents ...) is almost nonexistent. Furthermore, this gap in the teaching, this disregard for concrete realities, poses an enormous problem for those who would like to render themselves useful to economic and social actors.

They asked instead for: 'a pluralism of approaches adapted to the complexity of the objects and to the uncertainty surrounding most of the big questions in economics'.

Although the French students' protest was only national in scope, similar student petitions soon appeared in the UK, the US and Italy. More significant, the French initiative was the spark that ignited what has become known as Post-Autistic Economics (PAE), a broadly international movement composed mainly of professional economists, now numbering in the thousands. The movement seeks to change fundamentally the way *all* economics is practised, by introducing a pluralism such as one finds in the natural sciences. This both removes the intellectual legitimacy of neo-liberalism and carries immediate and radical everyday implications for policy-makers and politicians.

Despite all the hype about economics being a hard science like physics, it has always in significant part been an ideological pursuit shaped by a true-believer mentality. In particular, each of economics' many 'schools', not just the neo-classical, has tended to present its partial view of economic reality as if it were the whole view or at least the only one it is necessary to know. A similar situation would be one in which, for example, in the discipline of physics, micro-physicists tried to stop the teaching and application of general relativity with its radically different, indeed contrary, conceptual system, and macro-physicists in turn tried to bury quantum mechanics. Physicists do not do that, partly because they are not dealing with the social world, but also because they appreciate that knowledge accumulates by investigating reality from more that one conceptual point of view (Boyle, 1983). Nearly all economists, however, have tended to be 'paradigm warriors', seeking to establish their school's limited viewpoint as the only legitimate one and as being *the* economic truth. Inevitably this leads to political struggles and media positioning, as has been described in this essay, within and outside the institutions in which economics is taught and applied. Occasionally, as in the Soviet Union and in much of the developed world today, one school wins out over all the rest, with the consequence that open and informed discussion of economic issues is closed down and political decision comes to be dictated by dogmatic slogans broadcast from an inner sanctum.

The Post-Autistic Economics movement offers a way out of this impasse and one that people seeking to liberate the Labour Party from Tony Blair's neo-liberalism should grab hold of immediately. PAE is apolitical and concerns itself mainly with a matter of epistemology. That may sound like a singularly inadequate grounding for a political initiative. But remember that, according to my analysis, the curtailment of knowledge is, as was the case with Soviet Marxism, the ultimate powerbase of neo-liberalism.

PAE seeks to break down the our-and-only-our approach to economics that traditionally has characterised the discipline and currently underwrites neo-liberalism. It aims instead to bring about in university economics, in both teaching and research, an interacting and co-operative pluralism of approaches that, like the French students called for, is adapted to the complexity and uncertainty of economic reality and parallels long-established practices in modern physics and biology. Instead of aiming to indoctrinate students and the general public in a closed system of belief, it would bring to bear on economic issues a whole range of approaches, including neo-classical, institutional, post-Keynesian, intersubjectivist, Austrian, Marxian, anthropological, ecological, behaviouralist, feminist, systems analysis and complexity theory. Each of these approaches – and this is not an exhaustive list – reveals things about the economy that the others do not. With the spread of this knowledge base, the ignorance upon which neo-liberalism's hegemony depends would be voided.

Labour Party supporters can hook into this academic reform movement by demanding a corresponding analytical pluralism in the formation of Labour Party policies. An intra-party climate could and should be created wherein intellectual standards are such that attempts to fashion and justify policy on the basis of the slogans or the one-dimensional thought processes of neo-liberalism, *or any other ideology*, are, as a matter of course, ridiculed. To this end, consultation with a diverse range of economists should routinely be sought, so that decisions once again are arrived at through open political processes, rather than by de facto academic dictates, and are broadly knowledge-based rather than produced by the tunnel vision of a quasi religion.

Such intra-party reform, however, will not eliminate the primary source of the malaise. After Blair a dilution of the Labour Party's neo-liberalism may be possible, but without more fundamental reform, in the long-run the cause is lost. So long as the country's university economics departments are allowed to be operated as political propaganda centres and one-paradigm closed-shops, successive generations of citizens, including journalists and politicians, will be indoctrinated in the neo-classical-neo-liberal creed. This situation is not compatible with normal ideas of democracy. Alas, I do not sense within Labour circles a willingness to confront the problem. But not until it is can the madness of neo-liberalism, like Soviet Marxism, be laid to rest.

NOTE

The *post-autistic economics review* now has over eight thousand subscribers, the majority of whom are professional economists.

REFERENCES

Bernstein, M. A. (2003), 'Rethinking Economics in Twentieth-Century America', in Fullbrook, E. (ed.), *The Crisis in Economics*, London: Routledge, pp. 154-8.

Bohm, D. (1983), *Wholeness and the Implicate Order*, London: Routledge.

Coase, R. (1999), 'Interview with Ronald Coase', *Newsletter of the International Society for New Institutional Economics*, Vol. 2 No. 1.

Friedman, M. (1999), 'Conversation with Milton Friedman', in Snowdon, B. and Vane, H. (eds), *Conversations with Leading Economists: interpreting modern macroeconomics*, Cheltenham: Edward Elgar, pp. 124-44.

Gingras, Y. (2002), 'Beautiful Mind, Ugly Deception: The Bank of Sweden Prize in Economics Science', *post-autistic economics review*, no. 17.

Jevons, W. S. (1871), *The Theory of Political Economy*, Harmondsworth: Pelican, 1970 edn.

Leontief, W. (1982), Letter, in *Science*, 217, pp. 104-7.

Walras, L. (1874-77), *Elements of Pure Economics: or the Theory of Social Wealth*, Philadelphia: Orion Editions, 1984 edn.

What's wrong with the official future?

Richard Eckersley

Over the past several decades, we have witnessed a profound loss of faith in a future constructed around notions of material progress, economic growth and scientific and technological fixes to the challenges we face. This demise of the 'official future' is of utmost importance, but remains largely ignored in public and political debate.

The failure of the official future represents, at one level, a coalescence of various national and global issues - the periodic eruptions over the past fifty years of worries about nuclear war, technological change, social decline and environmental destruction. Of course, these concerns, singly taken, are well known and discussed; and the totality of their impacts informs futures studies and writing on post-modernity. However, the depth and breadth – and, most importantly, the political significance – of the loss of faith barely register in current debate and discussion. We are still to understand its full implications, especially that our situation is not just a reflection of the changed external 'realities' of life, but also of a profound destabilisation of our inner lives.

This chapter discusses material progress, its rationale and why this is flawed; the public's loss of faith and the credibility gap which flows from this; and the prospect of a paradigm shift from material progress to sustainable development. My main concern is not with the changes in the external world, but with the subtle and complex relationship between those 'outer' changes and the 'inner' world of thoughts and emotions, and what this means socially, politically and personally.

This loss of faith applies to a large proportion, probably a majority, of people in the developed, Western world. People in developing countries may still share a faith in material progress and have most to gain from what it offers. Nevertheless, the issues I discuss are still relevant to their world and the choices they make.

GOING FOR GROWTH

The 'official future' prioritises economic growth as the basis for improving quality of life. This position is shared by all governments and major political parties – a 'policy constant' largely beyond scrutiny or debate. Whether the leader is Bill Clinton or George W. Bush, Margaret Thatcher or Tony Blair, the belief that 'it's the economy, stupid' rules. As the Australian Prime Minister John Howard states repeatedly: 'Maintaining a strong, dynamic and growing economy is the ... overriding responsibility of government' (Howard, 2004).

The concept of material progress regards economic growth as paramount because it creates the wealth necessary to increase personal freedoms and opportunities, and to meet community needs and national goals, including addressing social problems. In public policy terms, economic growth means more revenue, bigger budget surpluses, and more to spend on health, education and the environment.

There are, on the face of it, good grounds for the equation of more with better. *The Spectator* magazine claimed in 2004 that 'we live in the happiest, healthiest and most peaceful era in human history' (Hanlon, 2004). And if now was good, it argued, the future would be even better. The belief that we live in the best of all times has been most famously and controversially articulated in recent years by Danish academic Bjorn Lomborg (2001) in *The Skeptical Environmentalist: Measuring the Real State of the World*. Lomborg concludes that mankind's lot has improved vastly in every significant measurable field and that it is likely to continue to do so: 'children born today – in both the industrialized world and developing countries – will live longer and be healthier, they will get more food, a better education, a higher standard of living, more leisure time and far more possibilities – without the global environment being destroyed. And that is a beautiful world'. Like many others, Lomborg credits this achievement largely to material prosperity resulting from economic growth.

It is true that, today, many more people are living richer, longer lives than ever before. In the year 1000, according to Angus Maddison (2001), the 270 million people in the world on average could expect to live about 24 years and earn US$400 a year (in today's dollars). Today there are over six billion people on earth who, on average, can expect to live about 67 years and earn almost US$6000 year. In the developed world in the past two hundred years, per capita GDP has risen about twenty-fold, and life expectancy has more than doubled. In the rest of the world, per capita GDP has increased more than five-fold and life expectancy has also more than doubled.

COSTS AND QUALIFICATIONS

However, there is growing evidence that quality of life is not the same as standard of living, and that how well we live is not just a matter of how long we live, especially in rich nations. Against the gains we have to set the following qualifications (Eckersley, 2005):

- The benefits have been unevenly distributed globally, and there have been recent reversals in both per capita income and life expectancy in some nations.
- The benefits of rising income to quality of life diminish as income increases, and in rich nations health and happiness are at best only weakly related to average income levels.
- Economic growth is not the only, or perhaps even the main, factor behind improving health and wellbeing. Increased knowledge, better education and institutional reforms have also made major contributions, even in the absence of sustained growth.
- Increases in life expectancy partly reflect biomedical advances and individual lifestyle choices that say little about changes in social conditions and may be offsetting adverse health impacts of these changes.

Beyond these qualifications of the benefits of material progress, we must also acknowledge several formidable and growing costs related to sustainability, opportunity and meaning, all which have real and potentially immense implications for human health and wellbeing.

- The destruction of the natural environment of which we are an intrinsic part. However we address local and regional impacts through increased wealth and technological innovation, the evidence suggests we are disrupting planetary system on an increasing scale.
- Increasing inequality, sustained high unemployment, growing under-employment and overwork, pressures on public services such as health and education, and the geographic concentration of disadvantage, leading to deeper and more entrenched divisions within society.
- Psychosocial costs of cultural qualities such as materialism and individualism, which are deeply embedded in the worldview of material progress. These costs relate to meaning in life and things that create meaning – purpose, autonomy, identity and hope.

In other words, advocates of material progress not only oversell the benefits of growth, they also ignore the social and environmental costs of growth processes, or at least assume they can be more than compensated. But if, in creating wealth, we damage the fabric of society and the state of the natural environment more than we can repair with the extra wealth, we are going backwards in terms of quality of life, even while we grow richer. Material progress depends on the pursuit of individual and material self-interest that, morally, cannot be quarantined from other areas of our lives.

TRENDS IN HEALTH AND WELLBEING

The flaws in the model of material progress become clear when we look more closely at trends in health and wellbeing (often measured as happiness or life satisfaction) and their relationship with wealth. Comparing nations, increasing income confers large benefits at low income levels, but little, if any, benefit at high income levels (Inglehart, 2000; Eckersley, 2005). Life expectancy levels off at a per capita income of about US$5000, and happiness at about US$10,000. Across countries, happiness is more closely associated with democratic freedoms than income, and is strongly linked to equality, stability and human rights.

Looking at the relationship between income and wellbeing within countries, population happiness has not increased in recent decades in rich nations (over fifty years in the United States) even though people have become, on average, much richer. However, the rich remain happier than the poor, especially in poorer countries, but even in rich nations. While it is often said that money cannot buy happiness, most surveys reveal the two are linked. They also show, however, that the relationship is strongest at low incomes, where money improves living conditions and alleviates hardship. Furthermore, above this level, wealth has a largely symbolic value as a measure of social status: status affects wellbeing through the social comparisons it defines. This means that income-related differences in happiness will persist no matter how far average incomes rise through economic growth.

The costs of progress are more apparent if we examine a wider range of measures of wellbeing. Take young people, whose lives reveal most clearly the tenor and tempo of our times (Eckersley, 2005; Eckersley, Wierenga and Wyn, 2006). While their health, measured by life expectancy and mortality, continues to improve, and most say in surveys that they are healthy, happy and satisfied with their lives, adverse trends in young people's health range across both physical and mental problems, and from relatively minor but common complaints such as chronic tiredness to rare but serious problems, including suicide.

The extent to which we are falling short of maximising human well-being, despite rising life expectancy and material wealth, was demonstrated in a large study of adult Americans, which examined mental health as 'a syndrome of symptoms of positive feelings and positive functioning in life' (Keyes, 2002). It found that 26 per cent of people were either 'languishing', depressed, or both – that is, mentally unhealthy; 57 per cent were moderately mentally healthy – neither mentally ill nor fully mentally healthy; and only 17 per cent of people were 'flourishing' – that is, enjoyed good mental health.

PUBLIC PERCEPTIONS OF QUALITY OF LIFE

Declining quality of life is also apparent in people's perceptions of life today. These perceptions are at the heart of the case against the official future. Studies over the past decade, both qualitative and quantitative, reveal levels of anger and moral anxiety about changes in society that were not apparent thirty years ago (Eckersley, 2005). They show that many people are concerned about the materialism, greed and selfishness that they believe drive society today, underlie social ills, and threaten their children's future.

About twice as many Australians say quality of life is getting worse as say it is getting better. The latest in a series of annual reports on 'the mind and mood' of Australians says there is growing concern that the state of Australian society - rougher, tougher, more competitive, less compassionate – is producing stress, edginess and a feeling of personal vulnerability (Ipsos Mackay, 2005a). Australians feel they 'seem to lurching from one difficulty to another with the prospect of a serious crisis emerging'. The blame is repeatedly directed at political leaders, who are accused of 'short-term thinking' and neglecting to invest in the country's future.

A British study, *Changing Britain, Changing Lives*, found that despite higher incomes, better health and greater opportunity for women, Britons were increasingly depressed, unhappy in their relationships, and alienated from civic society (Woodward, 2003). A report of the New Economics Foundation says that, for many people, politics and corruption have become almost synonymous (Walker, 2002).

Some studies make explicit the tension between concerns about quality of life and the political emphasis on growth. For example, surveys show that 87 per cent of Britons and 83 per cent of Australians agree that their societies are 'too materialistic, with too much emphasis on money and not enough on the things that really matter' (Hamilton, 2002: 2003a). An Australian survey revealed that 'having extra money for things like luxuries and travel' ranked last in a list of seven items judged 'very important' to success, well behind the top-scorer, 'having a close and happy family' (Bagnall, 1999). And in contrast to government priorities, 'maintaining a high standard of living' ranked last in a list of sixteen critical issues headed by educational access, children and young people's wellbeing, and health care.

A recent Australian survey which included questions asked in 1988 and 1995 provides striking evidence of the gap between economic performance and people's perceptions and preferences (Ipsos Mackay, 2005b). Despite an economic boom of more than a decade, the proportion of Australians who felt that their quality of life in about 15 years' time would be better fell from 30 per cent in 1988 to 23 per cent in 2005. The proportion that said it would worsen rose from 40 to 46 per cent.

Offered two positive scenarios of Australia's future – one focused on individual wealth, economic growth and efficiency and enjoying 'the good life', the other on community, family, equality and environmental sustainability – 73 per cent expected the former, but 93 per cent preferred the latter. This gap between preference and expectation has widened markedly since 1995. Optimism about the future of world has slumped. Asked to choose between two statements about the world in the twenty-first century, only 23 per cent thought it was likely to be 'a new age of peace and prosperity'; 66 per cent opted for 'a bad time of crisis and trouble'.

SUSPICIONS OF THE APOCALYPSE

Our perceptions of the future are increasingly shaped by images of global or distant threat and disaster: earthquakes, hurricanes, floods, disease pandemics, terrorist attacks, genocide, famine. While these hazards are not new, previous fears were never so sustained and varied, or so powerfully reinforced by the immediacy and vividness of today's media images.

Our responses to these apocalyptic suspicions about the century ahead involve subtle and complex interactions between the world 'out there' and the world 'in here' (in our minds). Evidence suggests that we are being drawn in at least three directions by the prospects of dramatic, even catastrophic, social, economic and environmental changes: towards apocalyptic nihilism, fundamentalism, or activism. If this categorisation seems too stark, think of the responses as tendencies or deviations from the norm, with subtle to extreme manifestations, and which can overlap, co-exist and change over time in individuals and groups. My intention is to highlight the way that people, individually and collectively, can respond very differently to the same perceptions of threat and hazard.

Apocalyptic nihilism: the abandonment of belief; decadence rules. At the extreme are young criminals whose apocalyptic language conveys a message that 'in a world stripped of meaning and self-identity, adolescents can understand violence itself as a morally grounded gesture, a kind of purifying attempt to intervene against the nothingness' (Powers, 2002).

Others respond in less dramatic ways to this sense that 'it's a late hour in the day, and nothing much matters anymore'. They could, for example, become even more determined to succeed, to be a winner at all costs, or lose themselves in the quest for pleasure or excitement. These lifestyles have their own hazards, including various forms of addiction. Nihilistic inclinations are evident at a more mundane level in a growing political disengagement: a focus on home and hearth, on tending our own patch. This can be an effective coping strategy, but there is a cost: a fraying of citizenship and democracy, and a vulnerability to the politics of self-interest and fear.

Apocalyptic fundamentalism: the retreat to certain belief (whether secular or religious); dogma rules. In an extreme form, this is 'end time' thinking, rife among fundamentalist Christians in the US, in which global war and warming are embraced as harbingers of the Rapture and Christ's return to Earth (Scherer, 2004). Commentators are unsure how influential 'end time' philosophy is within the Bush administration, but argue that hard questions about Bush's religious convictions need to be asked. Philosopher Peter Singer (2004, cited in McGinn, 2004) says that President Bush's religious outlook is best represented by the Manichean idea of a force of evil in the world, with an apocalyptic Second Coming imminent and America as the divinely appointed nation set to destroy the forces of Satan.

The growth in fundamentalist thought extends beyond religion. Neo-liberal economics, which underpins the official future, also represents a form of fundamentalism in its rigid adherence to an economic doctrine in the face of the growing evidence of its failure to deliver promised benefits. Fundamentalism produces a comforting certainty about life and a call to united action against threats, both moral and physical, but it also generates simplistic solutions to complex problems.

Apocalyptic activism: the transformation of belief; hope rules. This reflects the desire to create a new conceptual framework or worldview (stories, values, beliefs) that will make a sustainable future possible. The counter-trend that this 'activism' represents is exemplified by the so-called downshifters and cultural creatives: people who are making a comprehensive shift in their worldview, values and way of life, including trading income for quality of life. Rejecting contemporary lifestyles and priorities, they place more emphasis in their lives on relationships, communities, spirituality, nature and the environment, and ecological sustainability.

Nihilism and fundamentalism represent maladaptive responses to our situation, whatever their short-term or personal appeal, because they do not address its root causes. Activism is an adaptive reaction. So let me say a little more about this response.

AGENTS OF CHANGE

Studies by American researchers Paul Ray and Sherry Ruth Anderson (2000) reveal that about a quarter of people in Western societies are 'cultural creatives'. They represent a coalescence of social movements that are not just concerned with influencing government, but with reframing issues in a way that changes how people understand the world. Ray and Anderson say that in the 1960s, they represented less than five per cent of the population, whereas now they have grown to 26 per cent.

Surveys on downshifting show that 25 per cent of Britons and 23 per cent of Australians aged 30-59 had 'downshifted' in the previous ten years by voluntarily making a long-term change in their lifestyle and earning less money (Hamilton and Mail, 2003; Hamilton, 2003b). Contrary to the popular belief that they tend to be middle-aged and wealthier people, downshifters are spread across age groups and social classes.

Beyond those who are changing their lives are many more people who are thinking about it. Hugh Mackay (2003), while noting the social dangers inherent in the process of disengagement, says many people are using this 'retreat time' to explore the meaning of their lives and to connect with their most deeply-held values. Whether this search for meaning is expressed in religion, New Age mysticism, moral reflection or love and friendship, the goal is the same: 'to feel that our lives express who we are and that we are living in harmony with the values we claim to espouse'.

The revolt against the official future is also consistent with a development noted by some sociologists: a new moral autonomy and a more 'cooperative or altruistic individualism' (Eckersley, 2005; Beck and Beck-Gernsheim, 2002). This deep conceptual shift in how we construe the self has far-reaching social implications, not least for politics because it undermines the philosophy of narrowly defined self-interest and personal freedom and responsibility that currently dominates political thinking.

BEYOND GROWTH, TOWARDS SUSTAINABILITY

The activism I have described is closely associated with the concept of sustainable development, which is increasingly challenging material progress as a framework for thinking about human betterment. Sustainable development does not accord economic growth 'overriding' priority. Instead, it seeks a better balance and integration of social, environmental and economic goals and objectives to produce a high, equitable and enduring quality of life (Eckersley, 2005). A common theme is the perceived need to shift from *quantity* to *quality* in our way of life. Rather than casting the core question in terms of being pro-growth or anti-growth, we need to see that growth itself is not the main game.

We can also characterise the shift from material progress to sustainable development as replacing the outdated industrial metaphor of progress as a pipeline (pump more wealth in one end and more welfare flows out the other) with an ecological metaphor of progress as an evolving ecosystem – reflecting the reality that the processes that drive social systems are complex, dynamic, diffuse and non-linear.

In recent years, international bodies such as the OECD and the World Bank have acknowledged the need to place more emphasis on the quality – or content – of growth. As Vinod Thomas, the lead author of a 2000 World Bank report, *Quality of Growth*, remarked at its launch: 'Just as the quality of people's diet, and not just the quantity of food they eat, influences their health and life expectancy, the way in which growth is generated and distributed has profound implications for people and their quality of life' (Thomas et al., 2000).

The key challenge of sustainable development has usually been seen as reconciling the requirements of the economy – growth – with the requirements of the environment – conservation and sustainable use of natural resources. However, our growing understanding of the social basis of health and happiness can shift this perspective, making an important contribution to working towards sustainability. It provides a means of integrating different priorities by allowing them to be measured against a common goal or benchmark: improving human wellbeing.

If we were to make this shift in thinking, we would be forced to recognise that the basis of health and happiness is much more complex, and often less tangible and material, than current strategies presume. Of particular importance is the mounting evidence that money and what it buys constitute only a part of what makes for a high quality of life. And the pursuit of wealth can exact a high cost when it is given too high a priority – nationally or personally – so that it crowds out other, more important goals.

In other words, we need to think, politically, less in terms of a 'wealth-producing economy' and more about a 'health-creating society'. Confronted with the magnitude and global scale of twenty-first century challenges – population pressures, environmental destruction, economic equity, global governance, technological change – it makes no sense to continue to regard these issues as something we can deal with by fiddling at the margins of the economy, the main purpose of which remains to serve, and promote, our increasingly extravagant – and unhealthy and unsustainable – consumer lifestyle.

The current worldview framed by material progress and based on self-interested, competitive individualism has created a 'shallow' democracy (where citizenship involves voting every few years for whichever party promises the best personal deal) and has resulted in reduced social cohesion, weaker families and communities, and so diminished quality of life. Challenging this construction is a new worldview framed by sustainable development and based on altruistic, cooperative individualism. This encourages a 'deep' democracy (where citizenship is embodied in all aspects of our lives), leading to greater social cohesion, stronger communities and families, and so better quality of life. The former represents a vicious cycle, the latter a virtuous one.

POLITICAL IMPLICATIONS
The demise of the official future is causing a cascade of consequences. Our visions of the future are woven into the stories we create to make sense and meaning of our lives. This 'storying' is important in linking individuals to a broader social or collective narrative, and affects both our own wellbeing (by enhancing our sense of belonging, identity and control over our lives, for example), and societal functioning (by engaging us in the shared task of working for a better future).

Elections have rarely, if ever, been about deep desires and concerns about quality of life or the future; and, increasingly, election campaigns are manipulated through the use of sophisticated marketing tactics to focus on a few, often contrived, issues. With the loss of a wider faith, there is a retreat from the public realm to the private, with many people turning inwards to focus on their own lives. Trust in government and other 'official' institutions is eroded. As leaders learn they can get away with it, they pursue power and self-interest more ruthlessly.

It may even be that we are moving between paradigms depending on circumstances and occasions. Asked about social directions and preferred futures, we inhabit a new worldview defined by sustainable development; when it comes to voting in elections, we choose the old paradigm of material progress because we are aware that this is the framework within which government operates. Democracy is jeopardized because it continues to function in a paradigm that now alienates the people.

In other words, apocalyptic nihilism and fundamentalism are finding clearer political expression than activism, which has yet to find its voice in mainstream politics. We may be approaching a tipping point, at which one or another of the responses dominates. But is it impossible to predict when that point will occur and in which direction it will tip.

History and legend show that when the gap between the ideal and real becomes too wide, the system eventually breaks down (Tuchman, 1989). In the meantime, however, it tends to become more oppressive, as those whose interests are vested in the status quo strive to maintain their control and advantage. And today, these individuals and groups have enormous economic, political and technological power to call upon.

Our current worldview and lifestyle are neither inevitable nor optimal, but are culturally 'manufactured' by a massive and growing media-marketing complex. For example, big business in the United States spends over US$1000 billion dollars annually on marketing – about twice what Americans spend on education (Dawson, 2003, cited in York, 2004). This expenditure includes 'macro-marketing', the management of the social environment, particularly public policy, to suit the interests of business.

Cultures have been said to exert a pervasive but diffuse influence on actions, providing the underlying assumptions of an entire way of life, while ideologies exert a powerful, clearly articulated, but more restricted, basis for social action (Swidler, 1986). The increasing weight of public perception, scientific evidence and global events will – eventually – tilt the balance in favour of a new cultural order. However, how and when this new order becomes expressed ideologically remains unclear. We could see politics continue to be misguided for some time by nihilistic or fundamentalist responses; a new political force could emerge; or there might be a shift of the whole political spectrum in a new direction, with mainstream parties forced to acknowledge new cultural ideals, but in ways that move beyond the traditional socialist-left and conservative-right frame of reference.

Seen in a broad, cultural and futures context, the neo-liberal, market-based strategies that currently dominate government begin to look more like a political supernova: the final, flaring brilliance of a dying star.

REFERENCES

Bagnall, D. (1999), 'Reasons to be cheerful', *The Bulletin*, 29 June, pp. 36-39.

Beck, U. and Beck-Gernsheim, E. (2002), *Individualization*, London: Sage.

Dawson, M. (2003), *The Consumer Trap: Big Business Marketing in American Life*, Champaign: University of Illinois Press.

Eckersley, R (2005), *Well and Good: Morality, Meaning and Happiness*, Melbourne: Text Publishing, 2nd edn.

Eckersley R., Wierenga, A. and Wyn, J. (2006), *Flashpoints and Signposts: Pathways to success ands wellbeing for Australia's young people*, Melbourne: Australia 21 Ltd, Canberra, and Australian Youth Research Centre.

Hamilton, C. (2002), *Overconsumption in Australia: The rise of the middle-class battler*, Discussion paper no. 49, Canberra: Australia Institute.

Hamilton, C. and Mail E. (2003), *Downshifting in Australia: A sea-change in the pursuit of happiness*, Discussion paper no. 50, Canberra: Australia Institute.

Hamilton, C. (2003a), *Overconsumption in Britain: A culture of middle-class complaint*, Discussion paper no. 57, Canberra: Australia Institute.

Hamilton, C. (2003b), *Downshifting in Britain: A sea-change in the pursuit of happiness*, Discussion paper no. 58, Canberra: Australia Institute.

Hanlon, M. (2004), 'There's no time like the present', *Spectator*, 7 August.

Howard, J. (2004), 'Getting the Big Things Right: Goals and Responsibilities in a Fourth Term', Address to Enterprise Forum lunch, Adelaide, 8 July, Canberra: News Room, Office of the Prime Minister, Parliament House.

Ipsos Mackay (2005a), *Mind and Mood: The Ipsos Mackay Report no. 116*, Sydney: Ipsos Mackay Public Affairs.

Ipsos Mackay (2005b), *Where are we headed as a community?*, National Omnibus Poll, November, Sydney: Ipsos Mackay Public Affairs.

Keyes, C.L.M. (2002), 'The mental health continuum: from languishing to flourishing in life', *Journal of Health and Social Research*, vol. 43, pp. 207-222.

Lomborg, B. (2001), *The Skeptical Environmentalist: Measuring the Real State of the World*, Cambridge: Cambridge University Press.

Mackay, H. (2003), *The Wrap: Understanding Where We Are Now and Where We've Come From. The Mackay Report: 1979-2003*, Sydney: Mackay Research.

Maddison, A. (2001), *The World Economy: A Millennial Perspective*, Paris: Development Centre of the Organisation for Economic Cooperation and Development.

McGinn, C. (2004), Swaying in the political breeze, *Australian Financial Review*, 16 April, *Review* p. 12 (reprinted from *Washington Post Book World*).

Powers, R. (2002), 'The Apocalypse of adolescence', *The Atlantic Monthly*, March.

Ray, P.H. and Anderson, R.S. (2000), *The Cultural Creatives: How 50 Million People are Changing the World*, New York: Harmony Books.

Scherer G. (2004), 'The Godly must be Crazy', *Grist Magazine*, 27 October.

Singer, P. (2004), *The President of Good and Evil: The Ethics of George W Bush*, Melbourne: Text Publishing.

Swidler, A. (1986), Culture in action: symbols and strategies, *American Sociological Review*, vol. 51, pp. 273-286.

Thomas, V. et al (2000), *The Quality of Growth*, World Bank and Oxford University Press, Oxford (press release and briefing transcript, 25 September 2000).

Tuchman, B. (1989), *A Distant Mirror – the Calamitous 14th Century*, London: Papermac, (first published 1978).

Walker, P. (2002), *We, the People: Developing a new democracy*, London: new economics foundation.

Woodward, W. (2003), 'An affluent but more anxious society', *Guardian Weekly*, 27 February-5 March, p. 11.

York, R. (2004), 'Manufacturing the love of possession – The Consumer Trap: Big Business Marketing in American Life – Book Review', *Monthly Review*, February.

The next progressive political wave

Neal Lawson and Hetan Shah

Political movements rarely make the weather; instead they tend to respond to them. As Karl Marx said, men make their own history but not in circumstances of their own choosing. We can shape events but only in the context in which we find ourselves. The two most dynamic moments of post-war British politics – 1945 itself and then 1979 – bear witness to this. Neither Attlee nor Thatcher created the cultural, social and economic waves of their time, but they understood the potential political implications of what was happening around them. It is essential for the democratic left to grasp the political potential of this moment and this time.

Before we examine what sources of energy and vitality could give purpose and direction to a democratic left of the future it is helpful to reflect on the past. We need to look at Blair before we turn to political life 'after Blair'. A second famous quote is illuminating here, this time from Hegel, who said that the 'owl of Minerva spreads its wings only with the falling of the dusk'. We can perhaps only really understand Blairism as its day comes to a close.

The context of Blairism was clear. Blair governed in the wake of three successive (and connected) waves. The first – the political tsunami – was the fall of communism in the East, which took place at the same time as the puncturing of the post-war social-democratic consensus in the West. Actually existing socialism in both its revolutionary and reformist hues was a spent force. The second wave was neo-liberalism, which eagerly filled the vacuum that was left with its big-market small-state fixation, becoming the hegemonic political force of our era. By the time Blair had arrived on the scene, however, this too was under challenge, at least in its more aggressive Thatcherite strain. People had come to realise that 'there was such a thing as society'. The third wave was therefore the one that crashed on the rocks of Majorism and saw Labour back in office in 1997 after eighteen years in the wilderness.

It is essential to understand New Labour as a second, more humanised, chapter within the rise of neo-liberalism. It was a reaction to the excesses of Thatcherism – but only a partial reaction. The state would become enabling, in the sense that it would actively assist individuals in finding their feet in the new competitive economy that neo-liberalism had unleashed. Crucially, though, it would not challenge the supremacy of capital. You still could not 'buck the market'. What you could do was deliver social justice – not through the state, but through economic efficiency, i.e. by making people employable. Thus the break with Thatcherism was over means not ends. New Labour was an adaptive response to triumphant market forces. It never questioned the morality of market domination.

One area of debate on the left is of course about whether or not this strategy of social justice through efficiency works, or is good enough. This is something we are sceptical on. But there is a further question: whether or not New Labour purposefully undersold the mandate it received in 1997. Was the third wave, which finally led to the election of a Labour government, a phenomenon that could have delivered much more than has been attempted by Blairism: could more radical policies have been put in place? It is difficult to tell of course, but majorities of over 160 come along very rarely, and sit uncomfortably alongside the timidity of New Labour in office. And we know from opinion polls that, despite New Labour's repeated protestations to the contrary, many people who voted for change in 1997 expected the new government to introduce measures such as increases in taxes. So there are some indications that people expected more of New Labour, and would have supported a more ambitious programme after the election. Indeed, this expectation had been encouraged in Labour's election campaign, with its conjuring up of the image of a New Britain and a new politics.

What has New Labour achieved? Did they change the weather? It could be argued here that the political emphasis now, unlike in the 1980s, is on the quality of public services, not on tax cuts. This is a major achievement. But this mood was created before New Labour came to power, and is now under threat from the choice and marketisation agenda. The high point on this question was the 2001 election pledge to put 1p on National Insurance contributions to go to health. But this step in the right direction was never built on. The minimum wage was another achievement, and is an important underpinning of the economy, but it can easily be left to wither on the vine when the

Tories get back into power (they will not repeal it – they will just not up-rate it). The only positive lasting legacy of the decade will be devolution to Edinburgh, Cardiff and London – and all of those occurred despite Blair's objections. On many issues, the Liberal Democrats – and the reviving Cameron Tories – are now able to enthusiastically pose to the left of New Labour. Meanwhile Blairism refuses to countenance any shift to new territory. The needle is stuck in the groove of 1994.

Much more could have been achieved given the quantity and quality of New Labour's landslide. Of course the mandate was tentative, and many votes were tactical and conditional. But they always are. The objective of politics is to then mould them into something more. Politics and democracy could have been recast through electoral reform, an end to adversarialism and the opening up of real pluralism. A social Europe could have been grasped, localism allowed to flourish; we could have been as tough on the causes of crime as on crime itself.

The failure of New Labour to realise its full potential was caused by a mix of timidity and an unquestioning acceptance of globalisation and the market as benign forces. But the New Labour failure is about more than just its inversion of social democracy – which is supposed to make people the masters of the market rather than its servants. The big tent strategy was simply unsustainable. In politics you cannot have friends without making enemies. And without friends it is impossible to survive the bad times, and to make the political weather. For Blair definition only ever came against those to his left. As he tacked ever rightwards, guided by the lodestar of triangulation, it was inevitable that opposition on the left would eventually reach a critical mass. The fall to only 36 per cent of the vote in the last general election, with many natural Labour supporters either abstaining or voting Liberal Democrat or Green, is the result of New Labour's reluctance to make any move towards changing the terms of political debate.

It is partly testament to Tony Blair's incredible political skills that New Labour has lasted so long, but it is also a result of the shell-shocked party he inherited in 1994, which would do whatever it was asked to do to win again and stay in office. In many respects the years since have only served to remind us of how far we had fallen before 1997. Like a tanker slowly turning itself round, Labour can only now begin to think about making headway against the currents of neo-liberalism.

The New Labour wave has come and gone. For the future it leaves a legacy of economic competence and some new political structures. Neither is unimportant, as they provide a platform for future modern democratic left advance. But what are the next waves that will provide the vitality and energy for a post-Blair era?

There are a number of elements in this. Few of them are new or original – good strategy rarely is. Some of them are centred on policy, but politics is perhaps the more difficult problem. We begin by looking at the agents for change and the constituencies that need to be mobilised. We then look at the need to build vision, create narratives and set up new institutions that embed values. Finally we turn to the changing policy context.

NURTURING CHANGE

Who are the agents of democratic left advance: who is the 'we'? Political parties and their supporters have for a long time been the major focus of political discourse. But parties are now in decline – total membership of all parties is down from around 3.5 million in 1950 to around half a million today. There are probably less than 180,000 members of the Labour Party. This is not because people don't care about politics, however: membership of campaigning groups and the numbers of people volunteering are rising. And the success of campaigns such as Make Poverty History also show that there are many people who are interested in giving thought, time and resources to politics. What are the lessons from this? One issue here is trust: an ICM poll for BBC News 24 in 2005 showed that 79 per cent of people do not trust politicians to tell the truth. In contrast to this, polls show that campaign groups are regarded as far more trustworthy. Clear vision and demanding goals have also proved to be energising, as has giving people multiple ways to get involved. These are all things that parties need to learn from if they are to recover some semblance of ideological and coherent influence on the state and its relationship to civil society. And for the democratic left at least, we must ensure that the Labour Party (and not just a Labour government) does this.

However, it is not the case that political parties can simply imitate the practices of civil society groups. Partly this is because the role of parties is more complex. They have to balance a whole set of concerns, such as willing the means to pay for progress, whereas civil society groups tend to have a narrower remit. Furthermore, campaigns like Make Poverty History, however much attention they grab when they hit the news, tend to fade away without being able to tackle the difficult question of how to forge a tight and lasting grip on the final decision-makers. In addition, NGOs tend to be highly unaccountable, and, though there is much that Labour needs to do to improve its internal democracy, at least it has a notional framework for accountability, and one that can compel politicians to act.

Having said that, it needs also to be recognised that civil society is in itself a major change agent, something that has traditionally been underestimated by the left because of its overly statist conception of change. The next progressive political wave will emerge as much from actors outside the realm of formal party politics as from within. This will require a strengthening of civil society, a building of networks between party politics and other actors, and a clearer dialogue about the different roles of parties, state and civil society organisations.

A great deal of policy innovation happens through the voluntary and community sector, and through social enterprises. The democratic left needs to harness this energy. We are seeing signs of this through the formation of bodies such as the Young Foundation, which is designed to spin off institutions to deal with social needs, bypassing government entirely. In this sense the left should return to its trade union, mutual, co-operative and friendly society roots; this is particularly appropriate in a less deferential and decentralised world, where people are searching for autonomy – for the ability to self-manage their world. This kind of approach makes for socialism built from the bottom up, for and by people, and more localist than centralist. (We also recognise the role of a strong centre to legislate for equality, though at the same time having the confidence to allow local differences to emerge.) Organisations such as the Citizens Organising Foundation in London harness local anger about low wages and impossibly high house prices to campaign successfully for a living wage and affordable housing. They are doing so on their own terms, but are uniting and focusing the interests and anger of faith groups, trade unions, schools and community groups. There are also good examples of self organisation from the world of social enterprise, especially community-based enterprises such as development trusts, which earn an income from an asset (such as a building, for example, through providing a managed workspace) and use the profits for local benefit. But examples of self-organisation are not widespread, and many instances are fragile. There would need to be some kind of step change for these models to be a real force to be reckoned with, and at present it is not easy to see where this would come from.

Though all these civil society groups have important roles to play, a patchwork of progressive interests spanning social movements and consumer and producer interests is a necessary but insufficient basis for left advance. There needs to be an over-arching class alliance, that can act as the foundation for progressive advance. The left makes advances when the interests of the progressive middle classes and working classes coincide. This was the case for the welfare agenda post-1945 and again for the technocratic revolution of the 1960s. We know what the grievances of the excluded are, but what are the disaffections of the included? If the progressive consensus that came together to enable Labour to win in 1997 is not to totally wither away, what is the basis for a class alliance of the future?

The middle classes are certainly restless. Jobs may be well paid but anxiety abounds. Even where job security might exist, the desire for esteem through the corporate hierarchy is causing us to work longer and harder for the next promotion. Cultural pressure to conform to the demands of a consumerised society creates more pressure. The middle classes are living in a world beyond their control. As the celebrated American economist J. K. Galbraith said: 'there are many models of the good society, but the treadmill is not one them'. Millions are making the decision to down-shift their lives but formal politics is not leading the way on this; it is stuck in a time warp of growth and materialism.

One thought stands out. As the labour market continues to shape itself as an hour glass, with concentrations of work at the higher end and at the bottom, there is a potential unity to be forged between those that are cash-rich but time-poor and their alter-egos (often those who provide services for them), who have more time but less money. In both cases the system is not providing real well-being. So it may be in everybody's well-being interests to shift the system.

Demonstrating this is the political problem. New collectivist ideas, particularly from the environmental movement, which is premised on a notion of shared commons, could help forge this alliance. Within the context of a post-materialist culture for some, and with well-being overtaking wealth as a key concern, there is the possibility of a rebalancing or redistribution of wealth to where it would increase marginal utility the most. Here the Treasury notion of progressive universalism – that sees everyone getting something, but the most needy getting extra help – could be extended and built into a more transformative policy tool.

POLITICAL STRATEGY
Fundamental to the renewal of the democratic left is a clear vision and set of underlying values. This has been hopelessly missing from New Labour, and has led to a scattershot of policies: policies have flitted from authoritarianism to empowerment, from pandering to big business to being focused on poverty reduction, from programmes firmly based in evidence to those arising from back-of-the-envelope hunches.

And to the extent that there has been a vision it has been a neo-liberal one, but encased in a social democratic shell – what Stuart Hall has described as the New Labour 'double shuffle' (2003). Without a clear set of values and principles, it is easy for government to lose its way in the face of day to day political demands. We think those principles should include: the goal of freedom, as autonomy or self-management of our lives; the necessity to focus on the worst off and least powerful to achieve that goal; a recognition of the primacy of democracy as an instrumental good, not least to reconcile a belief in pluralism and solidarity; long-termism; a focus on prevention rather than dealing with symptoms; and a holistic approach to problem-solving.

Springing from these values are a set of stories or narratives. This is the real battleground of politics: to create the stories that we all believe in together. The Holy Grail is: how do we change culture and beliefs, not just policy? There is no clear answer to this. The struggle is won when something becomes absolute common sense, that is, the sense that is common. Thatcherism showed the way. Her kitchen table economics, that you cannot spend what you do not have and that people know best how to spend their own money, may have been transparently daft but they struck a chord. New Labour's narratives have been neither progressive enough or popular enough. The democratic left needs to think about what the narratives are that it wants to put forward, and, equally, to decide which of the narratives currently in play it wishes to neutralise.

In particular progressives need to create a story about equality, as the means both to use all our talents, and to limit the costs of social exclusion – costs that we all pay. Ultimately, though, the case for equality rests on the notion that inequalities of income and wealth distort our ability to be free. We can only be genuinely free when we are sufficiently equal. We also need a story about public goods that says that it is wasteful for individuals to have to retreat into providing their own private world, and that high levels of public investment are efficient. This can be married with a story that says that in the global marketplace the UK should invest in its comparative advantage as a good place to live and work. A small state is not necessarily good for economies – look at what is happening in failed states in Africa.

How do we put narratives into play? One way is to campaign around issues which are symbolic. For example, the Jamie Oliver campaign on school dinners did violence to the unconscious idea that value in public services comes from getting the cheapest price. Similarly, the Right in the US created a clever campaign which persuaded 70 per cent of the population to support the abolition of estate taxes, even though only 2 per cent of the population paid them (Graetz and Shairo, 2005). Where are the areas for which we need such campaigns? One space, quite clearly, is the question about the appropriate limit to markets and marketisation. For example, a campaign around banning commercial advertising aimed at children is something that would be popular (after all nobody benefits from it other than advertisers). At the same time such a campaign would carry embedded within it a deeper story about increasing commercialisation, and the need to put limits on this. New measures of progress can also serve to create change. For example, what would be the results of complementing existing school league tables with tables which look at well-being in schools?

Narratives and campaigns create the space for policy: policy cannot happen in a vacuum. This means that politicians cannot take citizens' preferences as given: they need to expend political capital to help change preferences. We have seen New Labour do this, but in general in a non-progressive direction – on issues such as Iraq, commercialisation of public services and ID cards. On progressive issues the approach has been either to proceed through stealth (such as the work on child poverty and tax credits) or to capitulate (e.g. backing down to fuel protesters rather than making the case for environmental taxation).

Another area of debate concerns the timing of our interventions. The raison d'etre of social democracy is to intervene to correct the injustices of capitalism – including damage to the planet. But should the democratic left intervene at the beginning, middle or end of the system of production, distribution and exchange? Intervention at the start of the process through measures such as macro-economic management, nationalisation or corporatism tends to focus on stopping things going wrong in the first place. Intervention at the end is more likely to involve clearing up the mess. In the middle there is regulation. New Labour has moved decisively away from any notion of early systemic intervention, towards a mix of regulation and sweeping up. The only decisive policy of intervention has been the minimum wage, but that has been fixed at a rate that causes little concern to companies trying to maximise their profits, and is in any case being undercut by those working outside the formal economy – most notably in terms of migrant workers. The democratic left needs to orientate itself around the need for early intervention.

If the left needs to have a narrative to popularise what it is for, it also needs to become much smarter at criticising and taking on the orthodoxies of neo-liberalism. For instance, there is a powerful argument to be made about the perversities and inadequacies of economic incentives (see for example Dawnay and Shah, 2005). In his classic work *The Gift Relationship* (1970), Richard Titmuss presented strong evidence on this, when he showed that it was more effective to obtain blood from donors (who were unpaid in England and Wales), than from those who were paid in various different ways (as in the US). Titmuss showed that proportionally more people gave blood in a voluntary system, and that the voluntarily donated blood was also of a higher quality. (It appeared that people who gave blood for financial reasons had a strong incentive not to be honest about any diseases potentially rendering their blood inadmissible.) He concluded that 'commercialisation of blood and donor relationships represses the expression of altruism': in terms of economic efficiency it was highly wasteful of blood; it was administratively inefficient and resulted in greater overhead costs; in terms of price per unit of blood the American (commercialised) system resulted in prices five to fifteen times higher than in the British (voluntary) system; and commercial markets were more likely to distribute contaminated blood. This kind of evidence needs to be circulated more widely.

Another important step in any political strategy is to build institutions which embed change and cannot be undone. Again, the teacher is Thatcher. She understood, perhaps like no other post-war politician, that institutions form the sites in which political values resonate and can outlast changes in government. So she established institutions which reflected her beliefs, through council house sales, privatisation and the deregulation of the city. Crucially, she attacked the institutions of the left, most notably the trade unions and local government. New Labour has done little to overturn this agenda, let alone to establish new progressive institutions: it has produced a mixed set of constitutional reforms, and a botched public service 'modernisation'. The Human Rights Act, which could have led to major institutional change, has been undermined by the very government that introduced it. Apart from the new sites of governance in Edinburgh, Cardiff and London, the best possibility for locally but potentially transformative self-help has been the Sure Start programme, but even this is dogged with problems of form, function and investment.

Then there is the issue of time. Any transformation of our society requires gradual but purposeful change. Sweden, where the left has been in power for most of the last seventy years, shows the way. They have slowly put together institutions which the right has been unable to dismantle even when in power (Taylor, 2005). Of course Britain is not Sweden, but we should remember that the Swedes started from a weak position. They were, however, consistent about their values base while being flexible about how these principles were applied. All this took them time, and similarly any transformation of Britain will take not years but decades. The crucial issue is whether we are heading in the right direction.

Finally, we have to recognise that there are major barriers to popular and radical democratic left narratives. Two substantial ones are the electoral system, which gives disproportionate power to a small number of voters, and the concentration of media ownership in the UK. These are fundamental institutional issues, which need to be tackled together. Our adversarial political culture and winner-takes-all electoral system lend themselves to a political system that can be dominated by media barons like Murdoch. It is essential that the supremacy of democracy is established, and with it a new political culture that welcomes not just pluralism, but the establishment of a long-term consensus with liberals, nationalists and environmentalists.

POLICY: FINDING A POPULAR POLITICAL AGENDA

Politicians in their Westminster bubble are often behind the political trends. Economic, social and demographic trends, as well as other developments, are changing the way policy needs to be thought about. There a number of emerging agendas to which the democratic left needs to respond. To facilitate this, Compass has been carrying out research around three broad areas for its programme for renewal: a vision of the good society; democracy and the public realm; and a new political economy. Some initial pointers about policy directions in these areas are sketched below.

The good society

The democratic left needs a clear vision of the good life that it can communicate. This needs to be based upon a strong conception of social justice and fairness, combined with an emphasis on people's quality of life and well-being. Social justice is well established as a concern for the left, but more work needs to be done to address the unequal chances in life that people face because of their background (Pearce and Paxton, 2005).The growing policy interest in well-being is a newer theme, and not traditional territory for the left. It is signalled by shifts in debates towards questions such as quality of work or childcare, and by the growth in 'downshifting', which is not confined to the middle classes (Hamilton, 2003). Research on well-being is well advanced, and provides a rich seam for policy (Shah and Marks, 2004). It shows that our relationships with others are fundamental to our well-being, and that policy should therefore be careful not to undermine them, through, for example, pushing towards longer working hours. It also shows that mental health is perhaps more important than physical health for our well-being. But, disturbingly, the trend seems to be for increasing mental health problems, with one in six people in the UK suffering at any given time. And it shows that a materialistic outlook on life is bad for happiness – going to the heart of questions about the kind culture that we want to develop.

One aspect of the good society that that the democratic left has not grappled with is the environment. The discourse of 'sustainable development' is much advanced but not very much within the democratic left. Given the serious problems we face around climate change, the task is to move towards environmental sustainability without being regressive. Sometimes the environment and social justice go hand in hand. For example, focusing on national home energy efficiency could end fuel poverty while simultaneously reducing energy demand. In other cases balancing the two will require intelligent policy framing – for example, congestion charges in cities tend to affect single parents regressively (other poor groups tend to travel during off peak hours). The democratic left has tended to see the environmental movement as primarily concerned with limits (to growth, to behaviour). We need to turn this round in two ways. Environmental issues need to be thought about in terms of social justice – for future generations. And they need to be promoted in a context focusing upon quality of life. The happiness research shows very strongly that rises in material standards in rich countries do not lead to overall gains in well-being, because people are primarily interested in relative consumption rather than absolute consumption. So there is a progressive agenda based on increasing quality of life through giving people more time rather than working them harder to shop more, and this simultaneously helps reduce the strain on the environment. But the democratic left will need to move fast. The ever-pragmatic Tories are beginning to occupy this agenda: Cameron has recently called for a focus on National Well-being and set up a policy commission on quality of life (*Independent*, 1.11.05). There is a real danger if the Tories occupy this space first. They can offer a seductive post-materialistic aspirational agenda in a simpler form than the democratic left, aimed solely at the better off.

Democracy and the public realm

Another crucial area lies in dealing with the democratic disconnect. The results from the POWER inquiry (an independent inquiry into Britain's democracy) suggest that the disconnect has been underestimated. People do not have a sense of influence in many areas of their lives. Whilst constitutional reform is worthy and important – and a move towards more devolved local power is fundamental – it could happen and yet leave untouched the broader sense of disconnection that people experience around politics. There are many ways to deal with this – and they don't necessarily involve the endless meetings that led Oscar Wilde to say that the trouble with socialism was that it would take too many evenings in the week. Real involvement of people in the policies that affect them is key, because often they know the solutions far better than the policy-makers. And involvement means they are not seen as passive recipients of policy, but as real actors, who will 'co-produce' the outcomes. In every major policy area it is more efficient to create change with the buy-in of the people who are affected. For example, to create a healthy population requires citizens to take charge of their own lives and change what they eat and how much they exercise. Progressives need to learn from bodies which are good at involving people – invariably civil society organisations – such as Community Links, a charity in East London, or timebanks, which are able to involve communities that are hard to reach.

Part of the democracy and governance question must focus on public service reform. The New Labour project is based on ideology about markets rather than on 'what works'. We need instead a clear framework for our public services. This is not necessarily to say that all public service delivery must remain in public hands. However, the widely acknowledged dangers about private sector involvement, and the less well understood but real dangers about voluntary sector involvement (e.g. compromise of independence from government, loss of their value-added), mean there needs to be thoughtful debate about where different kinds of providers add value, the regulatory framework and how to maintain accountability, and how all users will ultimately get the best experience.

A new political economy

Probably the most difficult area of all is political economy. One major question is how to run the economy in the face of the twin challenges of globalisation and climate change. It seems likely that globalisation is generally overestimated as a constraint on economic choices (Turner, 2001). We have choices about our level of public good provision without necessarily damaging our economic performance; thus, for example, Sweden has high levels of productivity and economic growth (and is ranked number 3 in the World Economic Forum competitiveness report) while sustaining tax levels at around 51 per cent of GDP, as opposed to approximately 38 per cent in the UK (Taylor, 2005). In fact it can be argued that the spectre of globalisation has been used by New Labour as way of escaping responsibility.

The democratic left conception of the economy needs broadening. Instead of seeing it primarily in terms of a division between the public and private sectors, it is important to acknowledge other important areas – the household sector (e.g. the care economy at home, or the production of meals at home), the informal economy and the 'third sector' (Purdy, 2004). Measures of economic progress tend to overlook the contribution of these other sectors, and this can lead to miscalculation. For example, policies which encourage the household economy to 'contract out' services (e.g. childcare, meals, care) register as a positive in economic growth figures, without registering that they can produce a corresponding negative in the household economy. The economy also needs to be understood as a subset of society and the environment: without either of these, the economy would cease to function. If economic growth is adjusted for social and environmental effects, we find that we are building a large amount of economic growth at the costs of social and environmental capital (Jackson, 2004).

CONCLUSION

The next progressive political wave will be greatly influenced by civil society movements and political developments which have happened outside of the democratic left movement. This is as it should be if we are to make history in conditions we did not choose. While the Labour Party is still the main vehicle we have for progressive politics, it is flawed, and democratic left politics should renew itself by looking outside of formal party politics.

All the old rules of the game apply. For progressives to win back ground after Blair they will need to be clear about what they are trying to do, and will need to organise intelligently to get there. We have taken these lessons to heart in organising Compass. Whilst maintaining a strong link with the Labour Party, Compass membership is open to non-party members. We work to provide a big tent for organisations and social movements who broadly share our democratic left values. We recognise the importance of policy but we know that politics is even more important, and so we are a pressure group not a think tank. Democracy is crucial to how we are organised, and this is why we have such an engaged membership. And learning from the way that social democracy has remained hegemonic in Sweden, we recognise that taking the long view is important. Our aim is to change the nature of progressive politics in the UK, and we will measure our success by the outcome not just of the next election but more importantly those beyond 2009. Blairism may have made Labour safe for unfettered capitalism, but to every action there is a reaction. As the tide ebbs from New Labour our job is to create the next wave for a new democratic left.

REFERENCES

Dawnay, E. and Shah, H. (2005), *Seven Key Principles of Behavioural Economics*, London: new economics foundation.

Graetz, M. and Shapiro, I. (2005), *Death by a Thousand Cuts*, Princeton: Princeton University Press.

Hall, S. (2003), 'New Labour's Double-shuffle', *Soundings* 24, accessed online at http://www.l-w-bks.co.uk/journals/articles/nov03.html

Hamilton, C. (2003), *Downshifting in Britain: A sea-change in the pursuit of happiness*, Discussion paper no. 58, Canberra: Australia Institute.

Jackson, T. (2004), *Chasing Progress*, Brighton/London: University of Surrey and new economics foundation.

Pearce, N. and Paxton, W. (eds) (2005), *Social Justice: Building a Fairer Britain*, London: Politico's.

Purdy, D. (2005), 'Markets and the mixed economy', *Soundings* 28.

Shah, H. and Marks, N. (2004), *A well-being manifesto for a flourishing society*, London: new economics foundation.

Taylor, R. (2005), *Sweden's New Social Democratic Model*, London: Compass.

Titmuss, R.M. (1970), *The Gift Relationship*, London: Allen and Unwin.

Turner, A. (2001), *Just Capital*, Basingstoke: Macmillan.

The next left: a transatlantic conversation

Jonathan Freedland and Michael Walzer

LONDON
23 May 2005

In the Clinton-Blair years, progressive parties in Britain and the US joined forces, trading electoral techniques and even the 'New' philosophy that saw them shed unpopular positions on welfare, crime etc in order to become more electable: New Labour, New Democrats.

In Britain that approach has weathered better than it did in the US: Labour is still in government while Democrats have been ejected from both Congress and the White House.

Could there be a new kind of transatlantic progressive dialogue that might heave the Democrats out of the hole – and rejuvenate a flagging Labour government? There are dozens of possibilities, including climate change and immigration, etc, but I propose three areas to consider:

1) 'Values': Can progressives construct a response to the 'values' agenda which has done so much to keep the right in power in the US and badly inhibits Labour in the UK? Can the left find its own language of morality, not merely to dress up old left positions in moral vocabulary, but to imagine new stances? Might there be some left shibboleths which have to go as a result, much as several shibboleths had to be discarded in the Blair/Clinton era? For example, might it fall to the left to call a halt to the sexualisation of the public sphere and mainstreaming of pornography, partly for traditional left reasons (feminism, anti-exploitation) but also for reasons that would strike a chord with social conservatives e.g. ensuring a public realm that is not off-limits to families, children, etc?

2) Domestic policy/welfare: Could the left rethink its own liberalism, adding a remodelled economic liberalism to its social liberalism? The right currently understands 'non-state actors', invited into provi-

sion of public or collective services, to mean private, profit-seeking companies. Could there be a refashioning of that non-statist approach that would involve actors that are not state but not commercial either? Actors from the voluntary or third sector: churches, charities, etc. This is not news in the US. Even in Britain this approach would revive Victorian notions of mutuality and even municipality. Nevertheless, spelled out coherently, it would count as innovative in the UK.

3) The left and the world: Is there a coherent, progressive response to the neo-con project? Currently it is the right who are articulating what used to be a left aim – a revolutionary plan to change the world, through force if necessary. Can those who opposed the Iraq war and the Bush method nevertheless craft their own doctrine which might hasten the demise of tyrannies around the world – without starting illegal wars or repeating the mistakes of imperialisms past?

Put together, might these ideas amount to an alternative Anglo-Saxon model? Right now, that model is understood – especially in Europe – to be neo-liberal on economics and neo-con on foreign policy. Might progressives in both the US and UK be able to construct a vision which would connect more easily with European approaches, thereby healing the current US-European rift and soothing Britain's own strained relations with its continental neighbour?

Yours,
Jonathan

PRINCETON
1 July 2005

Jonathan,

Thank you for your initial thoughts.

In response to your three areas.

1) 'Values': 'Values' on the American right today have to do almost entirely with sex: gay marriage, abortion, pornography in Hollywood, and so on. Of course, right wing opposition in these cases isn't serious: the number of abortions has increased during the Bush years, primarily because of the decline of welfare programs aimed at children; the spread of pornography is a market phenomenon, and the Bush people are not interested in regulation; they can stop gay marriage, though so many gay men and women are drawn to libertarian ideology that they may soon be a major presence in the Republican party. It isn't crazy to

think that this issue will pass to the Democrats – who shouldn't be eager to adopt it. The politicisation of sex is probably not in the interest of the left. We can't become the censors of movies and books, not even of billboards, and the internet is hopeless, short of the kind of controls that the Chinese government imposes. The right will always outbid us on these issues. Anyway, the truth is that morality is already the dominant discourse of the left, while on the right the dominant discourse is ideological (or theological). We have lost confidence in the old theories and the big picture; instead we talk endlessly about values: human rights, commodification, community, corporate corruption, equal respect ... The list goes on. Our primary task, it seems to me, is to make the value story coherent, to re-discover the big picture.

2) Domestic policy/welfare: I have been arguing for many years for leftist initiatives in this area. We should be the advocates of many different forms of civic action. The 'faith-based welfare' programs now being pushed by the Bush administration are not new in the US. Catholics, Lutherans, Jews, and others have for many years run mini-welfare societies – day-care, hospitals, nursing homes, etc – with access to tax money. The money spent by Catholic Charities, for example, is almost two-thirds state money. The trouble with these programs in the past is that the strongest groups collect and distribute the most money. If black Baptists were running welfare programs as extensive as those of white Lutherans, American society would look significantly different than it does. So what the state should do is to enhance the resources and capacities of the weakest groups first. But it shouldn't be only religious groups that provide these services. The actual legislation here in the US calls for community-based, not faith-based, welfare, so why haven't labour unions, say, rushed to develop programs? Why shouldn't there be day-care centres run by unions in factories and office buildings around the country, partially funded by the state? We have to oppose things like private prisons (a real danger to American justice), but we also have to support third-sector nursing homes. And we have to be able to explain the difference.

3) The left and the world: You are right. In this country, at least, the right is ideologically committed, single-minded, and radical, whereas the left, or the near-left, is cautious, prudent, and 'realistic.' I am less worried than you are about illegal wars. NATO in Kosovo was illegal, as was the Vietnamese intervention in Cambodia, India in Bangladesh, Tanzania in Idi Amin's Uganda. Any intervention in Rwanda would have been illegal, since the UN was not going to authorise it. The problem is with unnecessary and unjust wars. It seems to me that the best way to stop them is to recognise the value of force-short-of-war. We should be the advocates of new forms of collective security, which will

sometimes involve sanctions, embargoes, coercive inspections, no-fly zones, and so on – all the things that actually worked in Iraq and made that war unnecessary and unjust. In the face of actual aggression or massacres in progress, we have to be ready, as we mostly are not, to go to war. In the face of aggressive and brutal regimes, which have not yet attacked their neighbours and are not actually killing their own people, we need to open up a range of options. If collective security is to work, however, we have to resist the cant phrase about force being a last resort. It isn't; force-short-of-war obviously comes before war itself. Collective security is a 'realist' strategy, prudent, tough minded, and (we hope) unexciting. So, at the same time, we should be promoting a third sector radicalism. Groups like Human Rights Watch and Amnesty International actually work for regime change in places where state action would not be justified. The left generally should be engaged, and engaged enthusiastically, in this sort of work.

It is in the global arena, most importantly, that we should be putting forward an alternative to neo-liberal economics. We need a theoretical account of free trade and industrial production in the third world that factors in the environmental costs and the human costs – and points toward some way of dealing with both. Here, it seems to me, the US and UK need to move closer to European social democracy – conceived, however, in international rather than in domestic terms. But with regard to foreign policy, it is Europe that needs to move – not with reference to Iraq, where the US and UK are stuck and can't expect to be rescued, but on all sorts of other issues. What is important is that Europeans accept that they too are responsible for the way the world goes, in Iran, for example, or in Darfur, or in Afghanistan, wherever they have the capacity to act. I doubt that the rift with the Bush administration would be healed if the EU acted with greater responsibility and independence. But it would be a better rift, and some future American administration would recognise the improvement.

Michael

LONDON
2 September

Michael,

The summer hiatus in our correspondence may have brought a change in perspective. Bombs have gone off – and just failed to go off – in

London and, as I write, New Orleans is vanishing under floodwater. Both our countries have withstood some shocks.

To respond to your thoughts in those initial three areas. On values: one potent left tactic, at least, might be to do more often what you did in your last note – namely, to expose the right's failings to live up to their own rhetoric. As you say, abortion and pornography are both on the increase and the right are hobbled in their reaction – chiefly by the contradictions between their social conservatism and their free-market liberalism.

That's a useful debating point for liberals, but I would not yet want to give up on a left assault on some of this same ground. Sure, if that means the 'politicisation of sex,' with Chinese-style censoring of the Internet, the left would want to keep well away. But we are surely capable of a response which is somewhere between indifference and a Beijing-style crackdown. An example: *The Guardian* recently ran a story about a leading British store selling Playboy-branded stationery to young girls. There was an enormous response from all kinds of readers – young and old, male and female – almost unanimous in their condemnation of the store. These were self-described liberals and leftists who felt bereft of a vocabulary for speaking about this issue. They were not prudes or bigots, but they disliked the idea of big companies profiteering from the sexualisation of childhood. I don't think we can abandon that sentiment – or those people. We ought to be able to draw from feminism, amongst other ideas, to find our own language in this area.

More interesting though is your larger point about rediscovering the big picture. What might such an over-arching ideology for the left consist of? I once toyed with the slogan 'putting people in charge of their own lives' – which would capture everything from increased powers for local communities (a big issue for Britain which has little of the decentralised powers Americans take for granted) to women's reproductive rights and plenty in between. It would encompass democracy but also economic empowerment. Its central creed would be autonomy, the power to govern ourselves: that would extend to an internationalist belief in the right of self-determination, for Iraqis, Palestinians and, one might add, Israelis. But if that does not fly as a coherent left ideology, maybe it's 'dignity' or perhaps 'the equal worth of all human beings.' The right have 'markets and freedom'. We need a story of our own.

On domestic policy and welfare, I think we are in agreement. The US is much further down this third sector role than the UK. I can see that the challenge in the US is to ensure resources for the weakest groups. In the UK, we need first to establish the very idea! And that will mean a culture shift for the left. Since 1945 we have got used to seeing the state as the only legitimate actor – and have been suspicious of all other players as somehow presaging a return to pre-1945, Victorian-style 'charity.' On a specific: you condemn private prisons, which are pretty well an unchallenged part of the Blairite creed. Perhaps you could say more on your opposition to them?

Finally, on the left and the world. I take your point about legality. It chimes with my own view of the Kosovo war, which I believed was legitimate even if illegal under UN rules. So legitimacy is the issue. A very large challenge is to define legitimacy more precisely, and perhaps come to a new understanding of the very idea of sovereignty – one that would give us a clearer guide as to when nations can intervene in the affairs of other nations. I think the international commission which recently came up with the idea of a 'responsibility to protect', rather than a right to intervene, helped us along this path. But there's more work to do.

The force-short-of-war idea is similarly imaginative – and I cannot argue with your demand that the EU buries some of its pious inertia and starts taking responsibility for matters it currently dumps on the Americans. (Though this feels less likely now than ever. The defeat of the European constitution has brought the European project to a halt, while the internal woes of France and Germany leaves both those nations in little mood to shoulder global responsibilities.)

But, perhaps mindful of what happened here on July 7th, I think we need a left response to what feels like the great issue of our times: global Islamist radicalism. This movement is totalitarian and theocratic, but it clearly articulates the anger felt by those for whom the left would traditionally feel sympathy – the poor, the disadvantaged, the discriminated against, and, in some cases, the occupied. Are we to join Christopher Hitchens and others in branding this as Islamo-fascism – Nazism in a green bandana – or are we to join George Galloway et al in seeing it as the (perhaps unattractive) face of a global movement against imperialism? Or can we stake out some viable ground in between?

Jonathan

PRINCETON
8 September

Jonathan,

It looks like we are talking about three sets of issues, and I have organised my responses to fit that pattern.

Firstly, I certainly don't want to defend indifference to cultural pornification or to the sexual exploitation of children. Of course we should oppose that sort of thing, and we should identify it, accurately, with market freedom and corporate (also entrepeneurial) profiteering. This is capitalism unbridled. But what puzzles and disturbs me is that I don't see precisely how we mean to bridle it. With regard to child labour or factory safety or environmental damage, I know pretty clearly what constraints I want to impose on the market. But here I don't know. Where is the middle ground between Chinese style censorship and libertarian permissiveness? Or, better, what policies can you describe that are appropriate to this middle ground? Some feminists in the US are ready to defend censorship; I see their point, but given who the censors will be, I don't want to move in that direction.

As for the big picture – well, its creation can't simply be willed. The central ideas must respond to actual anxieties and aspirations. Individual autonomy is an aspiration, and it has great appeal these days, especially, I think, to younger and more affluent Americans (and Brits?). A student at Yale University wrote a piece for *Dissent* about the last elections in which he claimed that his classmates' overwhelming support for Kerry had more to do with gay marriage than with health care or social security or, for that matter, the war in Iraq. His sense of their emerging politics – a combination of cultural/social radicalism and neo-liberalism. That's not a good formula for the left's future.

My own sense is that we would do better right now to address anxieties. Hence the slogan I would adopt is an old one, first enunciated by Churchill and Roosevelt: 'Freedom from Fear.' The left has to address the question of security, and our way of doing that should be to talk about collective security both at home and abroad. I think that ordinary men and women (though maybe not the overprivileged young) feel very vulnerable these days – and not only because of terrorist attacks. Market forces produce their own terrors, and the steady erosion of all the forms of social protection exposes people to a new range of risk. The classic task of the left, I have always believed, is risk-reduction for the people most at risk. Egalitarianism is a commitment to make poor and poorer people as much at home in the world and as safe in it as rich people have always been. Well, that's a reductionist account, but maybe a useful one.

On domestic policy and welfare, twenty years ago I wrote an article (in *The New Republic*) against private prisons. I mean, private for-profit prisons; maybe the Blairites imagine prisons run by Amnesty International or Human Rights Watch. I would probably be against that too, but the other opposition is much easier. What's wrong with the private prison? 'It exposes the prisoners to private or corporate purposes, and it sets them at some distance from the protection of the law. The critical exposure is to profit-taking at the prisoners' expense, and given the conditions under which they live, they are bound to suspect that they are regularly used and exploited. For aren't the purposes of their private jailers different from the purposes of the courts that sent them to jail? All the internal rules and regulations of their imprisonment, the system of discipline and reward, the hundreds of small decisions that shape their daily lives, are open now to a single unanswerable question: Is this punishment or economic calculation, the law or the market?'

I still believe that the practice of punishment must be the responsibility of the state and that the agents of punishment must be officials of the state, bound in the first instance by its laws. You can privatise the prison's kitchen and its laundry, but not the prison itself. Surely the Blairites don't want to privatise the police – for that would raise very big questions about the legitimacy of just about everything the police do. But prison guards vis-à-vis prisoners are simply police, and their legitimacy, it seems to me, depends on their public role.

Finally, on the left and the world. Surely it is the responsibility to protect that gives rise to the right to intervene. If protection involves sending an army across an international frontier, then we might as well call it intervention. If you want to pose clearly the question of sovereignty's limits, then we might think of humanitarian intervention as the enforcement of human rights. Individual autonomy is limited by the rights of other people, and state sovereignty is limited by the rights of the state's own people. There is no sovereign right to massacre your own people, as the Khmer Rouge massacred the Cambodians, for example: sovereignty ends at the killing fields. How many people have to be at risk before intervention is justified? That is a hard question, and I don't know how to answer it. But it probably is a theoretical question. In so many places, from Cambodia and Uganda in the 1970s to Darfur today, the numbers were and are so great that the question isn't hard at all.

Does radical Islam in its terrorist versions articulate the anger of the poor, disadvantaged, and so on? We should not be too quick to accept that – given, first, that so many of the Islamist militants are neither poor nor disadvantaged and, second, that so many poor and disadvantaged people have found other articulations of their pain and anger. The causes of terrorism are no doubt deep and complex, but I would guess that they have more to do with resentment than with poverty. And for that reason I am tempted by the analogy with fascism – though it is

important to note that fascism was (except in Spain) a secular movement, so any religious likeness is bound to be unlike the original in
some respects. Still, authoritarianism, state-sponsored thuggery, daily
cruelty, and the cult of death (as evidenced most clearly in the Taliban
regime): all these argue for the analogy. And I am drawn to it for
another reason: in the past, anti-fascist politics, in contrast to anti-
communist politics, has tended to go along with a leftist domestic
agenda. Maybe opposition to radical Islam abroad will improve the
prospects of secular radicalism at home. Finally (we can talk more
about this), imagining the enemy as fascist-like doesn't entail an all-out
military response. Until 1939, there were forceful responses short of
war that would have contained the Nazi regime and would probably
have brought it down. And similar options certainly exist today.

Michael

LONDON
28 October

Dear Michael,

Usefully, I think, we are beginning to converge in those three areas.
Perhaps I'll say a little more on each – and then suggest another question for us to mull.

On values, we both agree on the need to restrain some of the most
directly exploitative consequences of capitalism: the challenge is to find
the means to bridle them. I share your fears about censorship. In
Britain just now we are getting an object lesson in how powers sought
for legitimate reasons – say the fight against terrorism – end up being
used to restrict our freedom. An 82-year-old heckler at the Labour
Party Conference was thrown out of the hall – and then detained under
anti-terror laws. So I don't doubt that if we handed to the state new
authority designed to thwart pornographers and child abusers, it
would not be long before it was used to gag the rest of us.

But maybe there is a mechanism which would entail collective, but
not state, action. I'm thinking of the consumer campaigns which have
punished corporations deemed guilty of unacceptable behaviour. In the
1980s it became financially damaging to trade with South Africa. No
right-thinking person wanted to have any association with apartheid.
Could we not demand that the software giants, the major search
engines and internet service providers do whatever it takes to ensure

they are not disseminating violent abusive porn – and withhold our custom from those who refuse to do the right thing? Something tells me that, faced with such a challenge, those companies would soon find a technological answer. It would be even easier to direct an equivalent campaign at shops (like my Playboy stationery example). We are being told all the time that we live in a consumer society: well, if that's so, what about some consumer politics? (Interestingly Britain's National Consumer Council is now run by Ed Mayo, a man who previously led one of the country's most radical think tanks: a hint, perhaps, that he sees consumerism as a political movement, potentially at least.) I like, too, the stories of pressure groups who have bought shares in financial companies – only to attend shareholder meetings, demanding the dumping of stocks in the arms industry.

This might feel like tinkering at the edges, but I think of the way big tobacco has had to change its tactics thanks to a marked shift in attitudes to its products. Could we not do the same about the corporations guilty of exploitation, both in the pornographic sense of that word – but also in the more traditional sense, by using, say, slave-wage labour abroad. Nor need this be solely the task of grass roots activism. With sufficient prompting, governments could surely put legal and tax obstacles in the path of corporate villains. But it is up to us to do the prompting.

On the big picture, the autonomy notion I flagged up earlier might be meatier if we link it to economics. We might say that an individual is not meaningfully autonomous if he is so poor that he merely exists rather than lives. In this way, and without reviving the old debate about positive and negative liberty, we could reclaim 'freedom' from the right – but endow it with a richer sense of possibility: freedom plus. (Though I concede that, on the page, that slogan looks uncomfortably close to positive freedom.)

In a similar vein, I would shy away from your line about 'Freedom from Fear.' The first objection is tactical: it sounds too negative. The left have often made the mistake of seeming like the gloom party: witness Ronald Reagan's monopolisation of optimism in the 1980s. Britain's Conservatives are set to choose David Cameron as their new leader, a young, smiling character whose face seems bathed in morning dew. It's a cliché that we should appeal to people's hopes not fears, but perhaps a sound one. It's partly for that reason that I am loath to disregard those quasi-libertarian instincts of the young (who voted for Kerry over gay marriage not health care). There is a rugged kind of confidence there that the left needs to harness, rather than shut out. Perhaps, then, instead of speaking about fear we might talk about opportunity. Admittedly tired from overuse, that word nevertheless might speak to those young Kerry voters. We don't merely propose risk-reduction for those at the bottom; we demand opportunities for them. Opportunities to work, to live, to express themselves.

Our discussion on domestic policy lighted upon the question of private prisons. I am wholly persuaded by what you say. I would add one note. I was speaking with a former British army officer this week who predicted a return to the Napoleonic notion of the mercenary garrison: the outsourcing of warfare. Already catering and other army functions have been privatised. He says it will not be long before a private security company offers a fighting unit for hire. All your arguments on prisons would apply to that in spades.

As for the left and the world, we agree on the responsibility to protect and the right to intervene – notions which merge in the most desperate circumstances. My fear is that the Iraq episode has tainted this just notion, perhaps for a generation to come.

On the question of whether we should describe Islamism as a mutation of fascism, I can see your logic – yet something holds me back. Perhaps it is the overlordism I associate with fascism – and yet which is surely absent in a worldwide Muslim community which regards itself as on the losing side in almost every sphere. It is true that Islamism has state power to call on in Iran, and had it in Afghanistan under the Taliban, but globally, Islam can make a strong case that it is under the boot-heel rather than wielding it. More candidly, perhaps my worry is that the f-word will demonise Muslim communities themselves. In Britain and Europe that is no idle risk: they are here in substantial numbers and, to paraphrase Rodney King, we have to get along.

The new area I want to mention is about politics itself. For this I'm afraid I have to resort to anecdote. This week I was speaking with an author friend now working on a book about the sex traffic industry across Europe and the Middle East. He interviewed women who had been abducted in Moldova and were now held by Russian hardmen under lock and key all night, until they were driven to a brothel where they 'service' up to 20 or 30 men at night, from 6pm till 6am. The women he interviewed were dead behind the eyes; their souls had been erased.

Driving back that night, I listened to the radio news: rows about a smoking ban in Britain, about the Valerie Plame affair in the US. It struck me that what passes for political discourse – the rows and arguments that dominate our media and our legislatures – bare scant relationship to the real injustices that scar our world. There is great cruelty going on everywhere, every day. And yet politics not only fails to stop it – it barely mentions it.

Others will say the same about climate change; our politics seems to miss the things that really matter. I'm not sure what the answer is, but I'm sure that the search for one is the work of the left.

All the best,
Jonathan

PRINCETON
7 November

Dear Jonathan,

Yes, we are, as you say, beginning to converge, but there are also some interesting differences, which make me feel a bit like an old leftist, even a very old one, sitting here in the New World. Let me focus on some of these disagreements, taking our broader convergence for granted.

Consumer politics is certainly better than state action on issues like media violence and pornography. But the South African example suggests to me that a leftist politics here might best begin with issues (which you mention also) like racial and gender discrimination, child labour, exploitative wages, and so on. The anti-sweatshop campaign among American college students is a useful example, aimed at forcing universities buying athletic equipment to deal only with companies that meet decent labour standards. I am not against directing campaigns like this against companies that use 'violent abusive porn' to sell their goods. However, I am a little more cautious here, because such campaigns will be adopted (here in the US at least) by right wing groups, and used against publishers who sell cheap editions of Lawrence or Nabokov, television stations that air scientific programs on evolution, and theatres and cinemas that cater to gay audiences. We may well end up longing for a free market in these areas.

You say that you are loath to disregard the quasi-libertarianism of the young: 'there is a rugged kind of confidence there that the left needs to harness, rather than shut out.' Maybe so, but the young Americans that I described in my last letter were students at one of our elite universities and I suspect that if you have similar British young people in mind they will also be from the upper or upper middle classes. Their confidence has an economic basis. But more and more people here, and probably in Britain too, are less and less confident about their futures.

I will write only about the US, where, in the last few days, the media have been pouring out stuff about the dangers of a bird flu pandemic. The anxiety is less about the birds and the flu than about the government's ability to cope in an emergency. It can't cope with terrorist attacks or hurricanes; it can't produce a decent health care system; it has visibly lost its 'wars' against crime, poverty, and drugs; it is providing fewer and fewer Americans with full-time jobs and adequate benefits. Why should anyone trust it to deal with the next crisis? A politics that offers some hope of dealing competently and successfully with terrorism, natural disaster, and joblessness seems to me the right politics for the left. I don't think that security is a negative idea, and the hope for security is the very opposite of gloom and doom.

I agree with what you say about opportunity, but the opportunities that people want are not focused only on individual careers, personal advancement, and self-expression. Of course, we have to talk to those ambitions, but people also want to be able to provide a secure environment for their children and their ageing parents. They want safe streets, and good schools, and available doctors, and clean air and water, and dikes and dams and bridges that won't collapse in a storm. Laissez faire government and free markets don't provide any of these. And this is what social democracy is all about – boring, perhaps, in ordinary times, but we are not living in ordinary times.

Yes, you have to get along with Muslim immigrants and fellow-citizens, and if a politics of recognition will help in that process, 'Islamic fascism' is probably not a useful term. But recognition by itself won't help enough unless it comes together with good schools and good jobs and, yes, 'opportunities to work, to live, to express themselves.' Another old left nostrum, but it is true, I think, that economic integration is the key to every other kind of integration. And if economic integration is effective, there wouldn't be much risk in arguing that supporters of terrorism, religious repression, and the radical subordination of women were near fascist in their politics. There would still be plenty of room for the recognition of Islam as one among other British or American religions.

Finally, our inability to focus British or American politics on 'the great cruelties that go on everywhere' is certainly something to worry about – though I can't resist pointing out that were we able to do that, we could hardly avoid seeming like the 'gloom party.' There is certainly a lot to be gloomy about, and angry about, in the world today. Most importantly right now: the murderous politics of the Sudanese government in Darfur, which the world watches (or doesn't watch) and does nothing. As you say, the Iraq war has gone a long way toward discrediting the idea of humanitarian intervention. But we have to insist on that idea, even when the US and UK can't be, shouldn't be, among the interveners. We need a programmatic response to the great cruelties, which means that we have to keep arguing about when and where the use of force is justified. People on the left who renounce the use of force are making their peace with cruelty. We should never do this.

Regards,
Michael

LONDON
11 November

Dear Michael,

The remaining disagreements between us are fascinating, not least because I suspect they evolve, indirectly, out of our wider convergence – or at least my assumption of it.

I agree, for example, with your insistence that a new kind of left consumer activism must begin by targeting companies guilty of what we might call 'traditional' exploitation – using child labour, paying slave wages and the rest – before campaigning against exploitative imagery in marketing. Of course that's the right way around. I realise that I hadn't written that from the outset because I assumed not only that we both thought that way, but that a left politics would always worry about the former – but suspected I had to argue for the latter. It's a useful lesson, reminding me that we should take nothing for granted. Left politics needs to remake its case anew for every generation and every era. And those college kids you describe will probably have to be persuaded of the case against basic economic exploitation as if for the first time. So, yes, let's get our priorities right. An anti-sweatshop campaign first; a campaign against Playboy stationery next.

Your next point is equally revealing about those things I took for granted. You write of Americans' fears over governmental competence: its simple ability to cope with crises, from avian flu to the war on drugs. After Katrina and five years of George W. Bush, I can entirely understand those fears. But I don't believe Britons share them, not when it comes to their own government. Now, heaven knows New Labour has made some calamitous mistakes and wasted some precious opportunities. But it can claim one remarkable achievement: it has rehabilitated the very idea of government.

Of course there are still complaints – about shortcomings in the health service or calls that go unanswered when you telephone the Passport Office – but the big picture here, after eight years of Labour, is that most people do feel they can rely on the state, more or less. Both Tony Blair and Gordon Brown still boast of their 'investment' (as opposed to spending) on schools and hospitals – and they do it because most people sense that their local school or hospital is pretty good now, and certainly better than it was.

In 1997 I suspect many Britons felt the way you suggest Americans feel today: that the public realm, the collective infrastructure, had been neglected so long that it was on the brink of collapse. People no longer feel that here. July 2005 brought two consecutive examples: London winning its bid to host the 2012 Olympics on July 6th and then showing tremendous skill and speed in its response to the bombs of the next day. My sense is that, in contrast with the US, people here do have a basic faith in government – and I think that counts as a genuine Labour achievement.

And yet, perhaps I had taken that too for granted. I can see from what you write that it is missing in the States – but I also realise that we may have to fight for it again in Britain. The story of this week is the arrival of David Cameron as the new leader of the Conservative Party. He is young, charismatic and winningly fluent. He presents himself as a 'compassionate conservative' – and we know who last used that phrase. It's at least possible that he, like Bush, will run from the centre, only to revert to right-wing type once in office. And then we will see once again the truth of your observation that those 'boring' staples of everyday life are not provided by free markets or laissez-faire governments. So we are going to have to fight anew for these first principles – ones I, and perhaps most social democrats in Britain – have come to take for granted. Labour's challenge now is both to keep making and to win the argument for social democracy – rather than taking it as read – but also to embed some of its core features so that they become a kind of Blair 'settlement,' a national modus operandi that is hard for any future government to unpick. FDR did that so effectively, the New Deal settlement endured for six decades. Brown calls it the 'progressive consensus' and aims for it at least to outlive this Labour government. Cameron's surge should remind all progressives why that is a worthwhile goal.

As for Muslim extremism, I'd like to believe that economics could reduce much of that danger – but I worry about it. It's a cliché now to note the wealth of the 9/11 hijackers, but Britain's own 7/7 bombers were also economically well-integrated. This is one area where the left's old nostrums only go so far. It may be that nothing less than a radical rethink of Western foreign policy can address this challenge. And when you hear the President of Iran doubting the truth of the Holocaust, you wonder whether even that would do the trick. In my darkest nights, I fear this is a rage that can never be put out.

On intervention, we wholly agree: the left cannot abandon this idea, despite the taint of Iraq, and Darfur is an object lesson in why not. But since we've been talking of old left nostrums, I thought I might conclude this final missive of mine by mentioning perhaps the very oldest.

I find myself appalled anew by the latest manifestations of old-fashioned economic inequality. There are hedge fund managers in this country whose annual bonuses run into the tens of millions. A group of bankers were recently reported to have asked a bartender to make the most expensive cocktail he could dream up: he prepared a drink costing £333 a glass. The bankers bought enough to run up a bill of £15,000.

I read about that in the same week that a new survey found that half a million British households are so cramped, kids have to sleep in the kitchen, on the floor or in the bathroom. It was as if the clock had turned back, to France in 1788. Despite all our progress, we are still a world of wild, extravagant gulfs between rich and poor – within societies and of course across the globe.

Do we raise taxes on the rich? Do we call for a Maoist style maximum wage? I don't know. But I think the left have to find again the confidence to rage with righteous fury at such a state of affairs – to discuss inequality in the moral terms it demands.

I don't expect a simple answer to that or any of the other questions we've raised over the last few months. Just to share them and discuss them together has been a privilege, for me at least. Sometimes the left can seem like an ageing beast, tired after so many bloody bouts. But after this exchange, I feel heartened: there's life in the old creature yet.

With comradely best wishes,
Jonathan

PRINCETON
27 December

Dear Jonathan,

There is, as you say, life in the old creature, but here in the US our health is not so good. We feel some revival as the Republican grip on power weakens. But this is more because of the corruption and incredible arrogance of the right than the courage or wisdom of the left. Now secular leftists pray for the truth of a biblical maxim: Pride goeth before a fall. The current 'spying on Americans' scandal may give the Democrats a boost, but at the same time it illustrates our difficulty: for no Democratic administration is going to give up searching the electronic mail for keywords that turn up, say, in Al Qaeda recruiting materials. I worry that the same thing is true of neo-liberal economic policies: in opposition, Democrats will attack the consequences of these policies, but none of the party's leaders have a real alternative in mind. It is probably true that no alternative can be merely national in scope; we need a global social democracy – you and I have touched on this before – and whatever is the case in Europe, American Democrats have barely begun to think about that. So, we are breathing, but we are not robust.

I agree that domestic inequalities should be a focus of liberal and left politics – of public anger and also of policy proposals. Our inequalities are probably worse than yours, since they extend dramatically to health care. Our upper classes (college professors are included here, so I can speak from experience) receive excellent care, addressing not only illness but also the prevention of illness. But millions of Americans get no preventive care at all; they depend on the emergency rooms of the local hospital; they live from one emergency to the next, and so do their children. I don't understand why this isn't a major issue in American politics, though I guess that we might find the answer in the voting statistics for those Americans who get their only medical care in the emergency rooms.

Since it is mostly poor people and members of minority groups who don't vote, American liberals and leftists have always believed that if we increased the turnout, we would win the election. That didn't work in 2004, when there was a six percent jump in the number of eligible voters who actually voted (the number is still shockingly low). For many of these voters, apparently, it was religion, not class, that determined their vote. We used to think that the old proverb about not living by bread alone was repeated most often by people who had plenty of bread, while the others were more likely to respond to Brecht's lines: 'First feed the face/And then talk right and wrong.' But it isn't so simple, and we do have to find a way of addressing the moral and cultural issues that you raised at the beginning of this conversation. Here, however, those questions are also religious, which makes them much harder. We have to persuade church-going Catholics and Protestants to vote for a liberal-left that is ideologically and often militantly secular. But I still believe, or cling to the hope, that with one or two more six per cent jumps, we would not only win, we would win strongly – even without compromising our secularism. But that's an old leftist talking. If I am wrong, well, then we need to begin a new conversation.

Regards,
Michael

Contributors

Zygmunt Bauman was a lecturer at the University of Warsaw from 1954, but was forced to leave Poland in 1968, eventually becoming Professor of Sociology at Leeds University. Bauman's international reputation has been built upon a considerable oeuvre which includes the following: *Legislators and Interpreters: On Modernity, Postmodernity and Intellectuals* (1987); *Modernity and the Holocaust* (1991); *Morality, Immorality and Other Life Strategies* (1992); *Modernity and Ambivalence* (1993); *Postmodernity and its Discontents* (1997); *Globalization: The Human Consequences* (1998); *In Search of Politics* (1999); *Liquid Modernity* (2000); *The Individualized Society* (2000); *Society Under Siege* (2002); *Wasted Lives* (2003); *Liquid Love* (2003); *Liquid Life* (2005); and *Liquid Risk* (2006).

Tom Bentley is Executive Director for Policy and Cabinet in the Premier's Department of Victoria, Australia. He is also a Director of the Australia and New Zealand School of Government (www.anzsog.edu.au), where he works on how to reshape government, public services and democracy. From 1999-2006 he was Director of Demos, the London based think tank (). His publications include *Learning beyond the classroom; education for a changing world* (1998); *The Adaptive State* (2003); and *Everyday democracy: why we get the politicians we deserve* (2005). Tom can be contacted at: tom_demos@yahoo.co.uk

Jake Chapman is a physicist from Cambridge, who previously worked at the Open University as Professor of Energy Systems. He was awarded a Royal Society gold medal for developing energy ratings for homes, a technology that formed the basis of the business he founded in 1983. Jake has applied the systems approach in academic, commercial and public sector contexts. His best known publications are *Fuels Paradise* (1975); *Tell Me Who You Are* (1985); and *System Failure* (2002). He is now semi-retired and a Demos Associate.

David Coats has been Associate Director-Policy at The Work Foundation since 2004. From 1999-2004 he was Head of the TUC's Economic and Social Affairs Department. He joined the TUC in 1989 as a Policy Officer on employment law, and later led the TUC's Partnership Team; he was also responsible for pay (including the National Minimum Wage), collective bargaining and human resource management issues. His recent publications include *Raising Lazarus: The Future of Organised Labour* (2005) and *Who's Afraid of Labour Market Flexibility?* (2006).

Colin Crouch is Chair of the Institute of Governance and Public Management at the Business School of Warwick University. He was previously professor of sociology at the European University Institute, Florence. He is a Fellow of the British Academy and chairman and former joint editor of *The Political Quarterly*. His most recent books include: (edited, with W Streeck) *Political Economy of Modern Capitalism: The Future of Capitalist Diversity* (1997); *Social Change in Western* Europe (1999); (with others) *Local Production Systems in Europe: Rise or Demise* (2001); *Post-Democracy* (2004); (with others) *Changing Governance of Local Economies: Response of European Local Production Systems* (2004); and *Capitalist Diversity and Change: Recombinant Governance and Institutional Entrepreneurs* (2005).

Richard Eckersley is a Visiting Fellow at the National Centre for Epidemiology and Population Health at the Australian National University, Canberra. His publications include *Well and Good: Morality, Meaning and Happiness* (2004); and he is co-author of a national index of subjective wellbeing, the first of its kind in the world, and the Australian Wellbeing Manifesto. He is a founding director of Australia 21, which aims to promote interdisciplinary and cross-institutional networks on important challenges facing Australia and the world this century.

Alan Finlayson is Senior Lecturer in the Department of Politics and International Relations, Swansea University. He previously worked at Queen's in Belfast for several years. He is co-editor of *Politics and Poststructuralism: An Introduction* (1998) and *Politics and Poststructuralism: An Introduction* (2005); and author of *Contemporary Political Thought: A Reader and Guide* (2003); and *Making Sense of New Labour* (2003). His current interests centre on the theory, history and practice of political rhetoric in the UK.

Jonathan Freedland is an award-winning journalist and broadcaster. He writes a weekly column in *The Guardian*, as well as a monthly piece for *The Jewish Chronicle*. He has written *Bring Home the Revolution: the Case for a British Republic* (1998), which argued that Britain needed a constitutional and cultural overhaul for which we could learn much from America, and *Jacob's Gift* (2005), looking at three generations of his own family. Before 1997 Jonathan was *The Guardian's* Washington Correspondent for four years

Edward Fullbrook is a Visiting Research Fellow at the School of Economics, University of the West of England. He is the founder and editor of the Post-Autistic Economics Review. He has written and edited a number of publications including *Intersubjectivity in Economics* (2002); *The Crisis in Economics* (2003); and *A Guide to What's Wrong with Economics* (2004).

Andrew Gamble is Professor of Politics at the University of Sheffield, and joint editor of *New Political Economy* and *The Political Quarterly*. He has published widely on political economy, political theory and political history. His most recent book is *Between Europe and America: The Future of British Politics*, which was awarded the PSA WJM Mackenzie Prize for the best book published in political science in 2003.

Sue Goss has wide experience of working with local, regional and central government. She works for the Office for Public Management and is Deputy Editor of the ideas journal *Renewal*. Sue is author and co-author of a number of books on local government and change. Her most recent publications include *Managing Working with the Public in Local Government* (1999); *Civic Entrepreneurship* (1999); and *Making Local Governance Work: Networks, Relationships and the Management of Change* (2001).

Gerry Hassan is a writer, commentator and researcher. He is a Demos Associate, and Head of the Scotland 2020 and Glasgow 2020 projects. He is also Associate Editor of the ideas journal *Renewal* and Honorary Research Fellow at Glasgow Caledonian University. Gerry is author and editor of a number of books, publications and pamphlets on Scottish and UK politics, the most recent of which include *Scotland 2020: Hopeful Stories for a Northern Nation* (2005), *The Political Guide to Modern Scotland* (2004), and *The Scottish Labour Party: History, Institutions and Ideas* (2004). Gerry can be contacted on: gerry.hassan@virgin.net.

Neal Lawson is Chair of Compass, the democratic left pressure group and Managing Editor of the ideas journal *Renewal*. He is a former researcher for the TGWU and for Gordon Brown. He is co-editor (with Neil Sherlock) of *The Progressive Century: The Future of the Centre-Left in Britain* (2001); and author of *Dare More Democracy* (2004). He is a regular contributor to *The Guardian, New Statesman* and radio and TV, on the Labour Party and a host of political and policy issues. He is currently researching for *All Consuming*, a book on shopping and politics to be published in 2008 (www.allconsuming.org.uk)

Ruth Lister is Professor of Social Policy at Loughborough University and is a former Director of the Child Poverty Action Group. She has served on various Commissions, most recently the Fabian Commission on Life Chances and Child Poverty. Her publications include *Citizenship: Feminist Perspectives* (2nd ed. 2003); and *Poverty* (2004).

Hetan Shah is policy director at Compass, the democratic left pressure group, where he has conducted a wide ranging policy review. He has co-edited three Compass books looking at progressive thinking for the long term: *The Good Society, A New Political Economy* and *Democracy and the Public Realm*, all published by Lawrence and Wishart in 2006. He was previously director of the New Economics programme at the New Economics Foundation, where his publications included *A Well-Being Manifesto* and *Seven Principles from Behavioural Economics*.

Michael Walzer has been Professor of Social Science at the Institute for Advanced Study, Princeton, New Jersey, since 1980. He has been co-editor of *Dissent* since 1976 and a contributing editor of *The New Republic* since 1977. His books include: *On Toleration* (1997); *What it Means to be an American* (1993); *The Company of Critics* (1988); *Exodus and Revolution* (1985); *Spheres of Justice: A Defense of Pluralism and Equality* (1983); *The Politics of Ethnicity* (1982); *Radical Principles: Reflections of an Unreconstructed Democrat* (1980); *Just and Unjust Wars: A Moral Argument with Historical Illustrations* (1977).

Index

About Compass

Compass is the democratic left pressure group whose goal is to both debate and develop the ideas for a more **equal** and **democratic** society, then **campaign** and **organise** to help ensure they become reality. We organise regular events and conferences that provide real space to discuss policy, we produce thought provoking pamphlets and we encourage debate through online discussions on our website. We campaign, take positions and lead the debate on key issues facing the democratic left. We're developing a coherent and strong voice, for those that believe in greater equality and democracy as the means to achieve radical social change.

We are:

- An **umbrella grouping** of the progressive left whose sum is greater than its parts.
- A **strategic political voice** – unlike thinktanks and single issue pressure groups Compass can develop a politically coherent position based on the values of equality and democracy.
- An **organising force** – Compass recognises that ideas need to be organised for and will seek to recruit, mobilise and encourage to be active, a membership across the UK to work in pursuit of greater equality and democracy.
- A **pressure group focused on changing Labour** – but recognises that energy and ideas can come from outside the party, not least the 200,000 who have left since 1997.

The central belief of Compass is that things will only change when people believe they can and must make a difference themselves. In the words of Gandhi 'Be the change you wish to see in the world'.

For more information or membership details contact:

Compass
FREEPOST LON15823
London
E9 5BR
t: 020 7463 0633
e: info@compassonline.org.uk
w: www.compassonline.org.uk